IMAGES
of America

ALONG THE MIAMI RIVER

On the Cover: This 1953 photograph of the Ebsary Foundation Company's *Cap'n Lew* shows the vessel returning to the firm's yard near Northwest Twenty-second Avenue from a task downriver. (Courtesy of Richard Ebsary and the Ebsary Foundation Company.)

IMAGES
of America

Along the Miami River

Paul S. George

ARCADIA
PUBLISHING

ISBN 978-0-7385-9888-8

Published by Arcadia Publishing
Charleston, South Carolina

Printed in the United States of America

Library of Congress Control Number: 2012949938

For all general information, please contact Arcadia Publishing:
Telephone 843-853-2070
Fax 843-853-0044
E-mail sales@arcadiapublishing.com
For customer service and orders:
Toll-Free 1-888-313-2665

Visit us on the Internet at www.arcadiapublishing.com

To my parents, Alice and Sargis George, who introduced their children to the Miami River; my sons, Paul Jr. and Matthew, who fished its waters with futility; and to those thousands of persons with whom I have been lucky to share the river and its rich lore amid tours of the stream.

Contents

ACKNOWLEDGMENTS

The Miami River is one of Miami's most intriguing elements. Of more than 60 different history tours that I offer, the river ranks at the top in popularity. In recent years, one of my most loyal tour-goers was Dr. Elliot Salloway, a dentist and professor at Harvard University. Salloway has photographed the river in all of its dimensions, and these photographs became the basis for presentations we have given before large audiences. Somewhere along the way, with Salloway's photographs and enthusiasm for the river in mind, I decided to create this pictorial history.

In addition to Elliot, many persons made this work possible, beginning with my supportive family—my wife, Laura, and children: Paul Jr., Matthew, and Maryrose. Others who have proved very helpful to the completion of this study include Larry Wiggins, who contributed many of the images that follow; historian Arva M. Parks; Scott Silverman; Dawn Hugh and Patty Barahona of HistoryMiami; Ronnie Hurwitz; Ben Torrens; Izzy Martinez; Sahir Iman; Richard Ebsary; Ruth Greenfield; Matthew George; Eileen Broton, whose late husband, Jim, had chronicled the long-ago communities bracketing the river; Don Gaby, who wrote the first full-fledged account of the river; Laura Morilla; Sara Leviten; Tom McAuliffe; Ronald Risner; Dan Hardie; Eveann Adams; Fred Stebbins; Janis Barrett; and Andrew Melick. All have contributed in a wonderful manner to the completion of this study.

The book was conceived when my boss, Dr. German Munoz, headed the Department of Social Science at Miami Dade College, Wolfson Campus. As usual, this singular human being was fully supportive of the project. Dr. Victor Vasquez, German's successor and a dear friend of mine, has been equally supportive of this effort. Special thanks also go to two reprobates and lifelong friends, Dr. Serge Martinez and Louis M. Jepeway Jr., esquire. Finally, Maggie Bullwinkel, my acquisitions editor at Arcadia Publishing, provided expert guidance (when it was requested) and prodding (when it was needed, which was frequently!).

INTRODUCTION

The Miami River is central to the story of Miami. In fact, a strong case can be made that the mouth of the river, especially the north bank, is the single most important historical element in all of southeast Florida. For it is here that a steady procession of people from dramatically different backgrounds have thrived for thousands of years. Among their ranks are Native Americans, called Tequestas by the Spanish; Jesuit missionaries, who ministered to the Indians; Seminole Indians, who came from Georgia in the 18th century; their white trading partners; slaves; US Army personnel; operators of boatyards and fisheries; pioneer homesteaders; and luxury-hotel guests. The north bank was home to Julia Tuttle, the "Mother of Miami," and her family; railroad baron Henry M. Flagler's stunning Royal Palm Hotel; Miami's first thoroughfare, Avenue D; and Fort Dallas Park, the city's early subdivision. At the mouth of the south bank is the site of the Miami Circle, one of the most celebrated archaeological discoveries of modern times. This serpentine stream, only four and a half miles in length and shallow in its original incarnation, was known in earlier times by the Spanish as Agua Dulce, meaning "sweet water," a reference to a freshwater stream.

The river has witnessed ceremonies of ancient times, fighting in wartime, interdiction by law authorities due to drug and alien smuggling, shoot-outs between the US Coast Guard and rumrunners during Prohibition; its shores, meanwhile, have welcomed a wave of vertical residential building as part of the latest real estate boom in a land of boom and bust.

Change has been the norm for the Miami River and for Miami, the city that brackets it. How else can one account for the fact that, as recently as 1895, the isolated wilderness surrounding the Miami River claimed only nine residents? But the following year, 1896, brought the entry of Flagler's Florida East Coast Railway and the settlement's first population boom, prompting incorporation on July 28. As a city was arising on the north bank of the river, the colorful Indian trade on the south bank was nearing the end of its three decades of activity.

As the river leaves the historic downtown sector, its configuration changes frequently while meandering west/northwest under a colorful variety of bridges and an imposing expressway span, past the site of boatyards where wartime vessels were manufactured, past lobster and stone crab fisheries, restaurants, and Lummus Park (one of the city and country's oldest parks). This six-acre green space hosts two of the area's most historical buildings, the William English Slave Plantation House/Fort Dallas and the William Wagner Homestead House, both clearly visible from the river.

About a quarter mile west of the old park, the historic neighborhood of Spring Garden nestles on the north bank. Carved out of a subtropical hammock, this quaint riverine neighborhood claimed famed author and environmentalist Marjory Stoneman Douglas as an early resident. Farther upriver, near the site of the new, $600 million Marlins Park that was built on the former grounds of the storied Orange Bowl stadium, stood the home of George Lewis, a blockade-runner during the Civil War. The home was torched by blockade enforcers upon the discovery of his activities in the region.

Nearby are the fabled "Indian Caves" that rise above the shallow waters of the Lawrence Canal, which runs perpendicular to the river west of Northwest Seventeenth Avenue. Tall enough for a person to stand upright in them, the caves are believed to have begun as solution holes in the oolitic limestone that undergirds the ridge overlooking the river in that area. Atop the caves is the striking new embassy of the Miccosukee Indians. Just west of that site, Coppinger's Tropical Garden, Indian Village & Alligator Farm, a popular tourist attraction featuring Indian alligator wrestling, stood for a half century.

Next to the old attraction, the south fork of the river breaks off from the main stream and roams for nearly a mile in a southwesterly direction before linking up to the Comfort Canal and continuing farther west. The north and south forks frame Durham Park, a picturesque peninsula community stretching from Northwest Nineteenth Avenue to Twenty-second Avenue. Picturesque though it may be today, its western edge was significantly different between World Wars I and II, owing to the presence of Gertie Walsh's famous bordello behind the tall, spreading trees in the immediate area.

The north bank of the river across from Durham Park has been the venue for many of the stream's most venerable businesses, including boatyards; engine-repair operations; marinas; and the Ebsary Foundation Company, which has laid the foundations for many of the most important building projects in Miami and south Florida for nearly a century and which maintains a presence on its original site overlooking the waterway.

At Northwest Twenty-fourth Avenue, the north fork splits in two, with the northern portion now connected to the Miami Canal, one of several drainage canals constructed by the State of Florida in the early 1900s as part of its ambitious effort to drain the Everglades. The peninsula, framed by the north fork and the canal and known as Martin's Point, developed primarily in the years right before World War II. Along with marine-related businesses, it contains homes whose occupants are affectionately referred to as "River Rats."

The Miami Canal extends close to 90 miles north to Lake Okeechobee. The beginning point of the canal is just east of the entrance to the Second Port of Miami, which hugs both banks of the canal from Northwest Twenty-seventh Avenue and is navigable west to approximately Northwest Thirty-seventh Avenue, where a railroad trestle crosses the stream. This bustling port accounts for billions of dollars in trade annually. Gritty and narrow, the Second Port of Miami is Florida's fifth-busiest port, hosting overage freighters that visit 110 ports of call in the hemisphere. During most days, small-but-powerful tugboats drag these freighters, laden with cargo above and below deck, up- and downriver. At times, the distance between the freighters and those vessels moored along the narrow canal is extremely tight, adding to the zest and excitement of the river.

This book, I hope, will provide a vicarious Miami River experience for the readers who will, upon finishing it, have sated at least some of their curiosity over one of Miami's most important elements, historically and otherwise.

One

An Edenic Wilderness

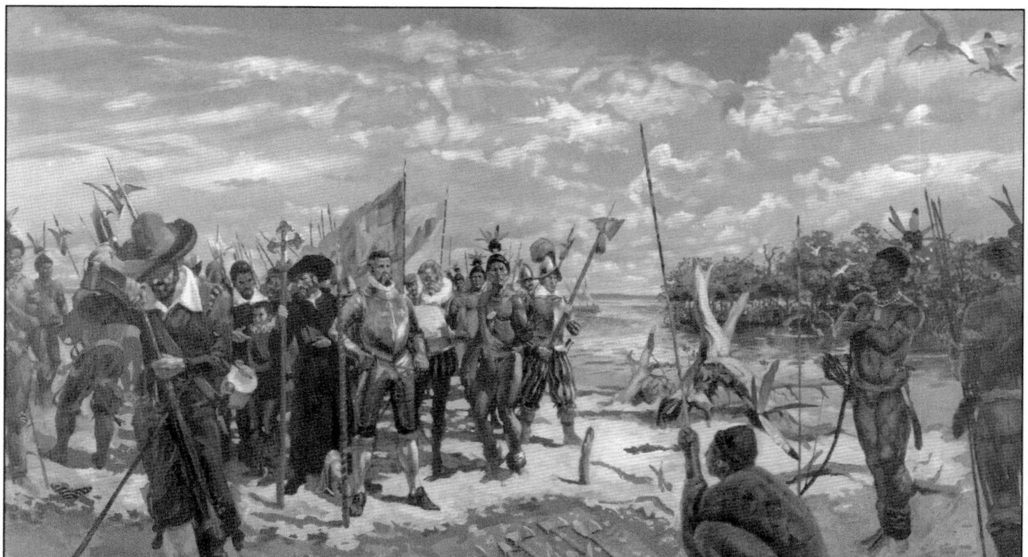

In 1568, Pedro Menendez de Aviles, the Spanish conqueror of Florida, visited the Tequesta Indian settlement on the north bank of the Miami River, at its mouth. Menendez is seen in the center of this painting, flanked by Spanish soldiers, as Tequesta Indians welcome him to the Spanish mission established among the natives the previous year. Menendez and his party stayed for four days and were entertained on one occasion by native children who performed a religious drama for him. (Painting by Ken Hughes, courtesy of HistoryMiami.)

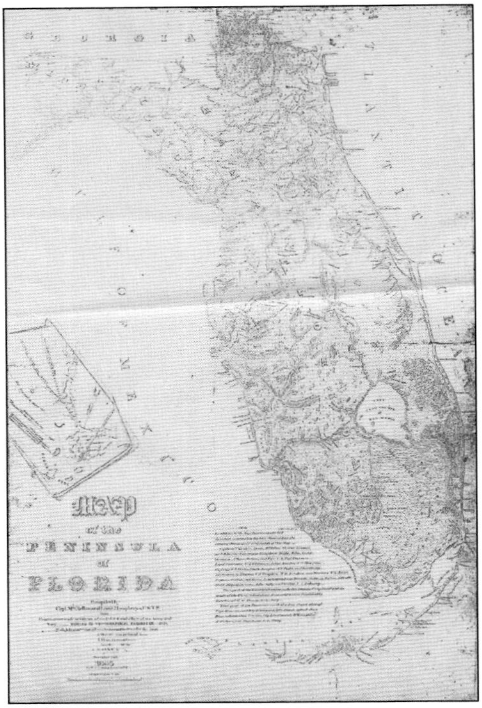

This survey by the US Bureau of Topographical Engineers dates to 1845, when the Territory of Florida was on the brink of statehood. The map indicates the topography of the land in southeast Florida, including hammock, prairie land, and, finally, Everglades swampland, which marked the earlier terminus of the Miami River. (Map by US Bureau of Engineers, courtesy of the author.)

On the cusp of statehood in 1845, Florida (especially its peninsula, depicted here) was a vast, often watery wilderness. In the lower right-hand corner of the map is Biscayne Bay. The Miami River, however, is not distinguishable. (Courtesy of the author.)

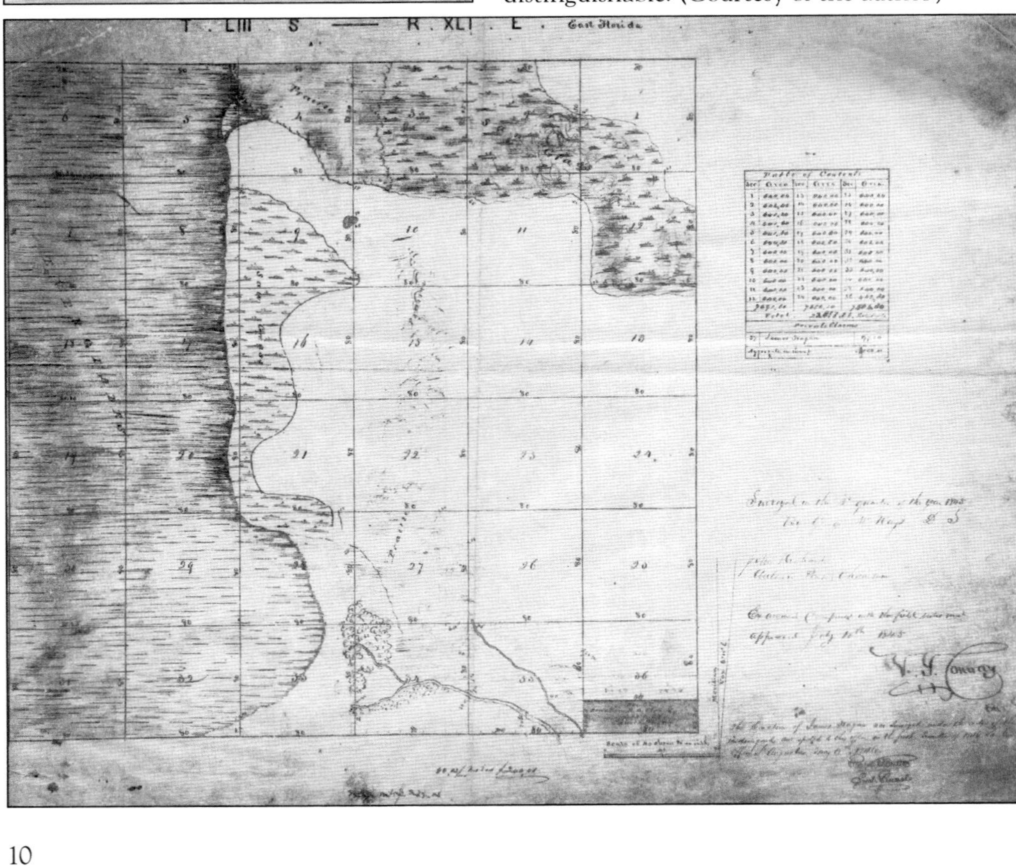

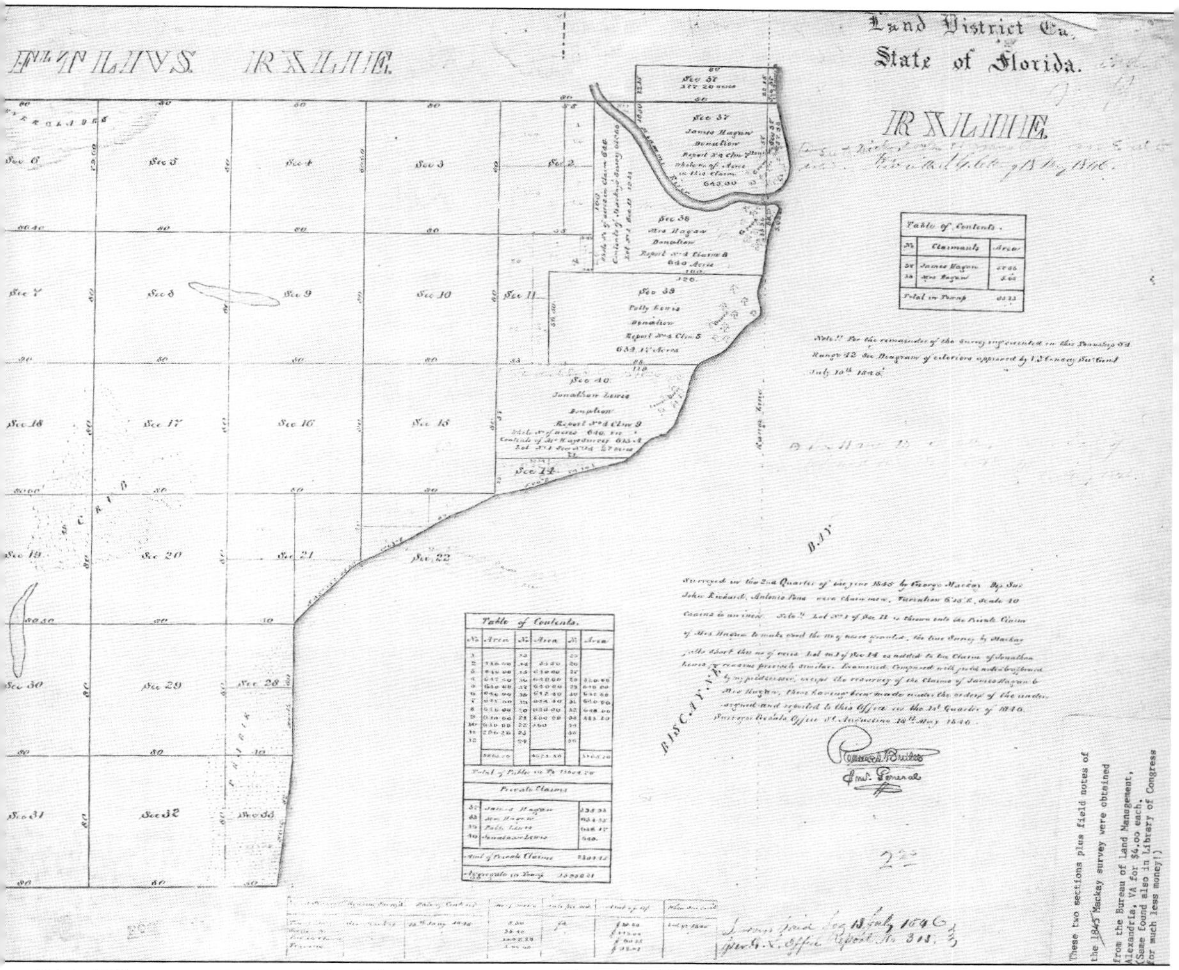

This US surveyor's map of the Miami area, created by the US Bureau of Land Management, dates to 1846. The "donations" refer to federal land grants given early families living on both sides of the Miami River and beyond. The grants dated back to the 1820s, when Florida became an American possession. (Courtesy of the author.)

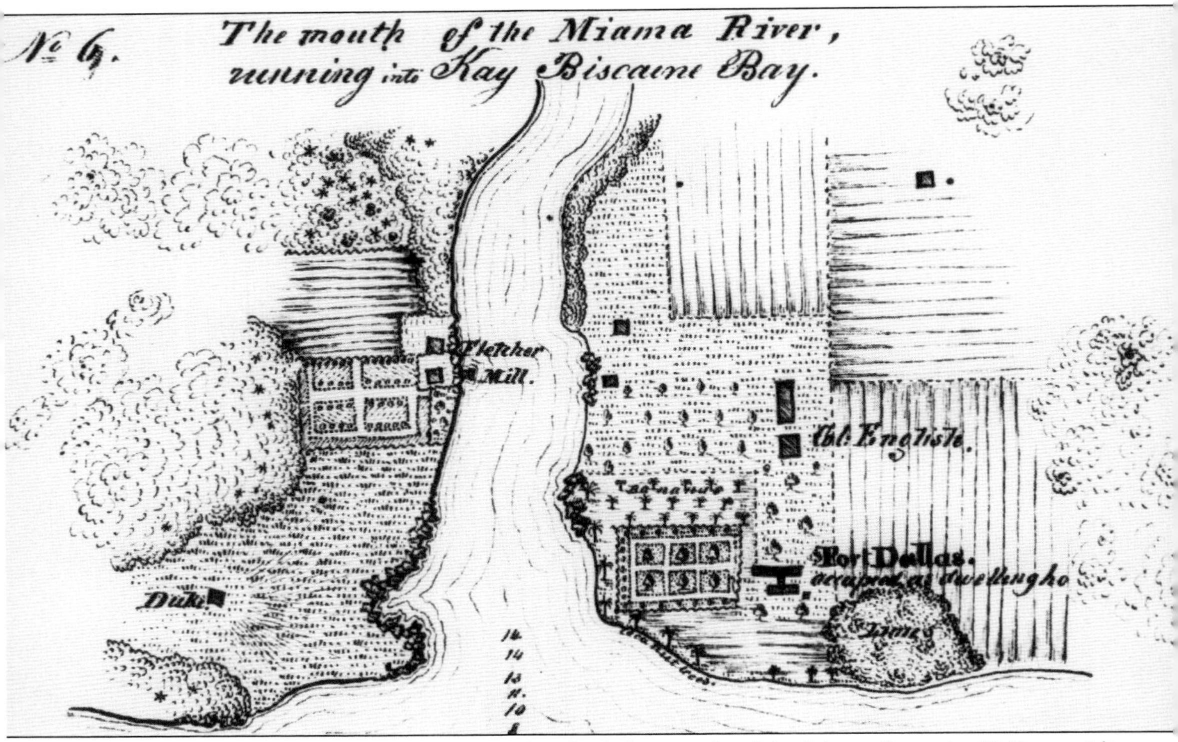

E.H. Gerdes of the US Coast Survey sketched the mouth of the Miami River in 1849, providing the first map of the area. Fort Dallas, noted on the lower right, was the Army fort that occupied part of William English's property in 1849. Fletcher's Mill, on the south bank of the stream, was a coontie starch mill operated by Dr. Robert Fletcher. Fletcher's property also hosted a store, a trading post, and even, for a time, the county courthouse. "Duke," in the lower left-hand corner of the image, refers to Reason Duke, who was once a keeper of the Cape Florida lighthouse on the southern tip of Key Biscayne. Note the spelling *Miama* River. (Courtesy of US Coast Survey, HistoryMiami.)

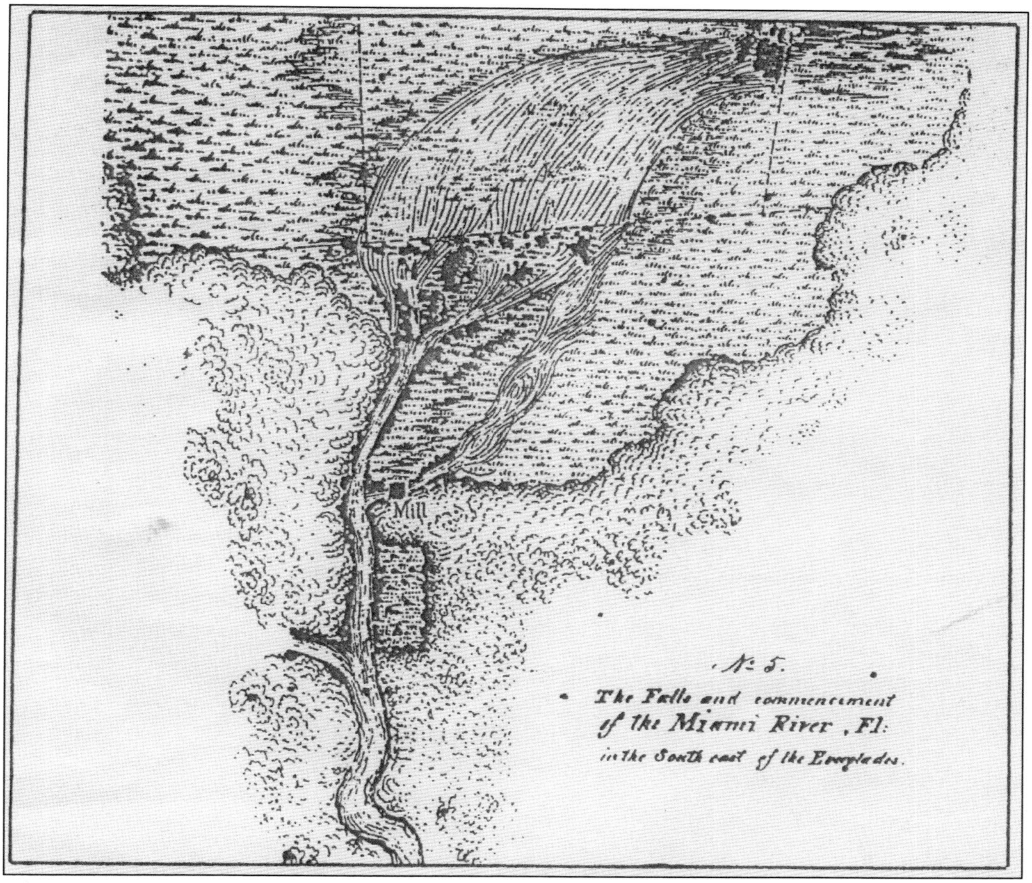

Also in 1849, E.H. Gerdes sketched the upper portions of the Miami River, including the falls and the headwaters, which, as noted, began at the eastern edge of the mysterious Everglades. (Courtesy of US Coast Survey, HistoryMiami.)

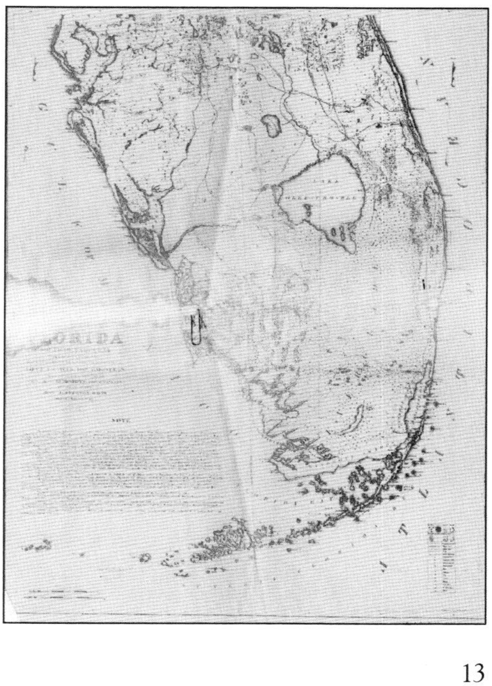

The J.C. Ives map of 1856, created just 11 years after Florida became the 27th state, outlines clearly the Everglades and Big Cypress, both lying south of Lake Okeechobee. A vast, intricate water system, emanating far north of the Everglades in the Kissimmee River basin, brought water to the Miami River and other streams in south Florida. (US Document No. 89. 82nd Congress, 1st Session; courtesy of the author.)

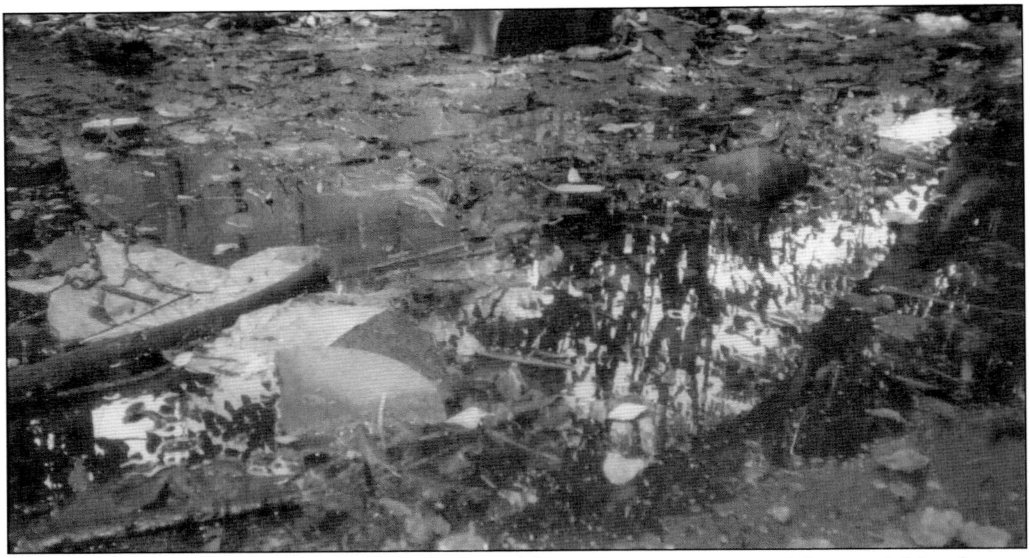

The former headwaters of the north fork of the Miami River are, as noted, but a trickle of water today since Everglades drainage, which began more than 100 years ago, radically transformed it by diverting water to the Miami Canal immediately to the north. Rocks, crab apple trees, and debris rise above the soft muck of the old riverbed. (Courtesy of Jim and Eileen Broton.)

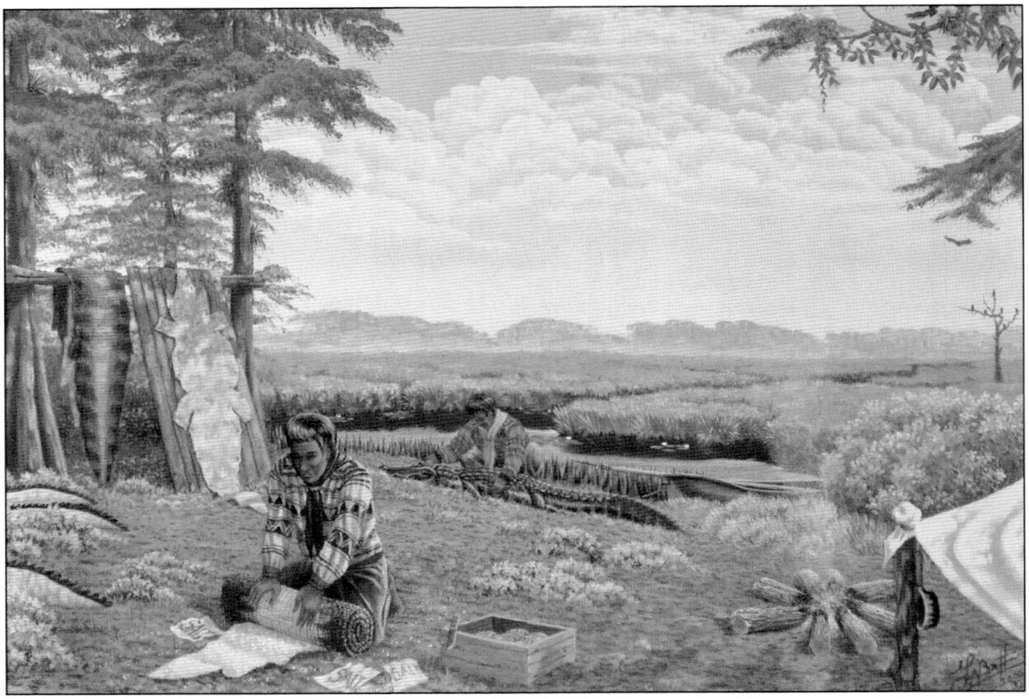

Guy Labree, the famed "Barefoot Artist of the Florida Seminoles," has painted these Native Americans for several decades. In this photograph of Labree's original oil painting, two Seminoles working near their wetlands redoubt are skinning alligators for their hides, which will be sold to Indian traders along southeast Florida waterways, including the Miami and New Rivers. (Courtesy of Ronald Risner.)

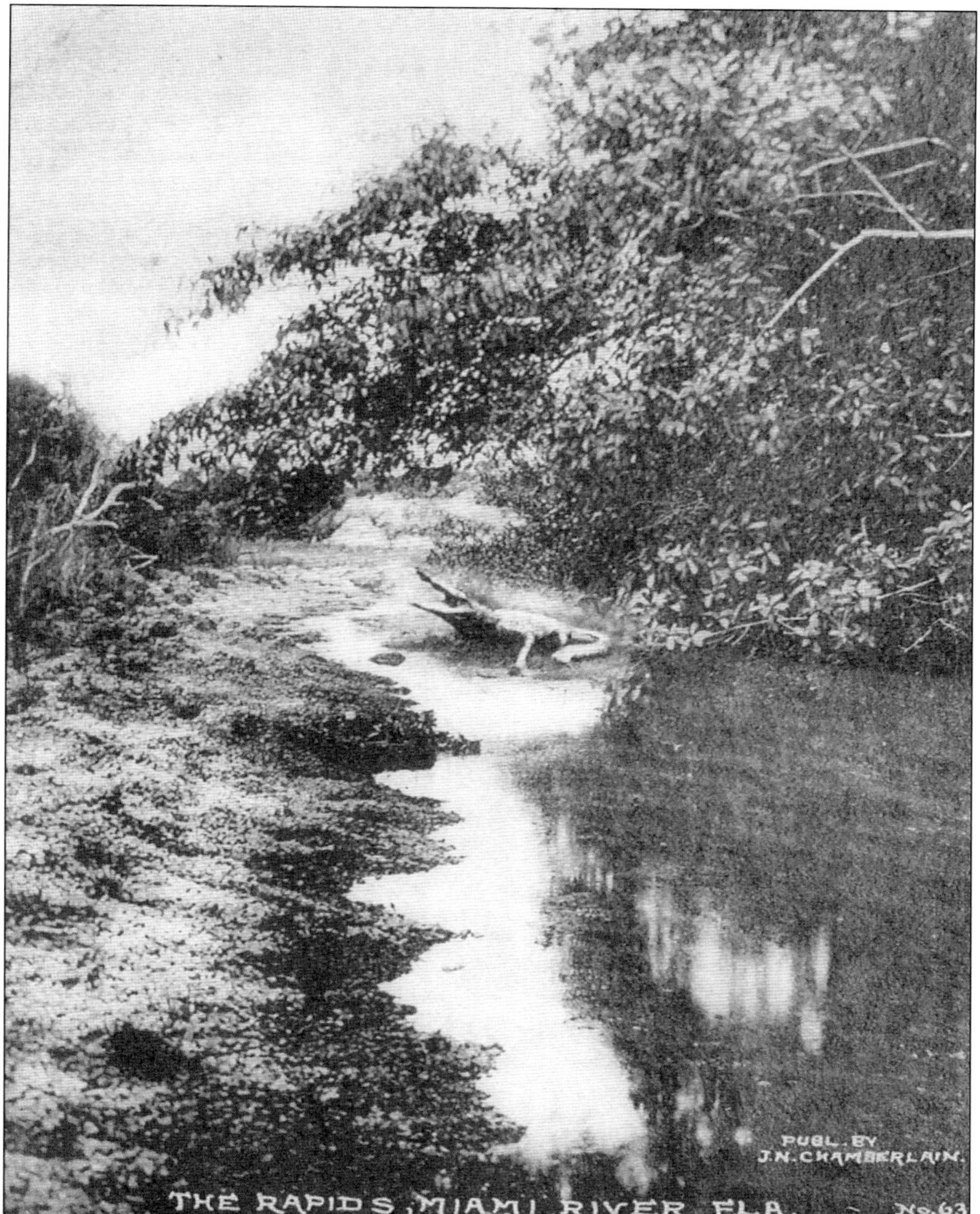

The Rapids of the Miami River represented a swift-flowing body of water just east of the falls, which marked the eastern edge of the Everglades. The rapids powered the Ferguson brothers' coontie starch mill, which was located along Ferguson's Creek (a contemporary name for the stream) in the 1840s and was Miami's largest business of that era. The rapids disappeared with Everglades drainage in the early 1900s. (Courtesy of Larry Wiggins.)

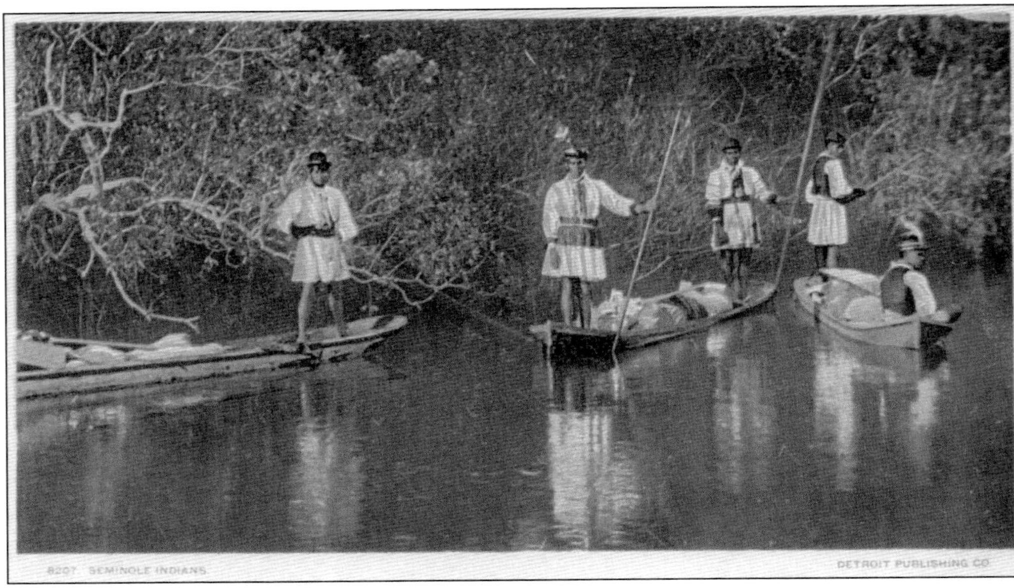

From the 1870s till the end of the 19th century, Native Americans—then identified only as Seminoles, but known today as Miccosukees (who lived in the far reaches of Dade County and beyond) and Seminoles (who lived in the future Broward and Palm Beach Counties, just north of Dade County)—poled downriver in their hardy dugout canoes, bringing goods from the nearby Everglades to traders like William Brickell and James Girtman near the mouth of the stream. Native American traders brought alligator eggs, steaks, skins, egret plumes, and coontie starch (used in baking and in thickening of soups and stews), all of which they exchanged for manufactured goods. This trade helped overcome decades of animosity and hostility between the races. (Both, courtesy of Larry Wiggins.)

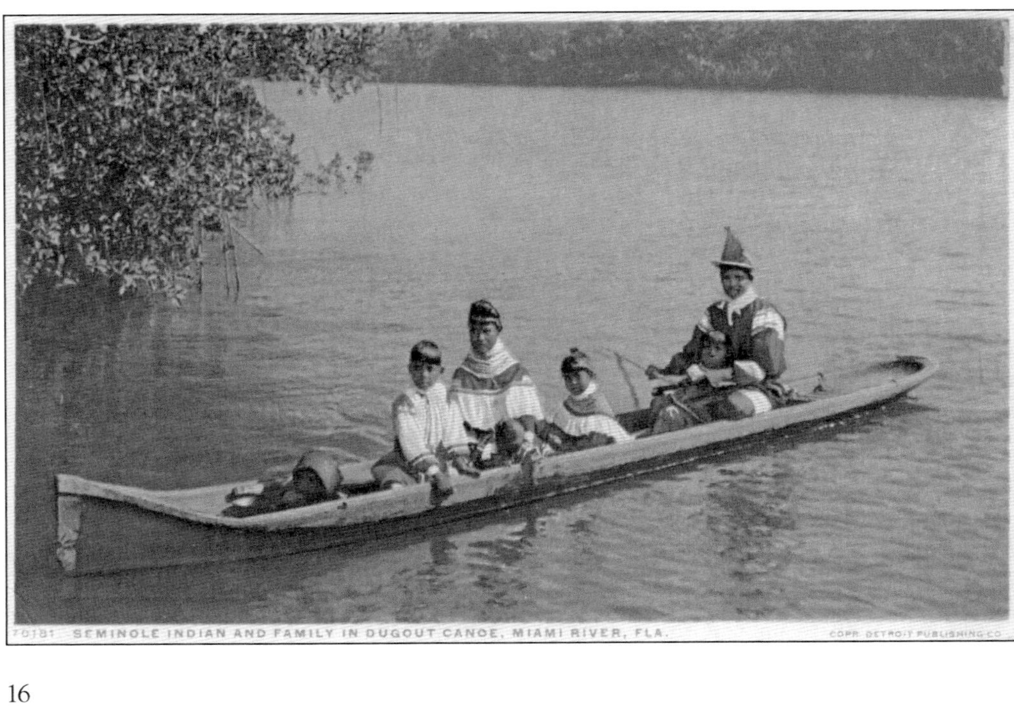

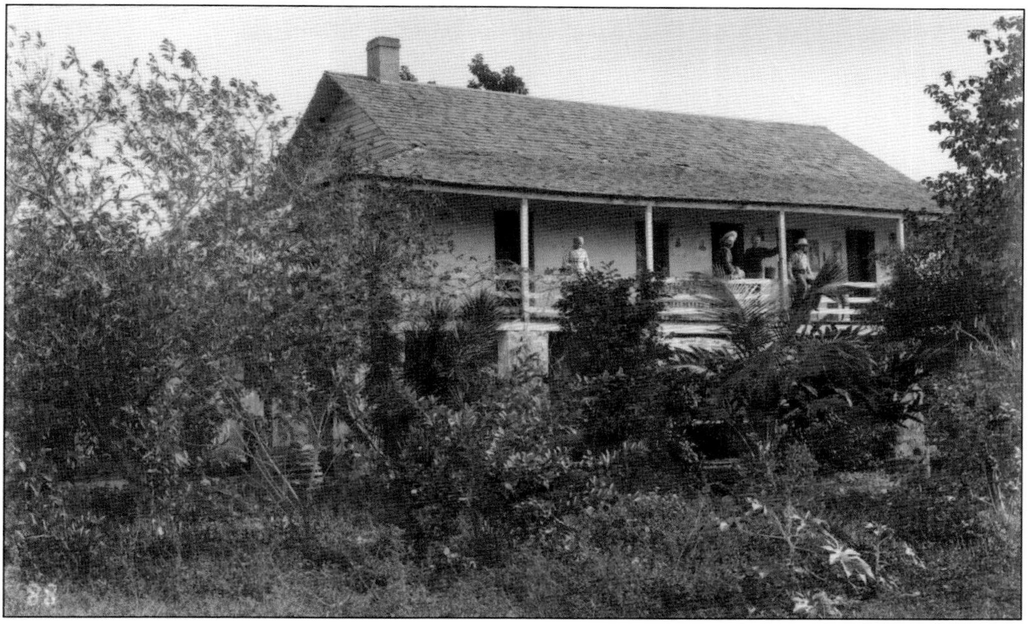

This slave plantation house, built by William English in the 1840s, hosted various occupants until Julia Tuttle and her two children moved there in November 1891. This photograph, by Coconut Grove Pioneer Ralph Munroe, dates from the 1880s. (Courtesy of HistoryMiami.)

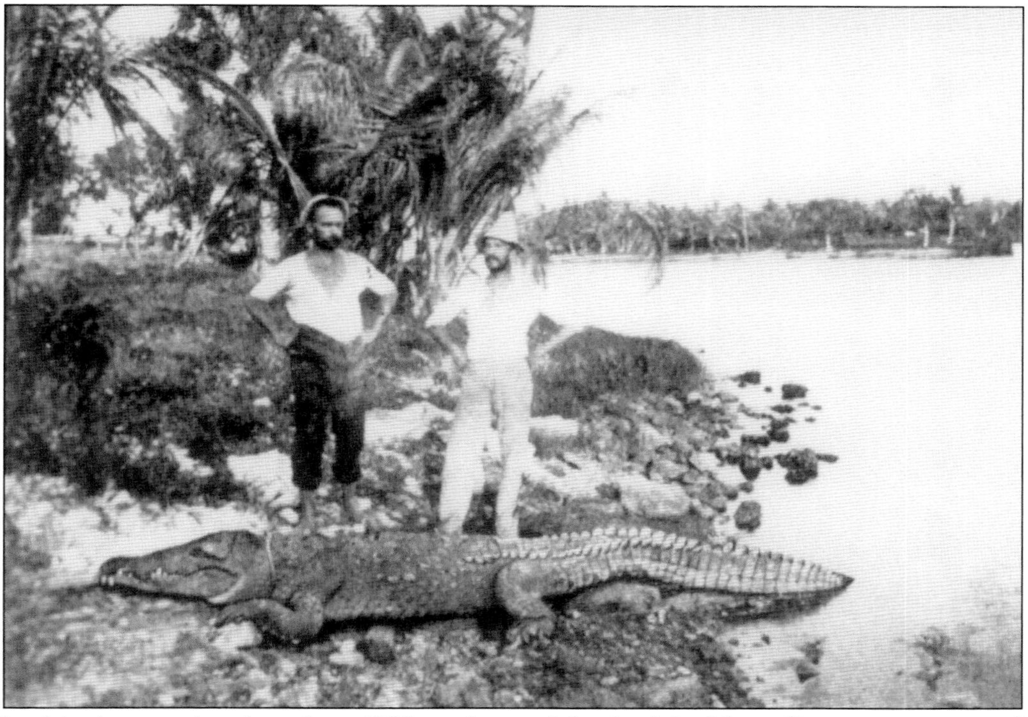

In this photograph, taken about 1890 on the north bank of the Miami River, two men stand triumphantly over an alligator they have captured in the stream. (Courtesy of the Arva Moore Parks Photograph Collection.)

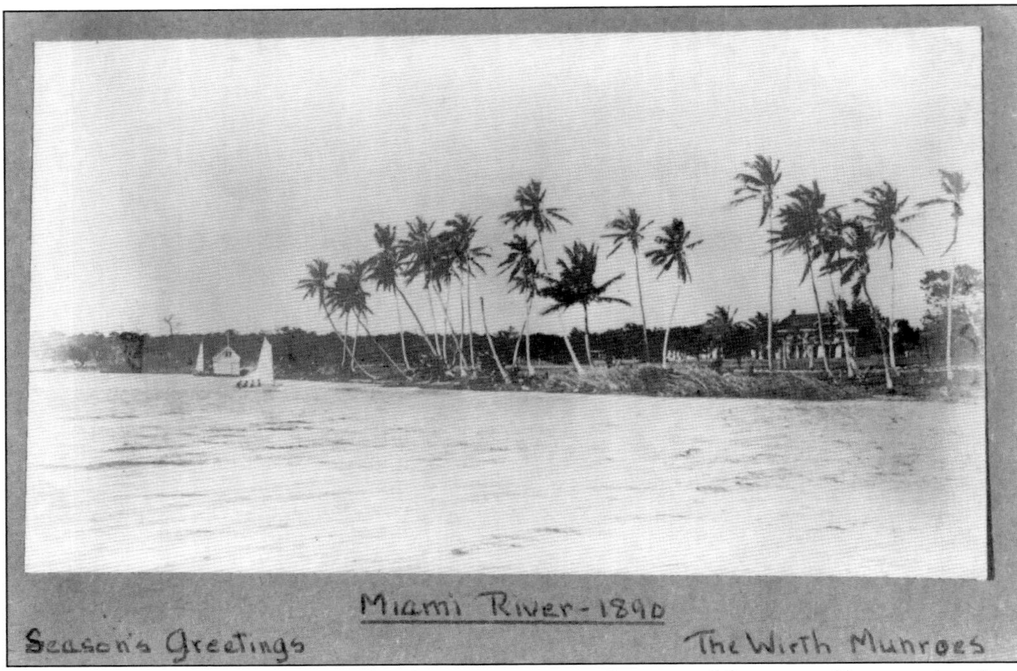

Although members of the Munroe family were prominent denizens of Cocoanut (the initial spelling of Coconut by the community) Grove, lying five miles south of the mouth of the Miami River, their "season's greetings" card for 1890 showcases the pristine stream. Taken from the south bank of the river, the photograph shows the old William English Slave Plantation House/Fort Dallas, which would be occupied by Julia Tuttle and her two children the following year. (Courtesy of the Arva Moore Parks Photograph Collection.)

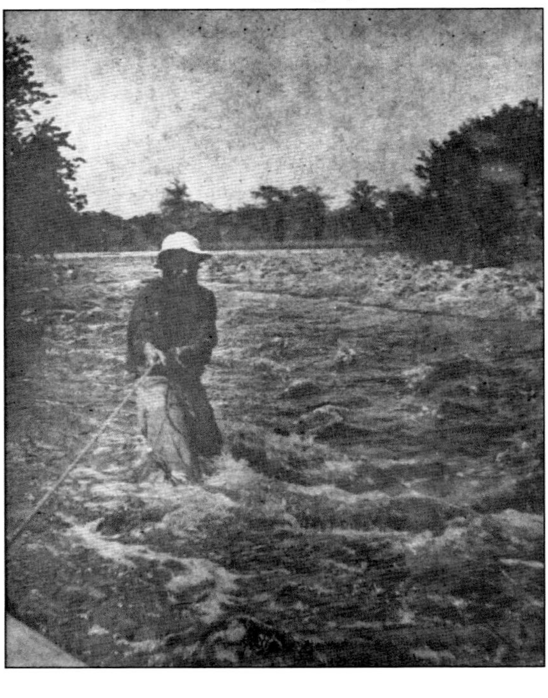

This photograph, taken at the outset of the 20th century, shows a lone figure amid the tumultuous rapids of the Miami River's north fork. The rapids powered a coontie mill in the mid-19th century, and the starch produced by the mill was the most significant trade item exported from sparsely settled Dade County. The rapids were gone about a half century later. (Courtesy of HistoryMiami.)

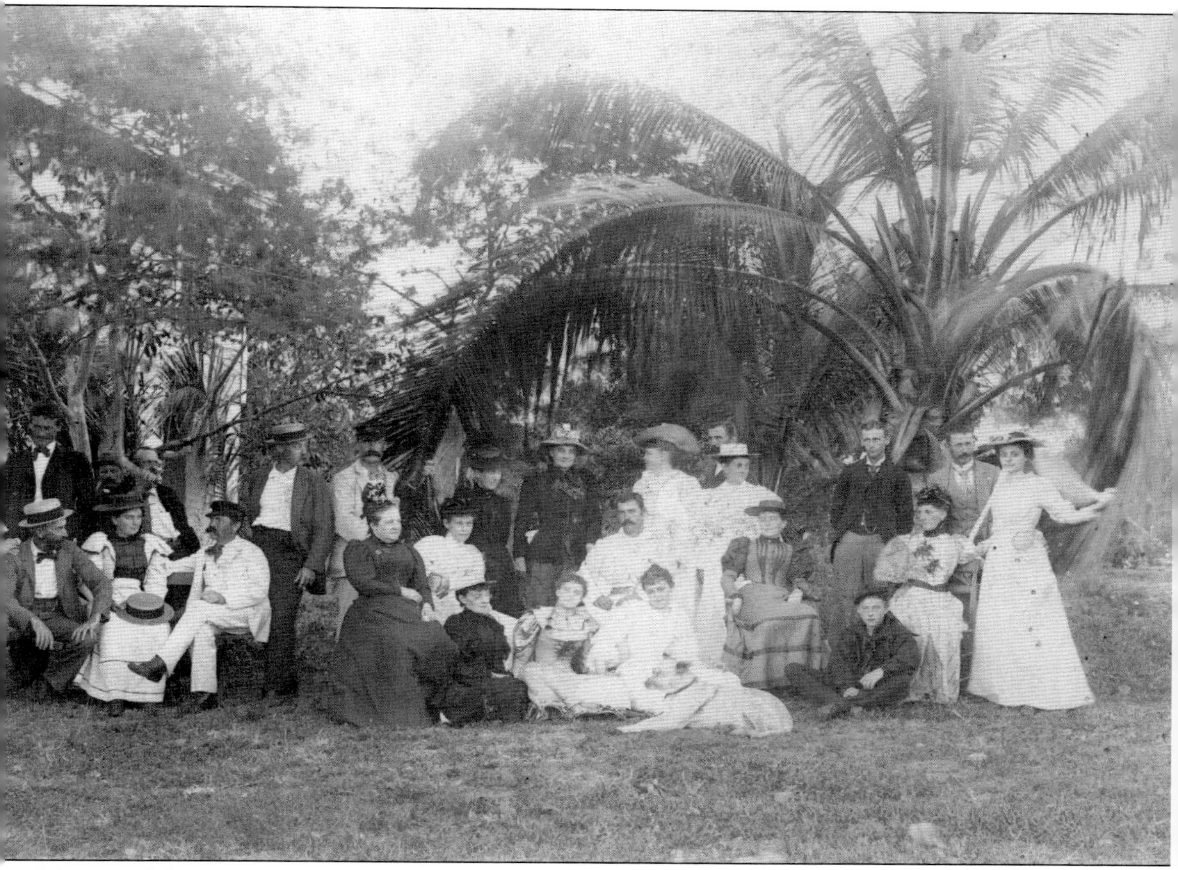

Miami and the communities flanking Biscayne Bay claimed few residents in the years immediately preceding the entry of the Florida East Coast Railway in April 1896, but the camaraderie between these communities was strong. Pictured in the mid-1890s on the lovely grounds surrounding the former officers' quarters of Fort Dallas (by then the home of Julia Tuttle, the "Mother of Miami") are members of Tuttle's family, along with many of the leading lights of Coconut Grove, a robust frontier community south of Miami. Included in the photograph are Isabella Peacock (in front, dressed in black), who, along with her family, managed the Peacock Inn in Coconut Grove. Julia Tuttle, wearing a white dress, stands behind son Harry and daughter Frances, both also adorned in white. Seated near the right-hand corner of the photograph, in white with a black headdress, is Flora McFarlane, an important figure in Coconut Grove. The Miami River runs just south this site. (Courtesy of HistoryMiami.)

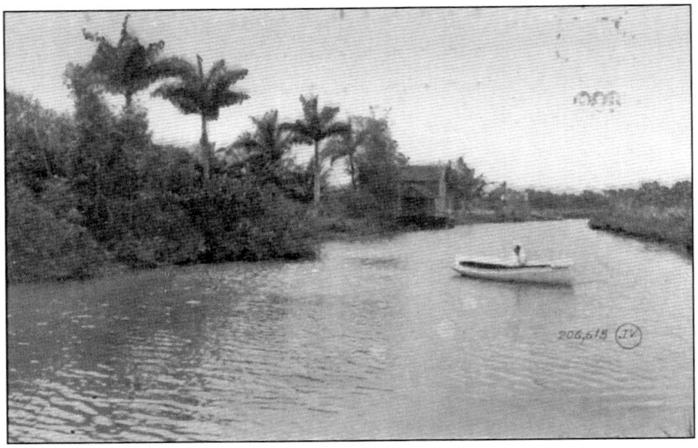

This 1909 postcard finds a lone mariner upriver while a nearby wood-frame structure sits by itself amid a profusion of foliage on the south bank of the river. The back of the card contains a paean to the beauty of Miami and its river, as the writer observes that his vessel was "winding in and out of the Everglades." He also notes that alligators on the banks were sunning themselves. (Courtesy of Ronald Risner.)

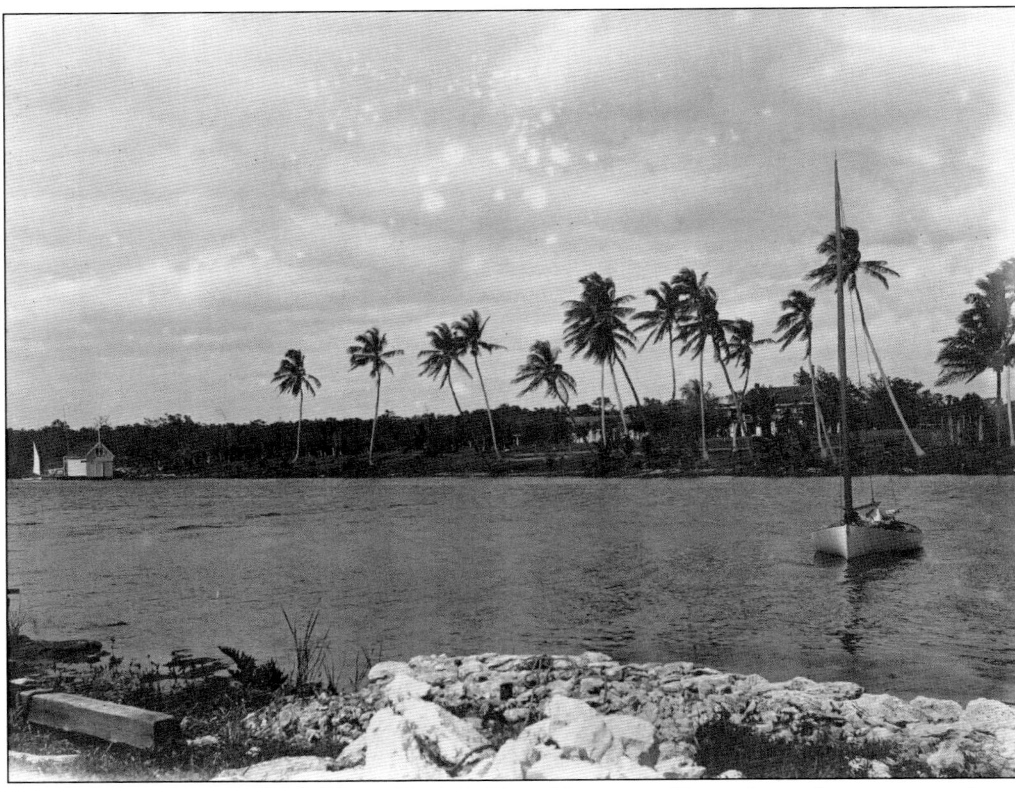

This view is of Fort Dallas/William English Slave Plantation House from the vantage point of the south bank of the river, an area owned by the land-rich Brickell family. Julia Tuttle's move to the old fort in 1891 represented a transformational moment in the history of Miami. (Courtesy of Ralph Munroe, HistoryMiami.)

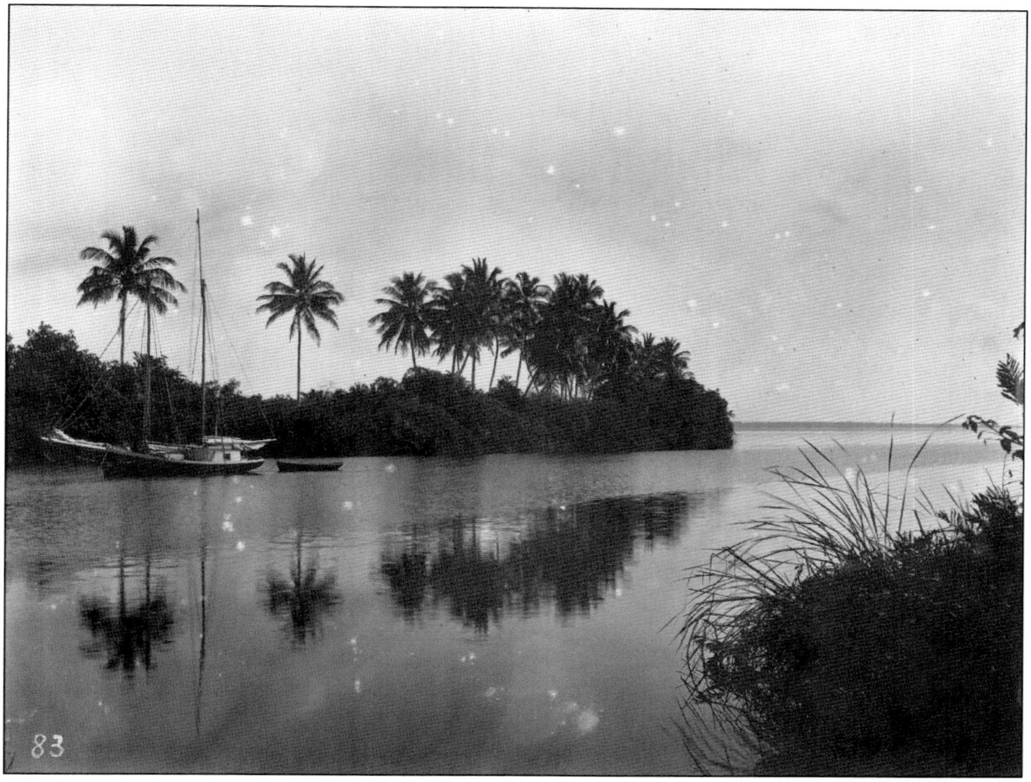

The beautiful Miami River is seen here through the lens of Ralph Munroe's camera in the 1880s. The north bank, in the upper part of the photograph, was verdant with coconut palms and other trees. Biscayne Bay lurks beyond the mouth of the river. The man-made islands that fill the same segment of the bay today are nowhere to be seen in this image. In the distance is a barrier peninsula, known today as Miami Beach. (Courtesy of HistoryMiami.)

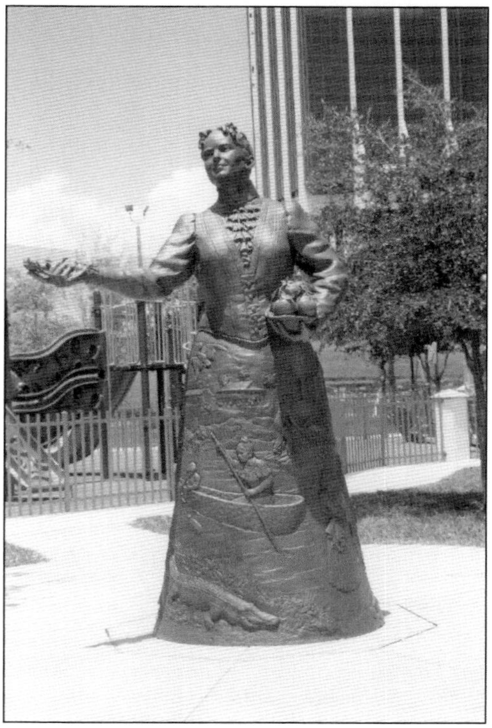

This handsome bronze statue of Julia Tuttle, the "Mother of Miami" (so named for her role in bringing Henry M. Flagler's Florida East Coast Railway to the settlement in 1896), stands tall in Bayfront Park, where it was dedicated on the city's 114th birthday, July 28, 2010. Built on landfill, Bayfront Park stands just north of the Miami River and a few blocks northeast of Julia's riverfront home. (Courtesy of Laura Morilla.)

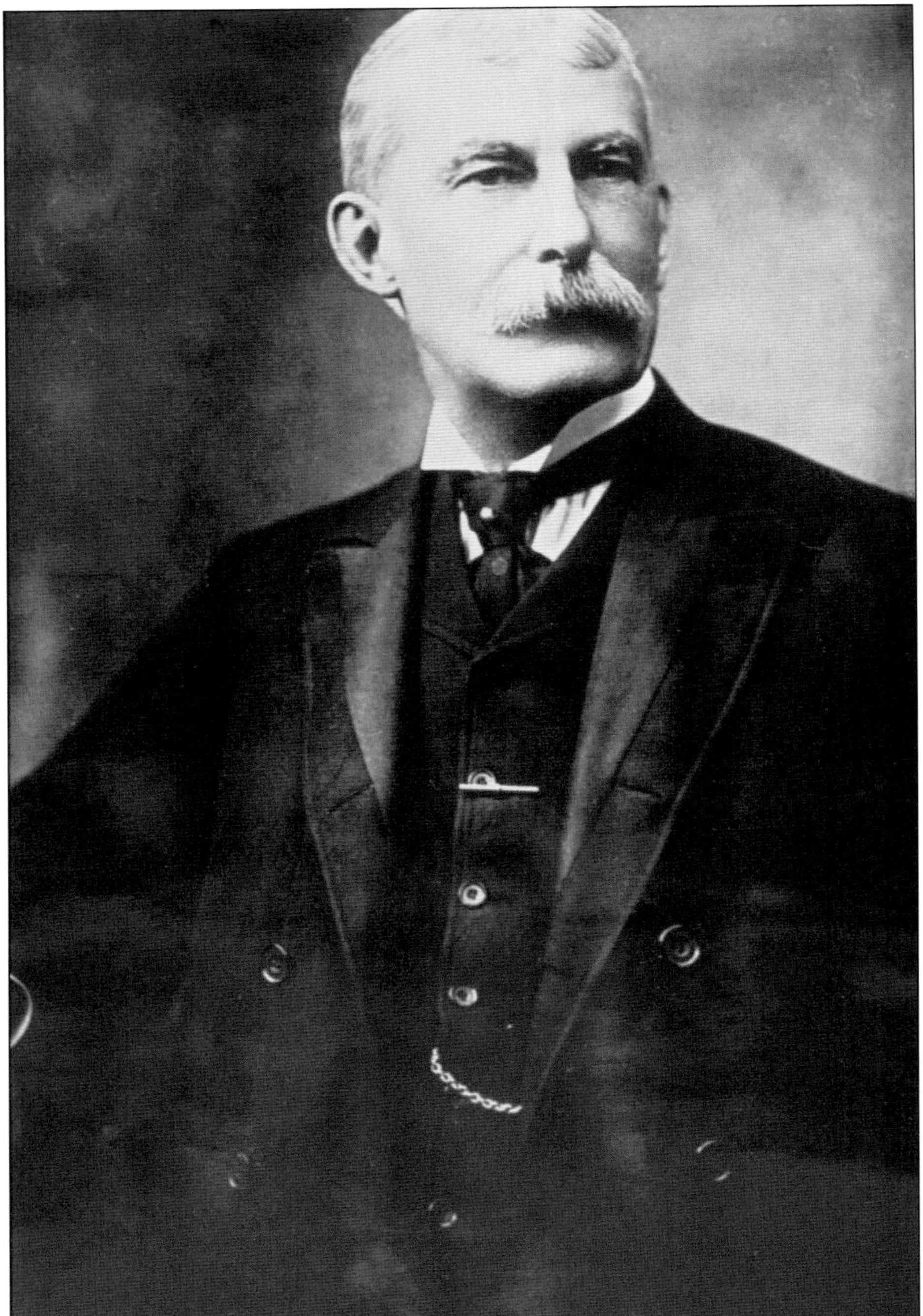

Henry M. Flagler, the great oil baron and railroad mogul, brought his Florida East Coast Railway to Miami for the first time on April 13, 1896, transforming a wilderness into a city within a few months of the train's arrival. Flagler quickly built several important components of the fledgling city, positioning it to become both a tourist haven and a shipping center. This striking photograph depicts Henry Flagler in the twilight of his splendid career. (Courtesy of Andrew Melick.)

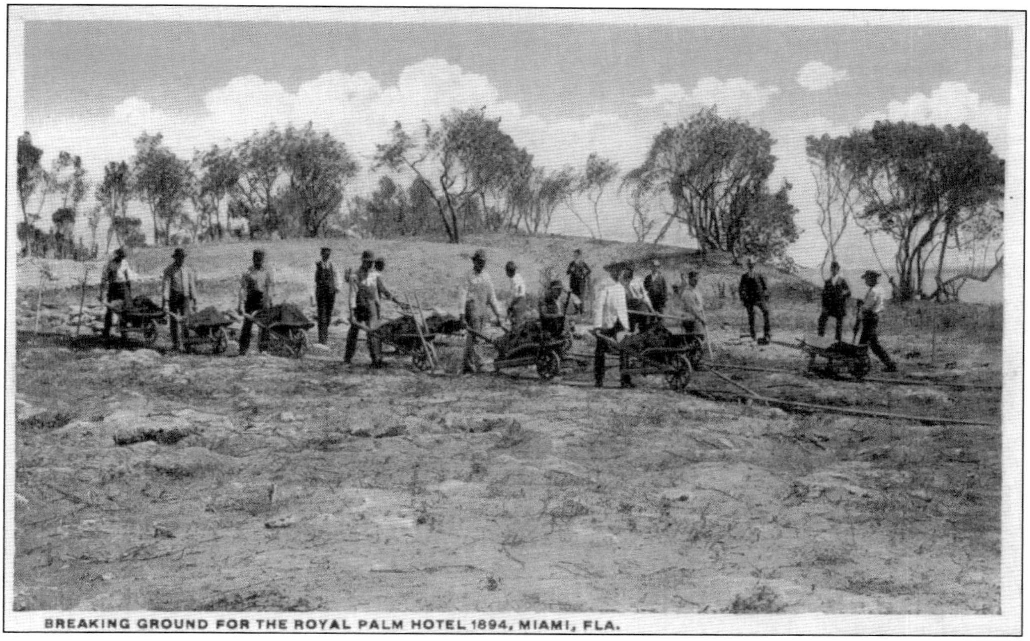

Joseph Chamberlain took this picture on March 3, 1896, marking the day workers began clearing land for Henry M. Flagler's Royal Palm Hotel, located near the confluence of the north bank of the Miami River and Biscayne Bay. The workers (many of whom came to Miami from West Palm Beach, where they were working on other Flagler projects) are carting away the remains of bodies found in the Indian burial mound that had previously occupied a portion of the site. The Royal Palm Hotel opened in January 1897 and closed for the final time after the 1927–1928 season. It was razed two years later. (Courtesy of Larry Wiggins.)

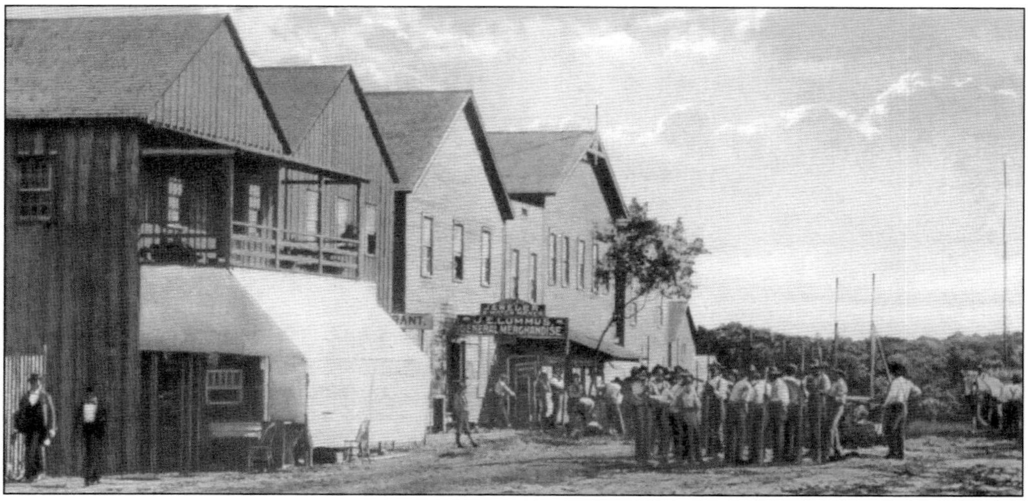

Miami was a barren wilderness in 1895, with just nine people living along the Miami River, according to the Florida State Census. That year, however, when assured by Henry Flagler that he was prepared to bring his Florida East Coast Railway to Miami, Julia Tuttle began preparing to develop her land around the river. This 1896 photograph shows a large workforce gathered on the first street, Avenue D (later known as Miami Avenue), stretching north from the Miami River on its north bank. (Courtesy of Larry Wiggins.)

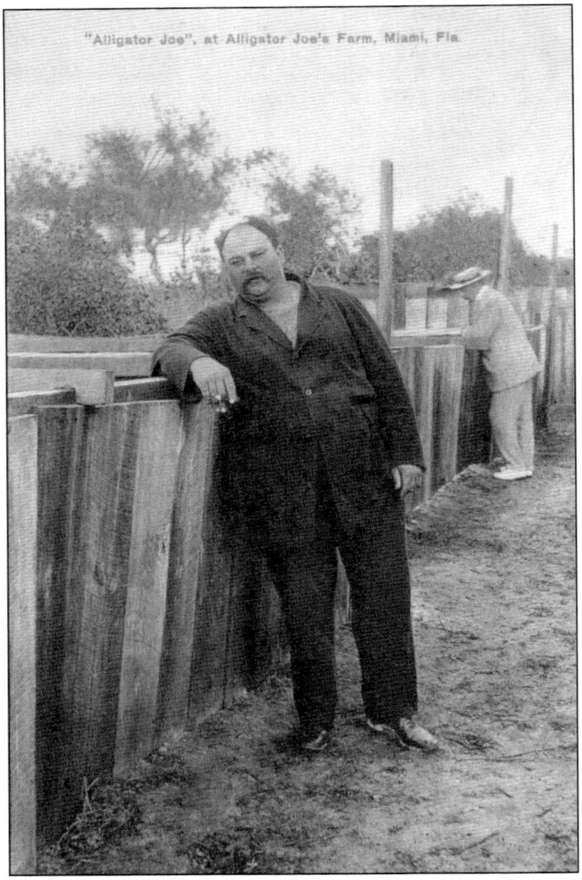

Warren Frazee, also known as "Alligator Joe," opened one of Miami's first tourist attractions at the juncture of the Miami River and Wagner Creek, just beyond the edge of the city limits, in 1898. Alligator Joe's Crocodile & Alligator Farm became a popular tourist attraction, featuring this burly, fearless man wrestling alligators and crocodiles in front of boatloads of tourists dressed to the nines in the formal attire of that era. The attraction operated on a portion of today's Spring Garden Point Park till 1910. The photograph at left shows Alligator Joe standing by one of his crocodile pens, while the picture below depicts the proud showman with a recent catch. (Both, courtesy of Larry Wiggins.)

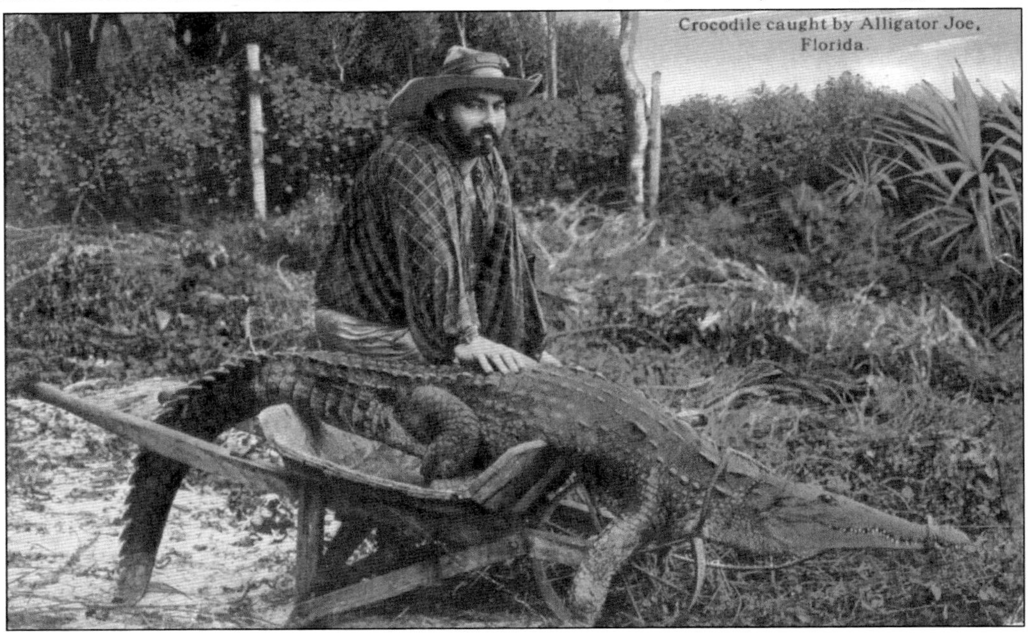

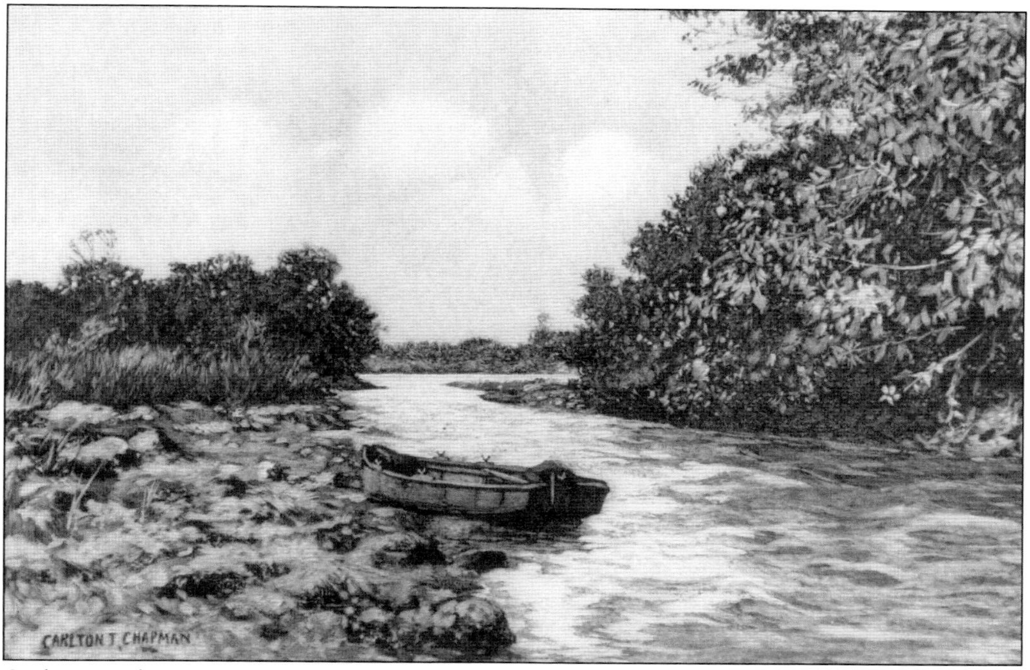

Carlton T. Chapman's painting of the rapids of the Miami River appeared in an issue of *Scribner's Magazine* around 1900. (Courtesy of the Arva Moore Parks Photograph Collection.)

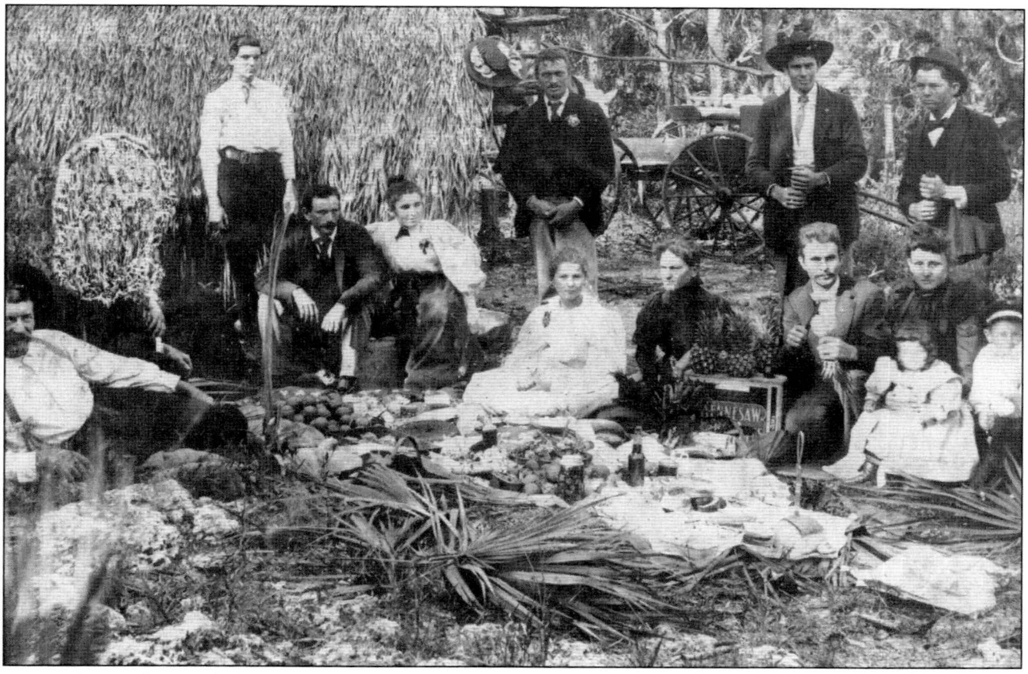

Several members of the pioneering Coates family, along with their neighbors, are pictured in the late 1890s, enjoying an outing near the headwaters of the north fork of the Miami River and Ferguson's Creek. Just west of them stood the eastern edge of the Everglades. (Courtesy of the Florida State Photographic Archives.)

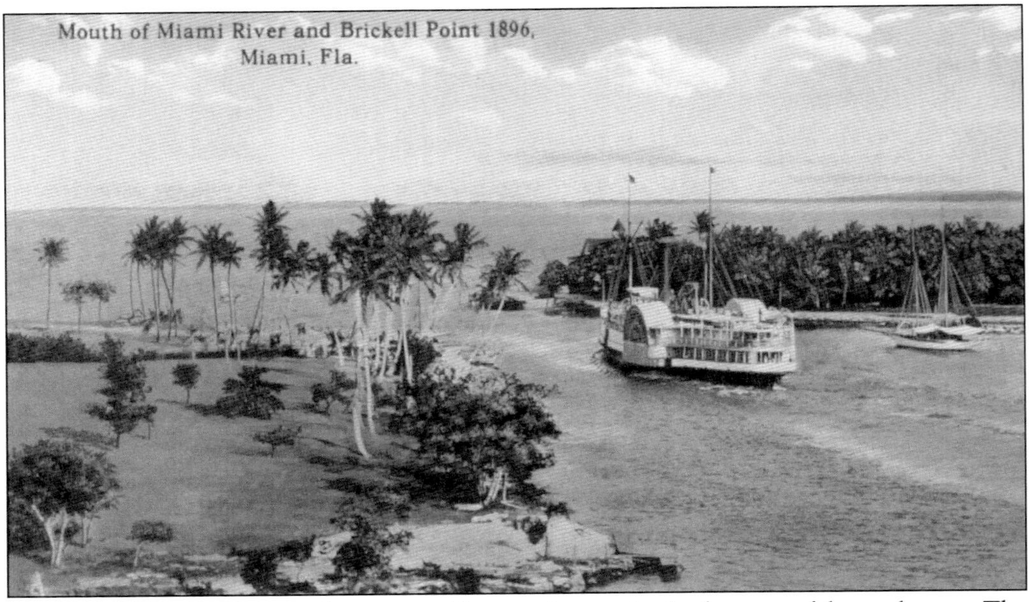

Miami's birth year, 1896, was characterized by vast changes in the fortunes of the settlement. The hand of Henry M. Flagler, the "Father of Miami," was seen in many elements of the fledgling city. He employed the small side-wheeler *St. Lucie* (pictured here in 1896 near the mouth of the Miami River) to carry the first materials for construction of his Royal Palm Hotel. Later, Flagler chartered a larger vessel for the same purpose. (Courtesy of the Arva Moore Parks Photograph Collection.)

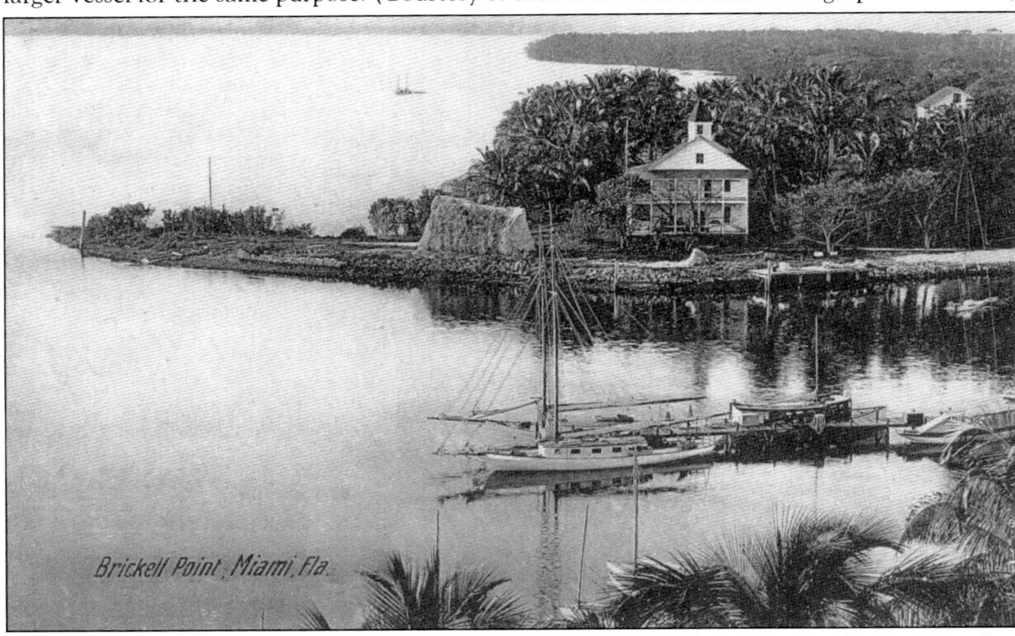

This turn-of-the-20th-century photograph finds the Brickell trading post, on the south bank of the Miami River near its mouth, still standing. It would not be for long, however, as the family's vast landholdings brought a new stream of revenue and great prosperity. The upper portions of the photograph indicate how verdant today's booming Brickell Avenue neighborhood once was. (Courtesy of Larry Wiggins.)

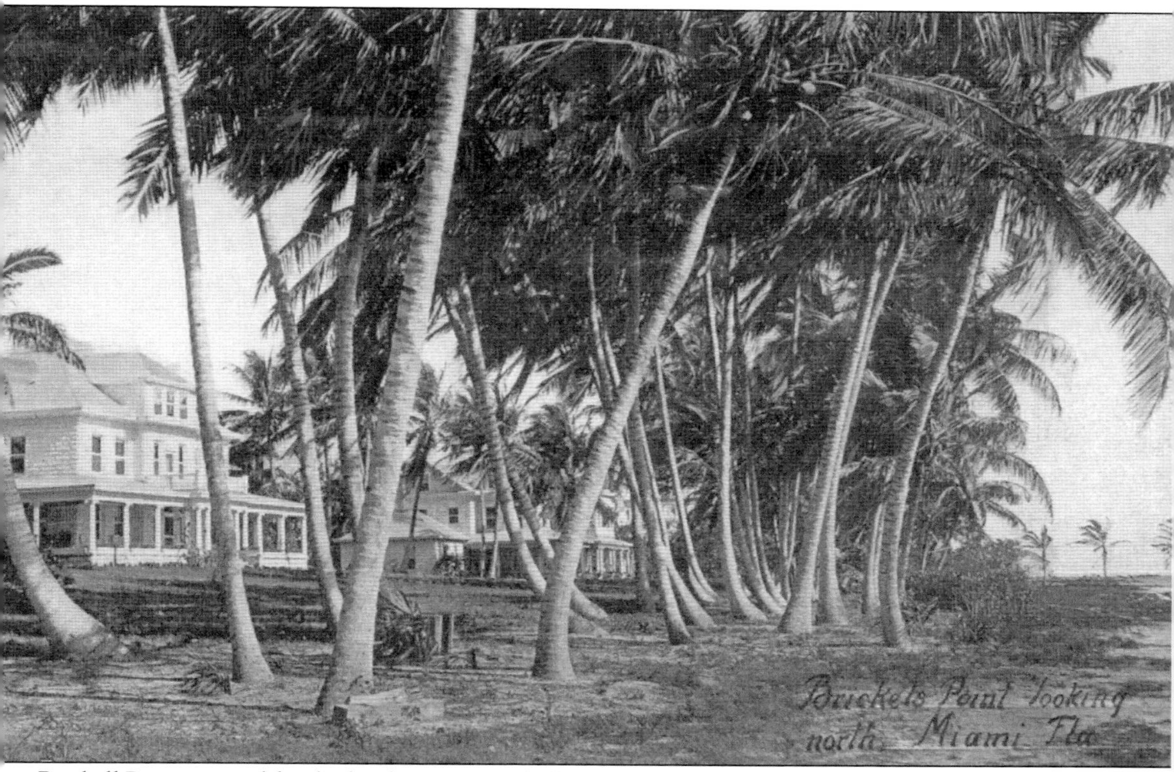

Brickell Point, named for the landowning Brickell family, references the south bank of the Miami River at the mouth of the stream. The homes in this early-1900s postcard image were among several built by the Brickells, who earlier had operated an Indian trading post on the site. (Courtesy of Larry Wiggins and Ronnie Hurwitz.)

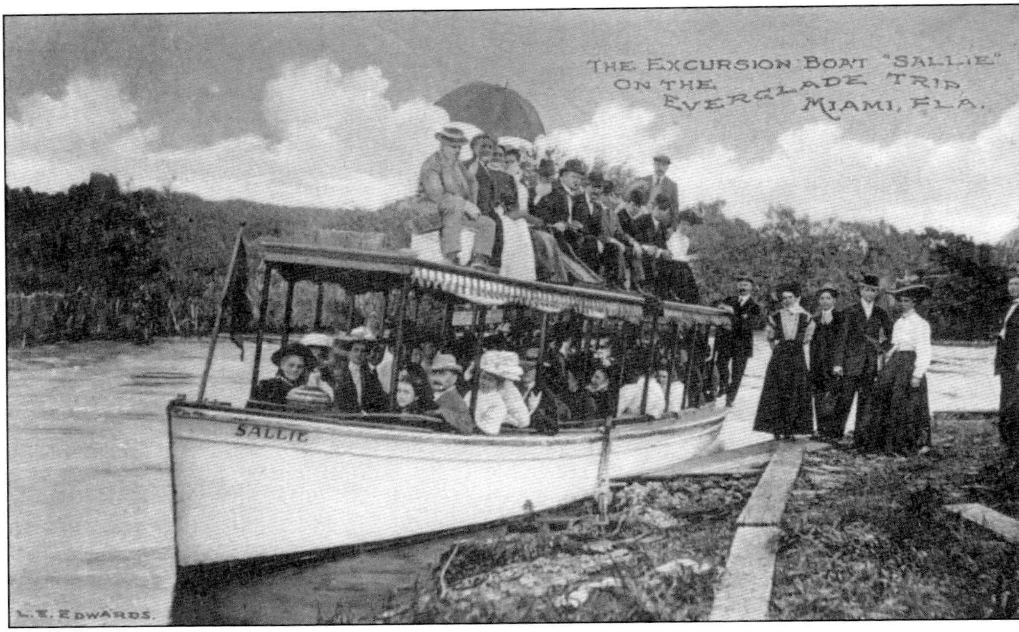

Beginning in the early 1900s, excursions on the Miami River were a favorite activity for visitors. The *Sallie* was the most popular of the vessels taking tourists upriver to the eastern edge of the Everglades. In the background of both photographs, tall mangrove trees stand at water's edge. (Both, courtesy of Larry Wiggins.)

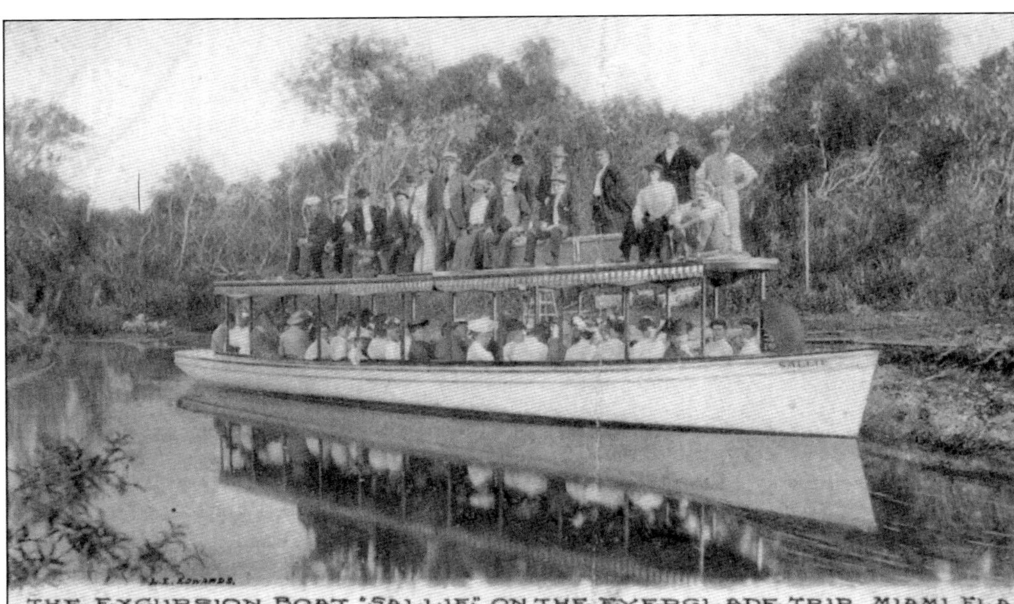

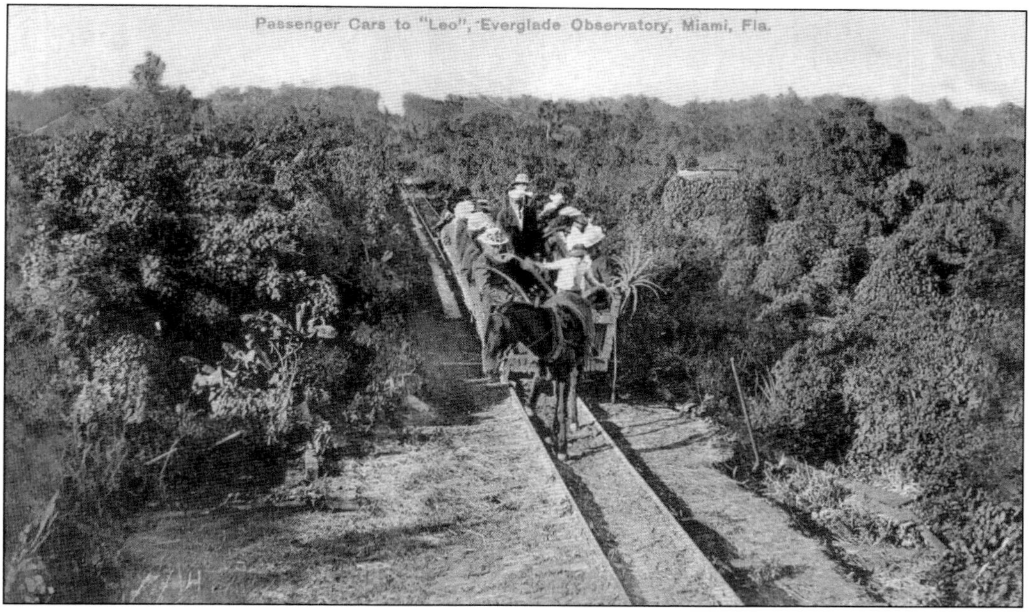

Pictured around 1903, these passengers are traveling the "Everglades Railway" to a large house on the edge of the Everglades. The building featured a second-floor viewing area, called the "Leo Observatory" after the *Leo*, the double-decked boat that brought passengers to the Everglades. The service operated till 1908, when the construction of a low fixed bridge at Northwest Twenty-seventh Avenue rendered it impossible for the vessel to proceed farther west to the edge of the Everglades. (Courtesy of Larry Wiggins.)

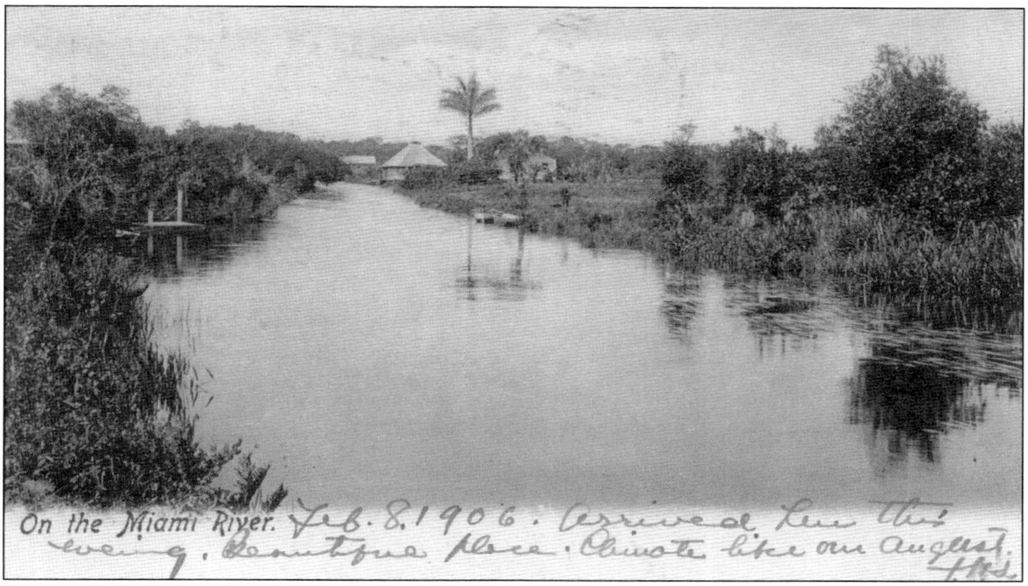

Postcards depicting the Miami River were popular almost from the time of the city's inception in 1896. The shoreline of the stream was verdant with subtropical trees as late as the mid-20th century. This photograph shows the north fork of the Miami River near its headwaters, while the structure next to a royal palm tree is believed to have been an Indian trading post. (Courtesy of Larry Wiggins.)

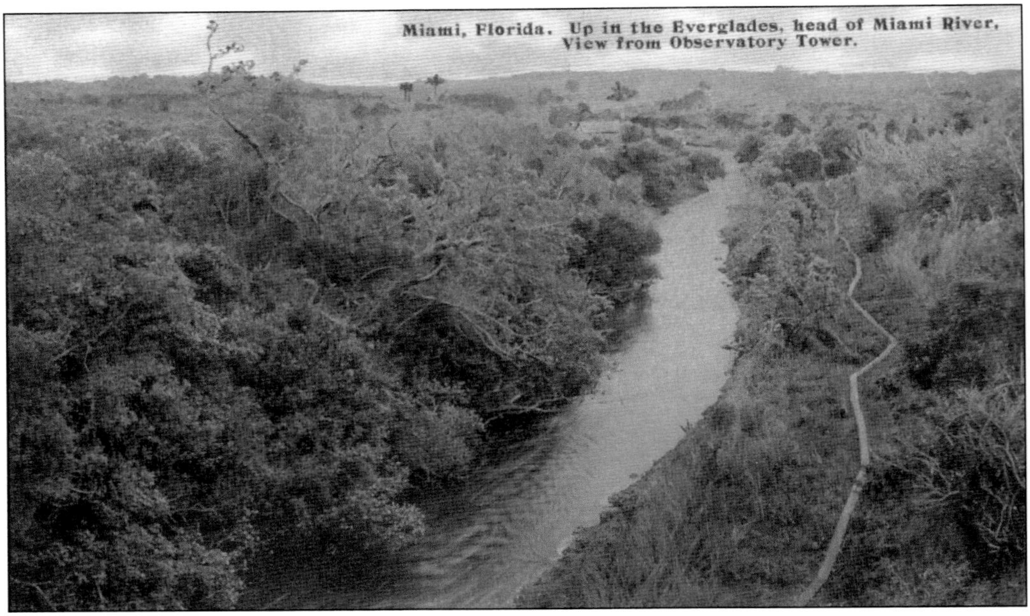

By 1912, Musa Isle was also hosting the Cardale Resort, which offered a skating rink and dance floor in a large building shaped like a Quonset hut. Standing adjacent to the structure and at the edge of the river was an approximately 90-foot-tall observatory tower. Known as the Cardale Tower, it attracted many climbers who peered west at the vast Everglades beyond them. Their view is captured in these photographs from the structure. (Both, courtesy of Larry Wiggins.)

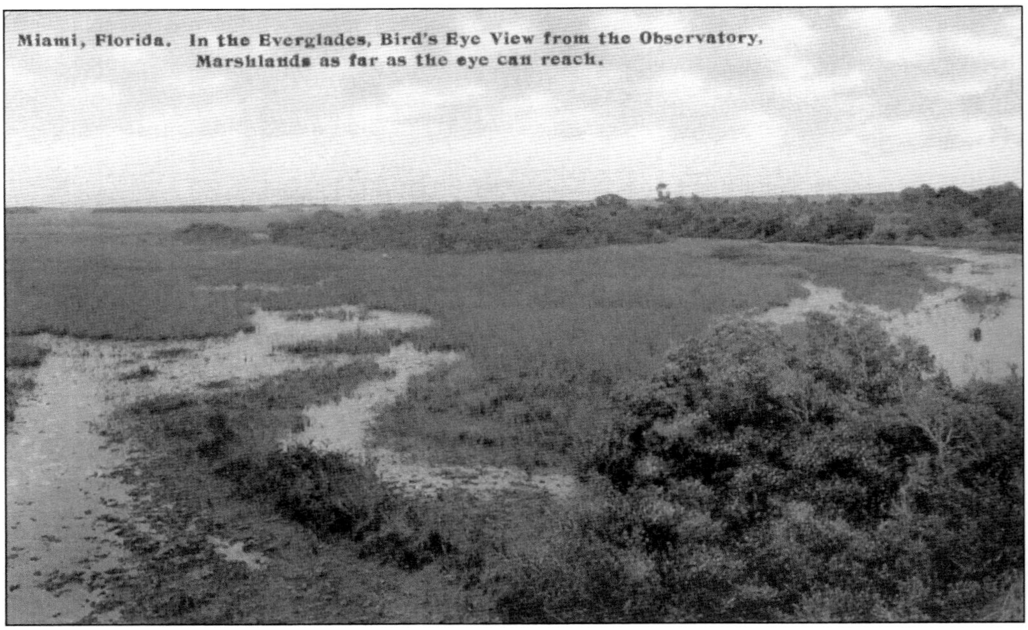

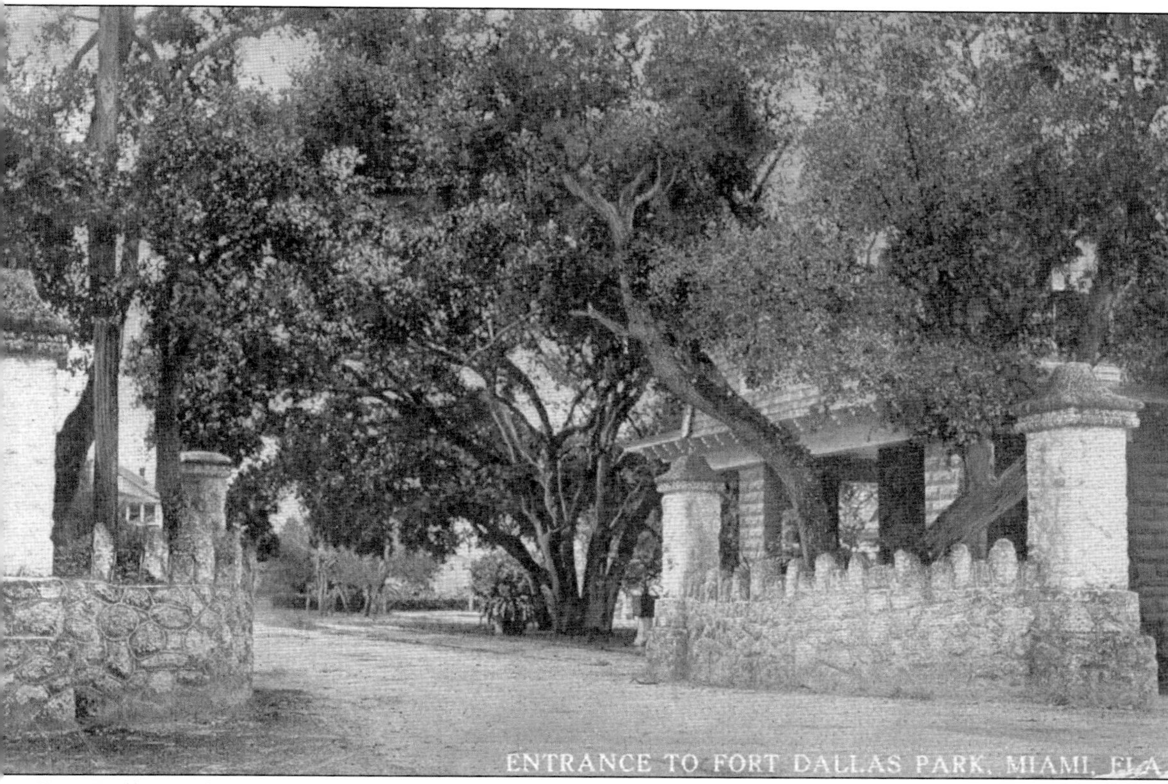

Fort Dallas Park arose at the outset of the 20th century on property owned by the Tuttles. Developed by Harry Tuttle, the son of Julia Tuttle, Fort Dallas Park ("Fort Dallas" being an early name for Miami) was a beautiful subdivision stretching from the north shore of the Miami River to Southeast Second Street and from Miami Avenue to east side of Southeast First Avenue, near the western edges of the Royal Palm Hotel property. The elaborate entrance stood on Southeast First Avenue. Many of early Miami's most prominent residents lived in elegant wood-frame homes in Fort Dallas Park, and the neighborhood remained viable till the end of the 1960s. (Courtesy of Ronnie Hurwitz.)

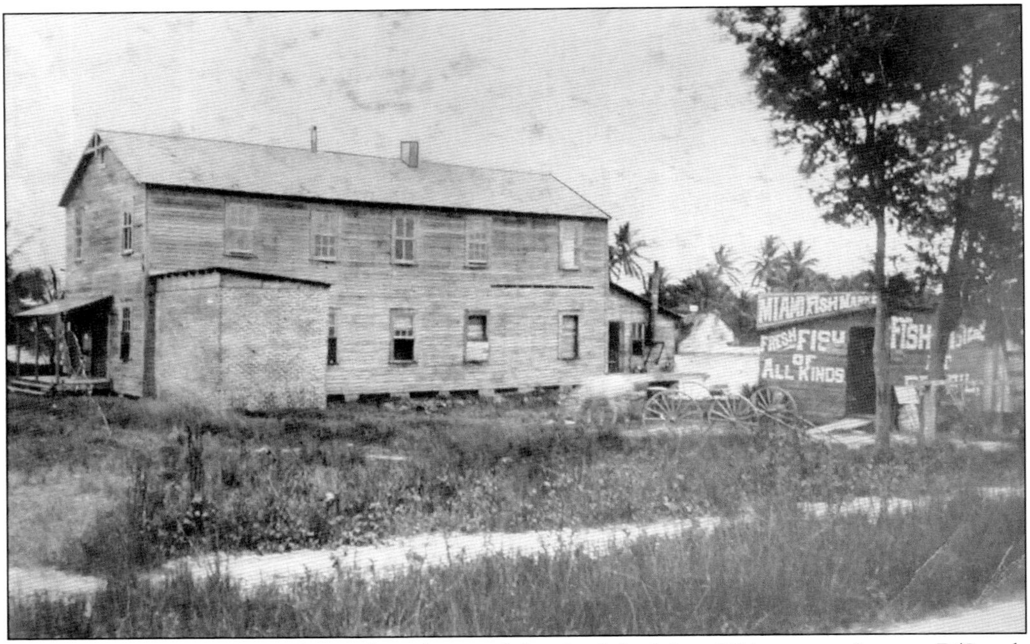

This unimposing building, located on the north bank of the Miami River near Avenue D/South Miami Avenue, served as the Dade County Courthouse after Miami again became the county seat in 1899. A new courthouse, on the site of today's Miami-Dade Courthouse on West Flagler Street, replaced it in 1904. (Courtesy of Scott Silverman.)

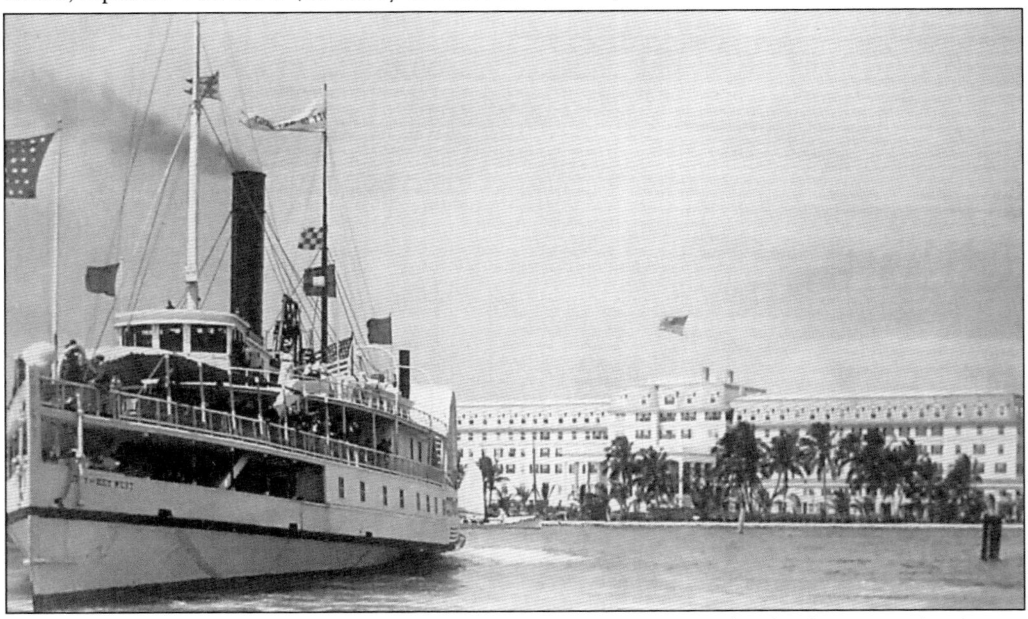

Henry M. Flagler's *City of Key West*, seen here around 1900, was a side-wheel steamer that began carrying passengers between Miami and Key West in 1897, after the railroad baron dredged a deepwater channel from the mouth of the Miami River to Cape Florida. The *City of Key West* operated thrice weekly. In this photograph, the vessel is moving south away from the mouth of the Miami River. In the background is Flagler's Royal Palm Hotel. (Courtesy of Andrew Melick.)

Two

The Magic City

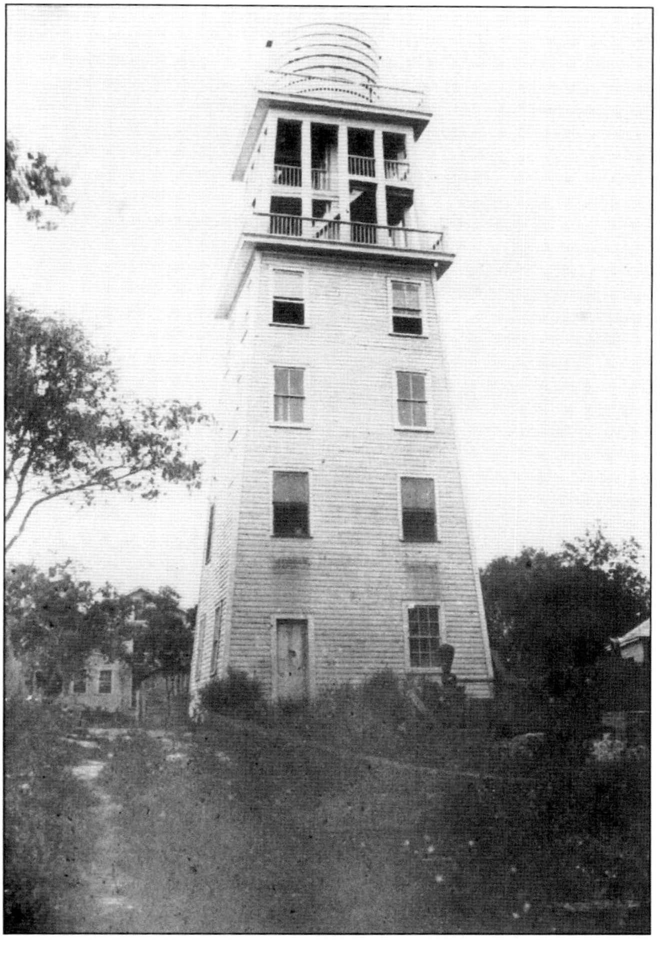

Standing east of today's South Miami Avenue on the north bank of the Miami River, Julia Tuttle's water tower was a landmark in the nascent city of Miami. This late-1890s photograph is found in John Sewell's *Miami Memoirs*. (Courtesy of the Arva Moore Parks Photograph Collection.)

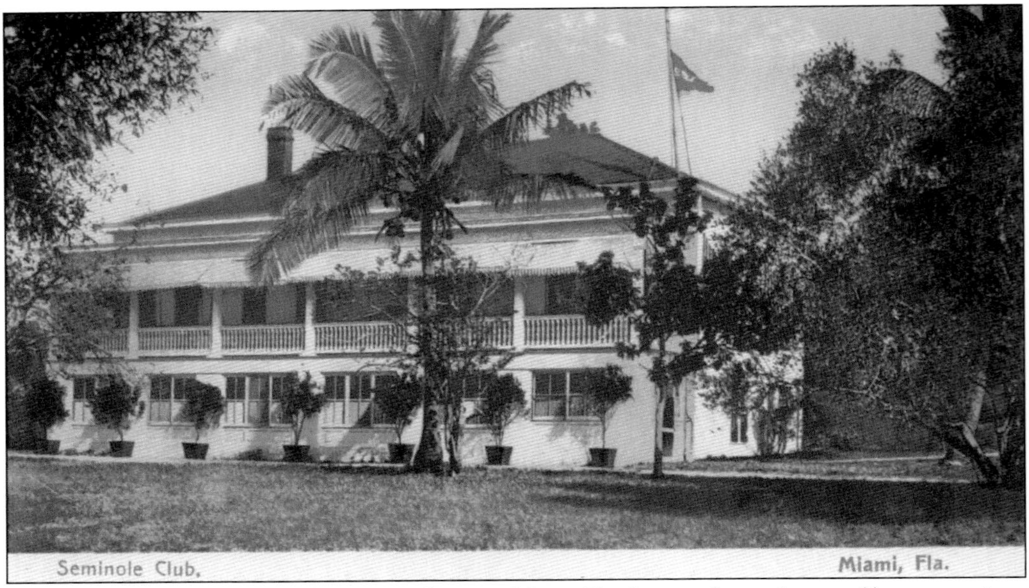

Soon after Julia Tuttle's death in 1898, her son Harry Tuttle transformed part of her estate into the posh subdivision of Fort Dallas Park. The Tuttle home, seen here, became the Seminole Club, which offered gambling, a development that would likely have saddened Harry's straitlaced mother. (Courtesy of Larry Wiggins.)

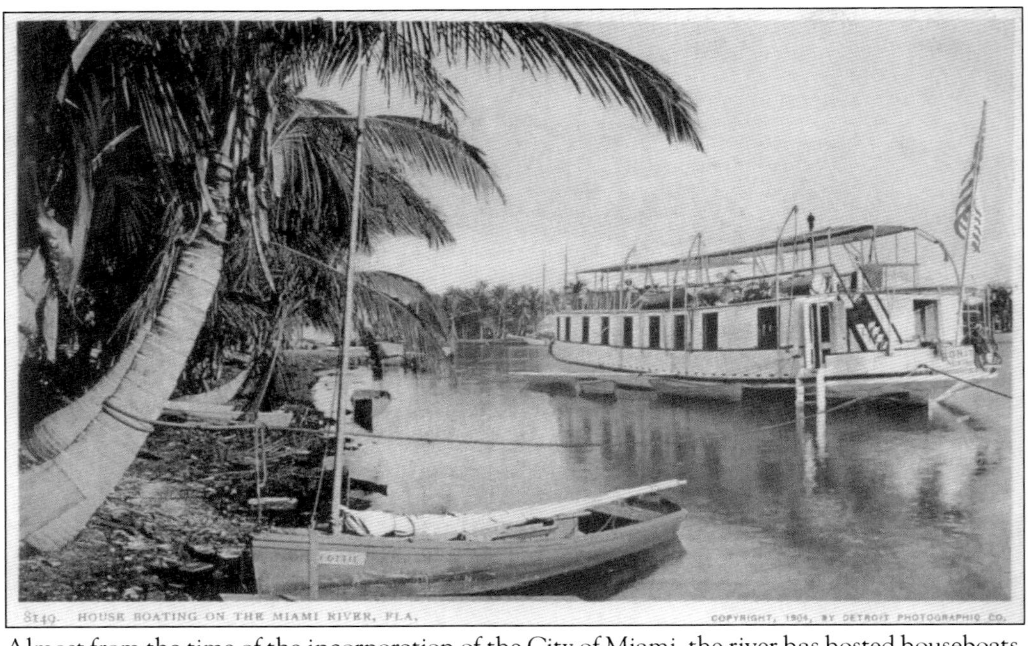

Almost from the time of the incorporation of the City of Miami, the river has hosted houseboats, as seen in this 1904 photograph. The *Bonita,* pictured here, is moored on the north bank of the stream. The river's banks hosted large stands of coconut palm trees for many years following the city's formation. (Courtesy of Larry Wiggins.)

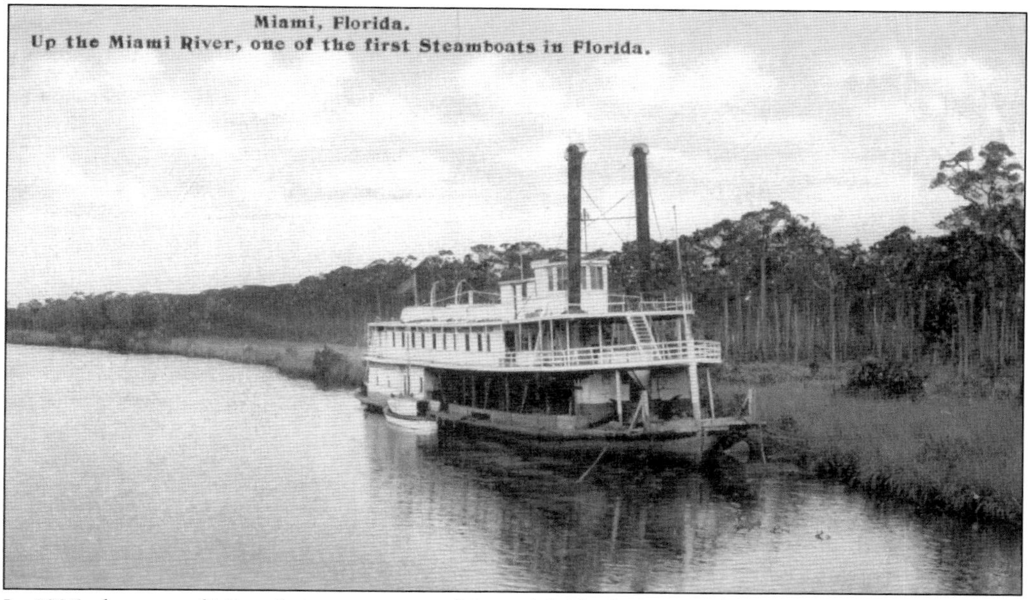

In 1896, the year of Miami's incorporation, Henry M. Flagler's steamboats served as early versions of cruise ships, plying the Miami River near its mouth. Pictured here, though, is a steamboat of a different kind. Moored upriver, it was possibly a quarantine vessel carrying yellow fever patients during Miami's battle with that disease in the final months of 1899 and the beginning of 1900. Note the dense Dade County pine forest just beyond the shoreline. (Courtesy of the author.)

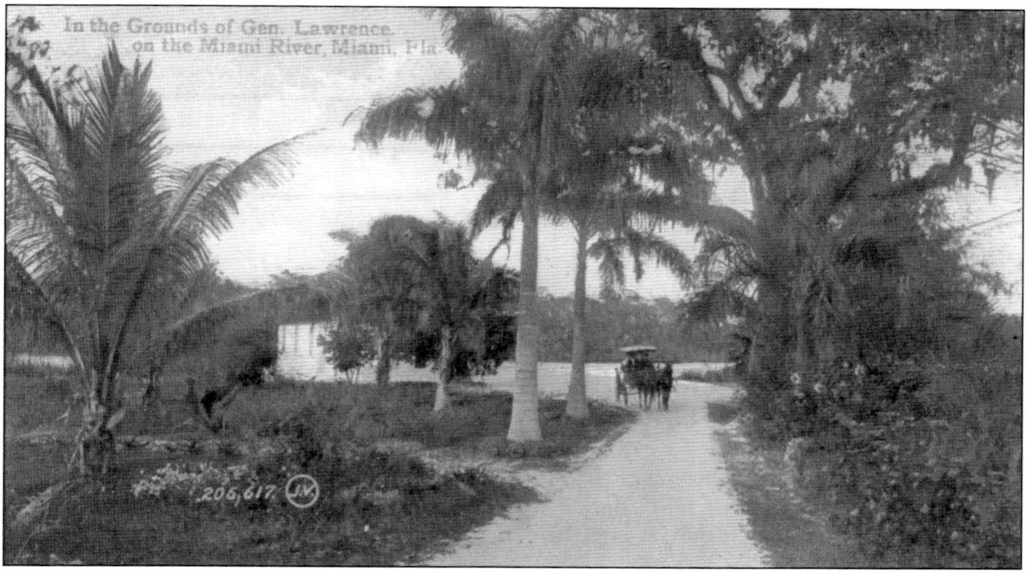

Gen. Samuel Lawrence, a native of Medford, Massachusetts, was a Union general in the Civil War. Lawrence moved to Miami soon after the city's incorporation in 1896. He owned a large tract of land extending from the south bank of the Miami River deep into today's Little Havana. His estate, seen here, later became beautiful Everest G. Sewell Memorial Park, which is located just west of the south entrance to the Northwest Seventeenth Avenue Bridge. Lawrence loved the subtropical ambiance of Miami and created a vast garden on his estate, including a stand of royal palm trees, many of which remain standing. (Courtesy of Larry Wiggins.)

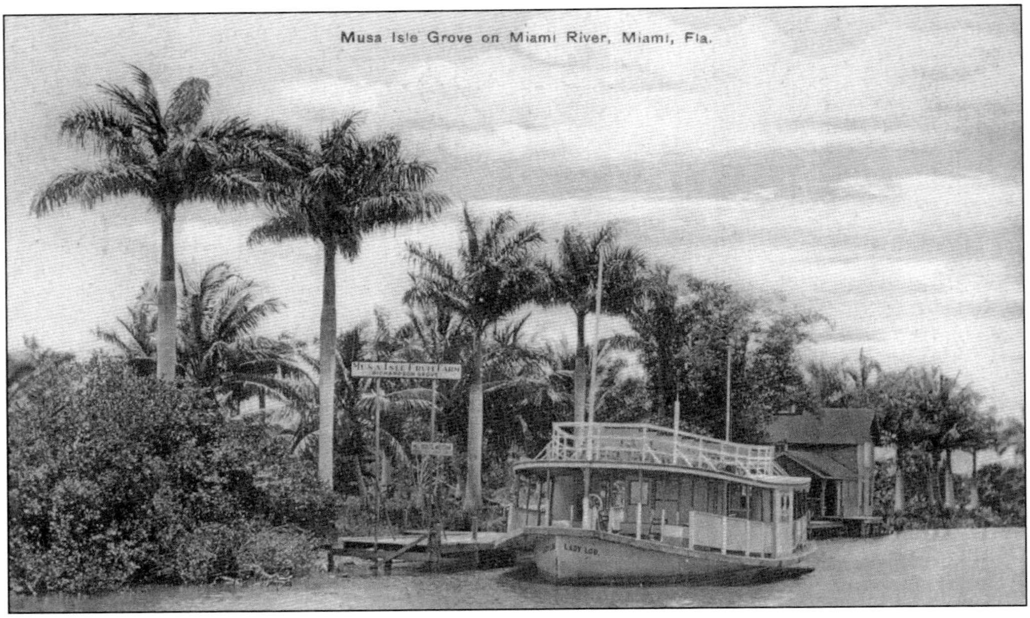

Before there was the Musa Isle Indian Village, there was, on the south bank of the north fork of the river near Northwest Twenty-fifth Avenue, the Richardson family's Musa Isle Fruit Farm, which, like its successor, was a tourist attraction. Opened in the late 1890s, the attraction drew the likes of Henry M. Flagler. The *Lady Lou* (seen here), the *Sallie*, and other tourist vessels brought visitors upriver to its docks. The Richardson family sold tropical fruits cultivated on their farm, which dominated the site. Many tourists, as seen here, enjoyed viewing the exotic subtropical plants and trees that filled the site. The term *Musa* is the botanical name for genus of bananas, which could be found growing at the entrance to the farm. (Both, courtesy of Larry Wiggins.)

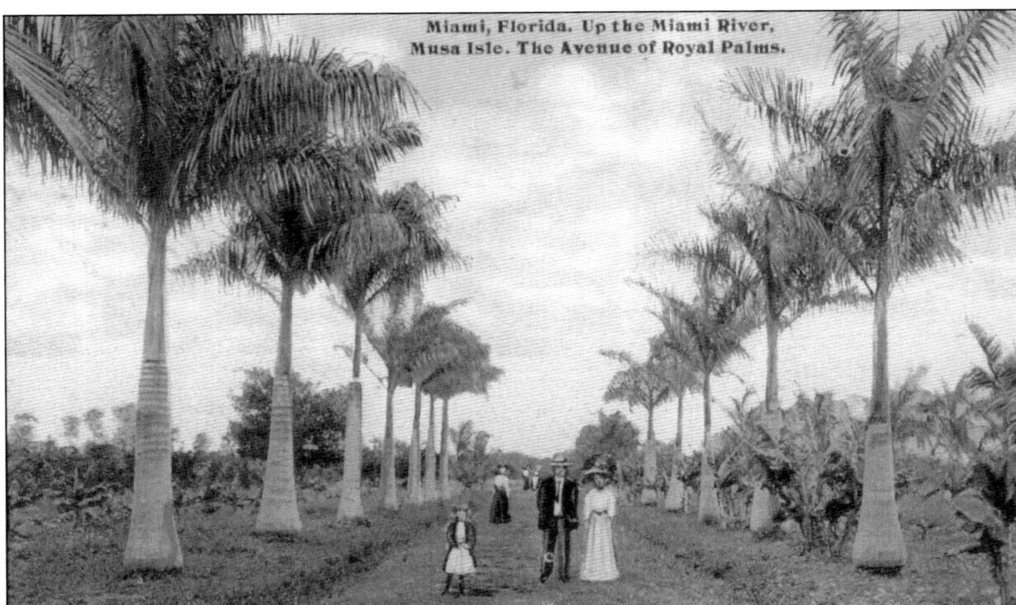

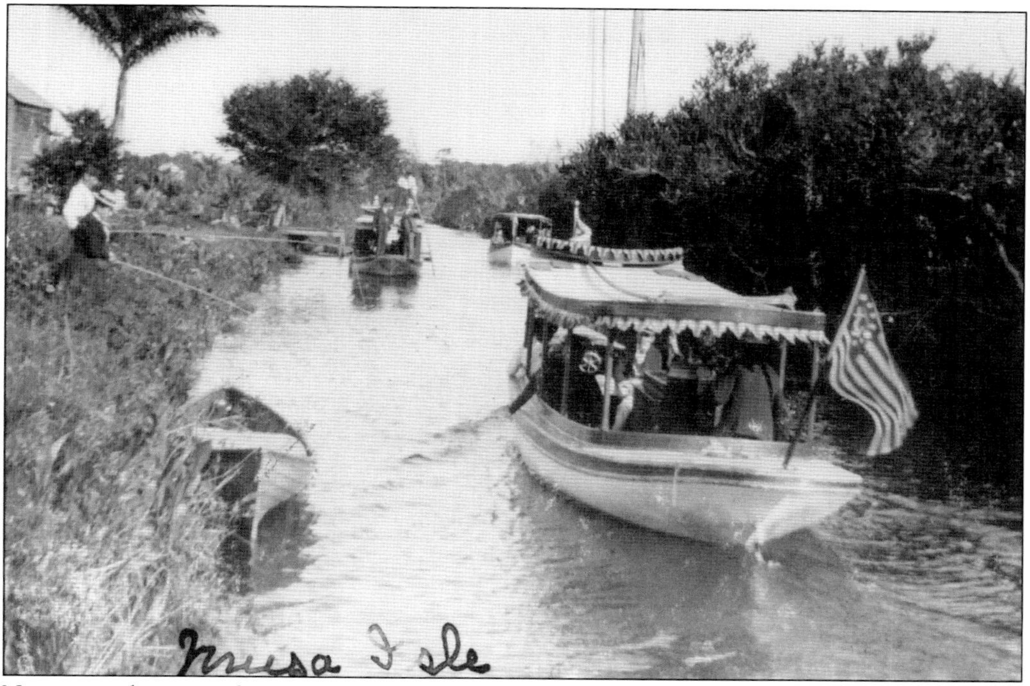

No matter the year, after Miami became a city in 1896, wayfarers were boating up and down its namesake river. Most of them headed west along the stream. A favorite destination was Musa Isle, which has gone through a few iterations in the past century. In this photograph, taken in the early 1900s, Musa Isle is the destination for many visitors attracted by its plants, trees, and tropical fruit for sale. (Courtesy of the author.)

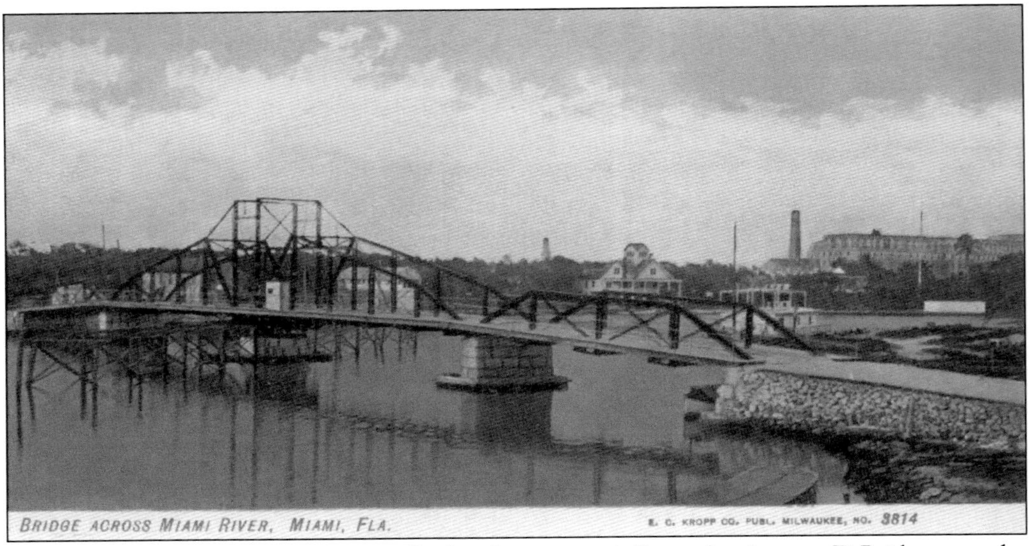

Erected in 1903, the Miami Avenue Bridge, known initially as the Avenue D Bridge, was the second span to cross the Miami River. The first was the Avenue G Bridge (today's Southwest Second Avenue). Miami was nearly two decades of age at the time of this photograph, but the river was already swelling with activity. Near the upper right-hand portion of the photograph sits Henry M. Flagler's beautiful Royal Palm Hotel. (Courtesy of Larry Wiggins.)

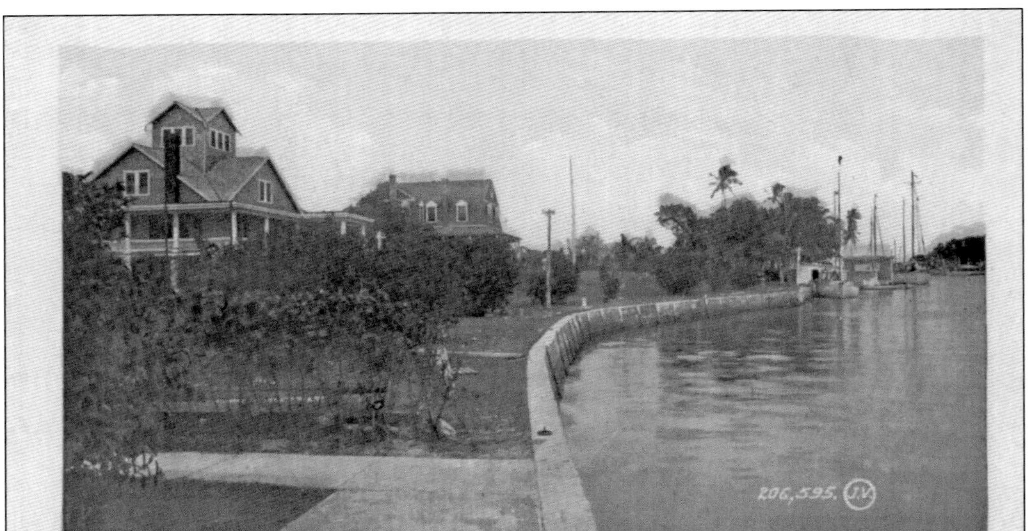

While today's downtown Miami is bereft of single-family homes, that was not the case in the city's early decades, when residences lined the river as well as areas farther inland. The grand wood-frame homes seen in this photograph stood on the north bank of the river, close to the lovely Fort Dallas Park neighborhood. (Courtesy of Larry Wiggins.)

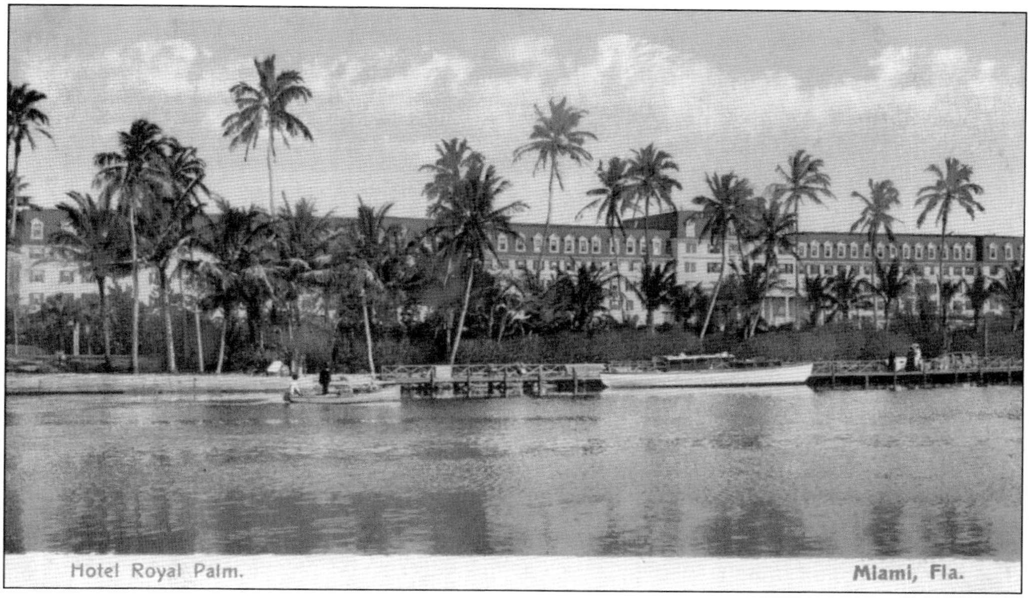

Although Henry Flagler was unable to build his Royal Palm Hotel at the confluence of the river and the bay (Julia Tuttle held that it would block her view of the waters beyond), he maintained the bower of trees at the edge of the river, seen to the left in the early-1900s photograph above, thereby creating a rustic entranceway to his hotel for those arriving by yacht. The image below, taken around the same time, looks across at the Brickell property on the south bank of the stream. (Both, courtesy of Larry Wiggins.)

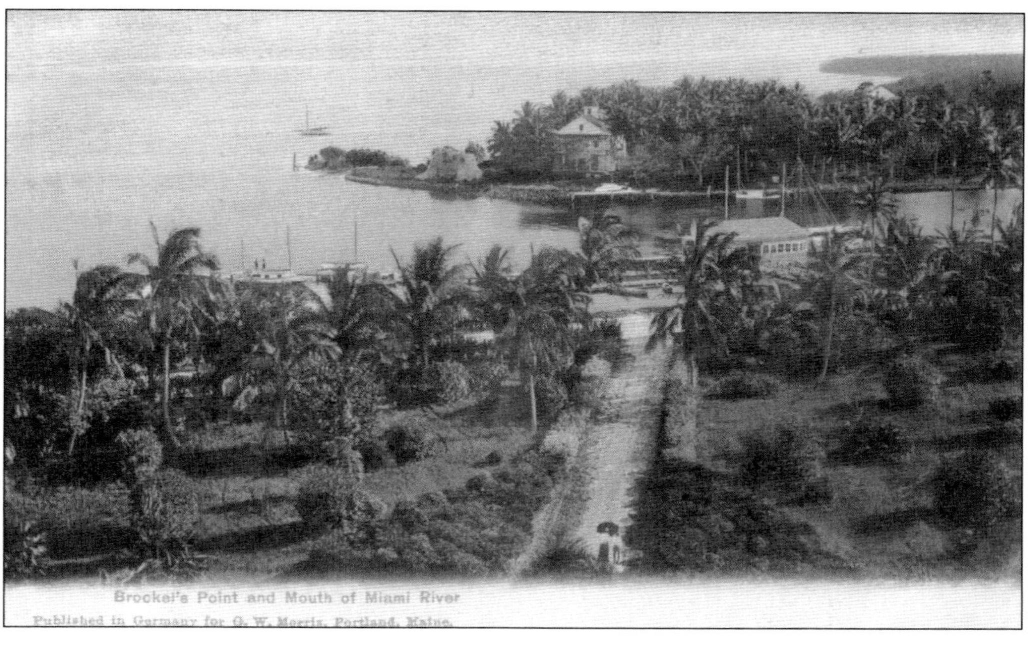

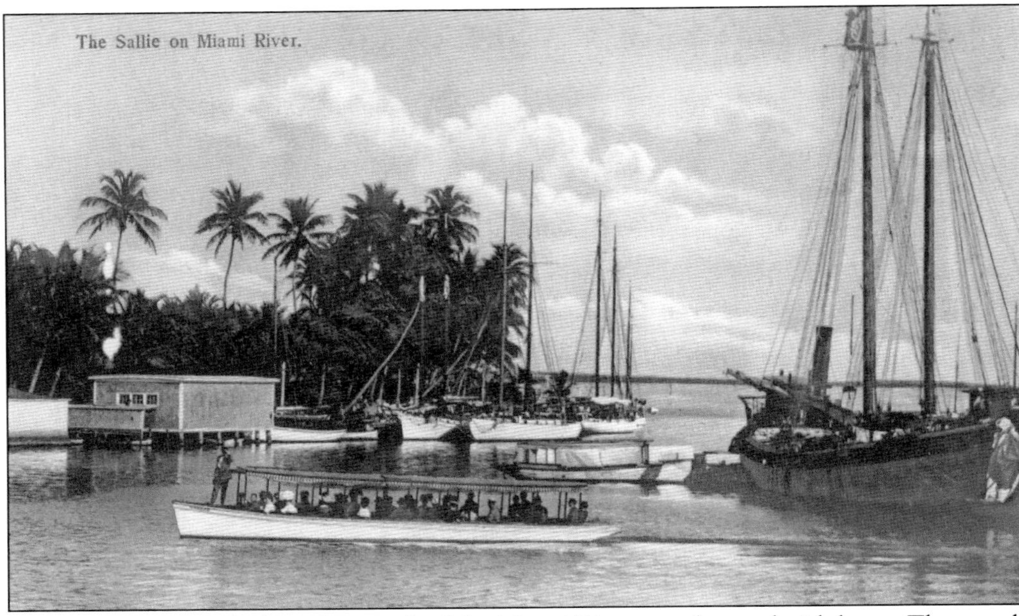

Even in the city's early days, the mouth of the Miami River was cluttered with boats. The vessels in this early-1900s photograph include fishing and pleasure boats. (Courtesy of Larry Wiggins.)

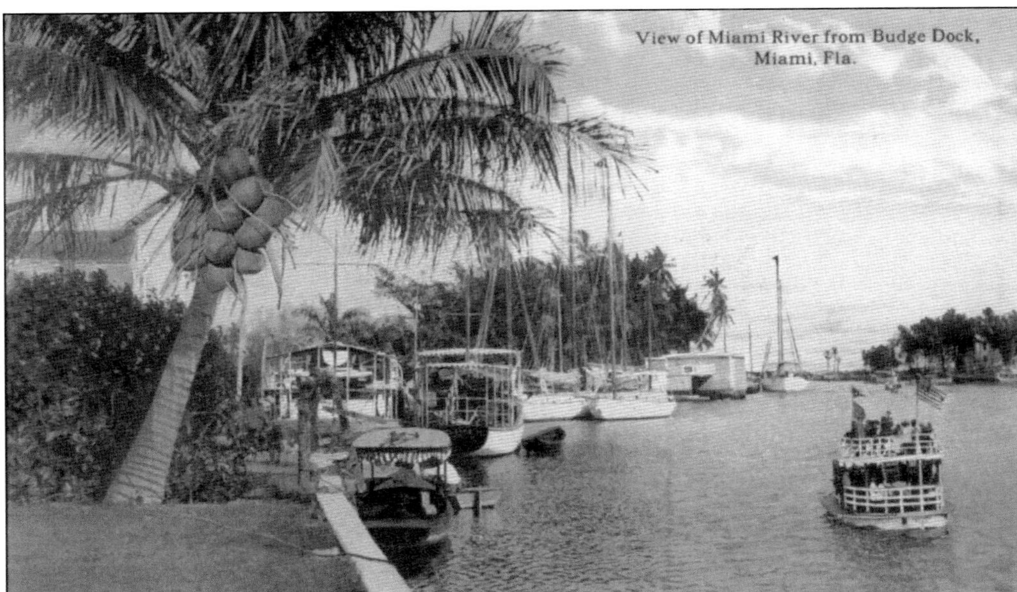

The Budge Dock refers to the property of Frank T. Budge and his family, who lived in beautiful Fort Dallas Park in the early 1900s. Budge's Hardware, which the family owned and operated at the bustling intersection of today's East Flagler Street and North Miami Avenue, was one of the young city's premier businesses. This picture indicates how important the north bank was as a maritime-related venue in the city's early years. The vessel in the lower portion of the photograph is a tour boat, demonstrating that, even then, the river evoked a strong curiosity on the part of the public. (Courtesy of Larry Wiggins.)

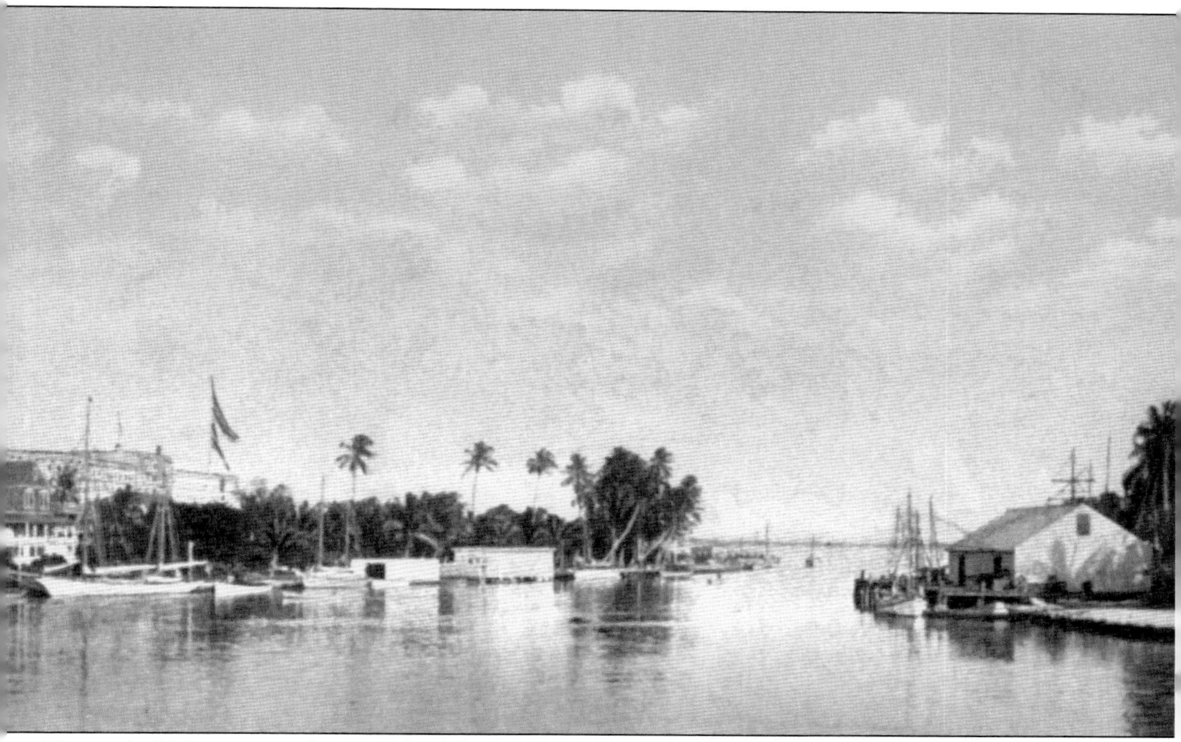

This early-20th-century photograph of the Miami River was taken from the south bank before the Avenue D/Miami Avenue Bridge was built in 1903. The shoreline is dotted with coconut palm trees, while the looming Royal Palm Hotel stands at the left center of the photograph. (Courtesy of Scott Silverman.)

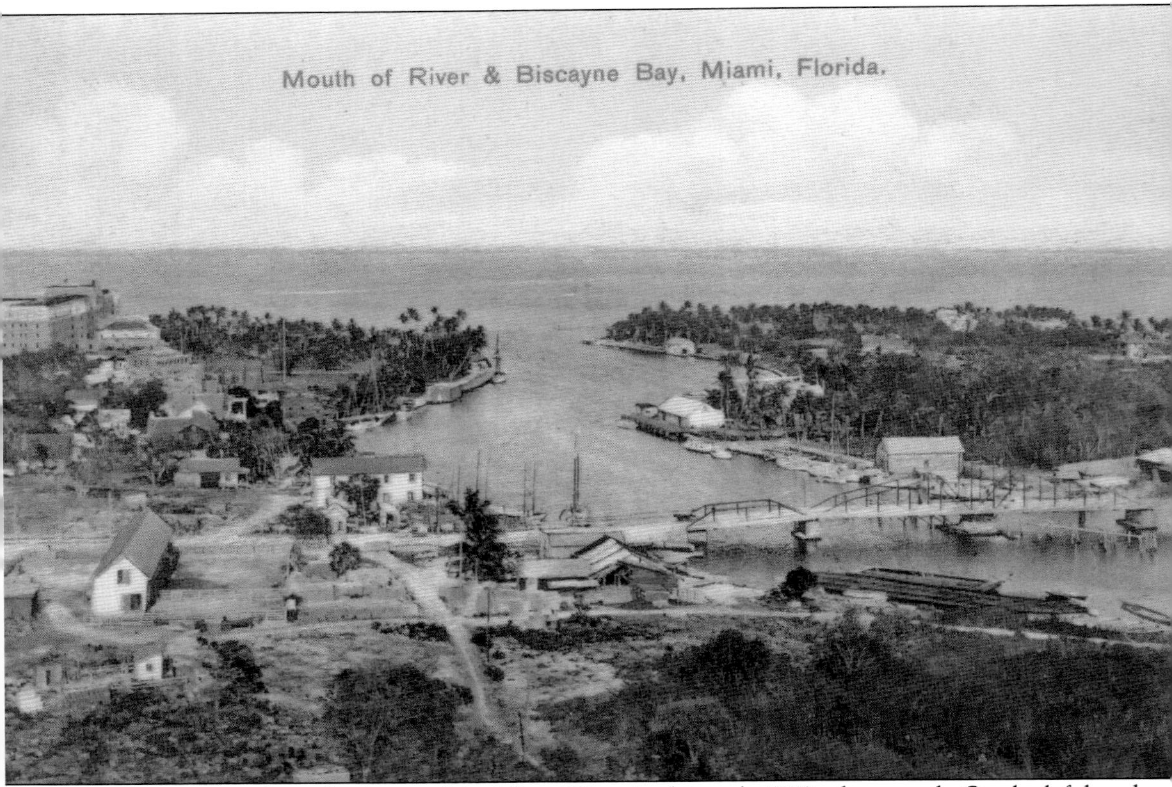

A city arises along the shores of the Miami River in this early-1900s photograph. On the left-hand side of the photograph, which corresponds to the north bank of the stream, is the downtown side of Miami, while on the opposite bank is the less developed Southside, or South Miami, neighborhood. The Avenue D Bridge, later known as the Miami Avenue Bridge, is visible in the lower portion of the photograph. To the left of the bridge is the two-story, wood-frame Dade County Courthouse, which served the county briefly from 1899 till 1904. (Courtesy of Larry Wiggins.)

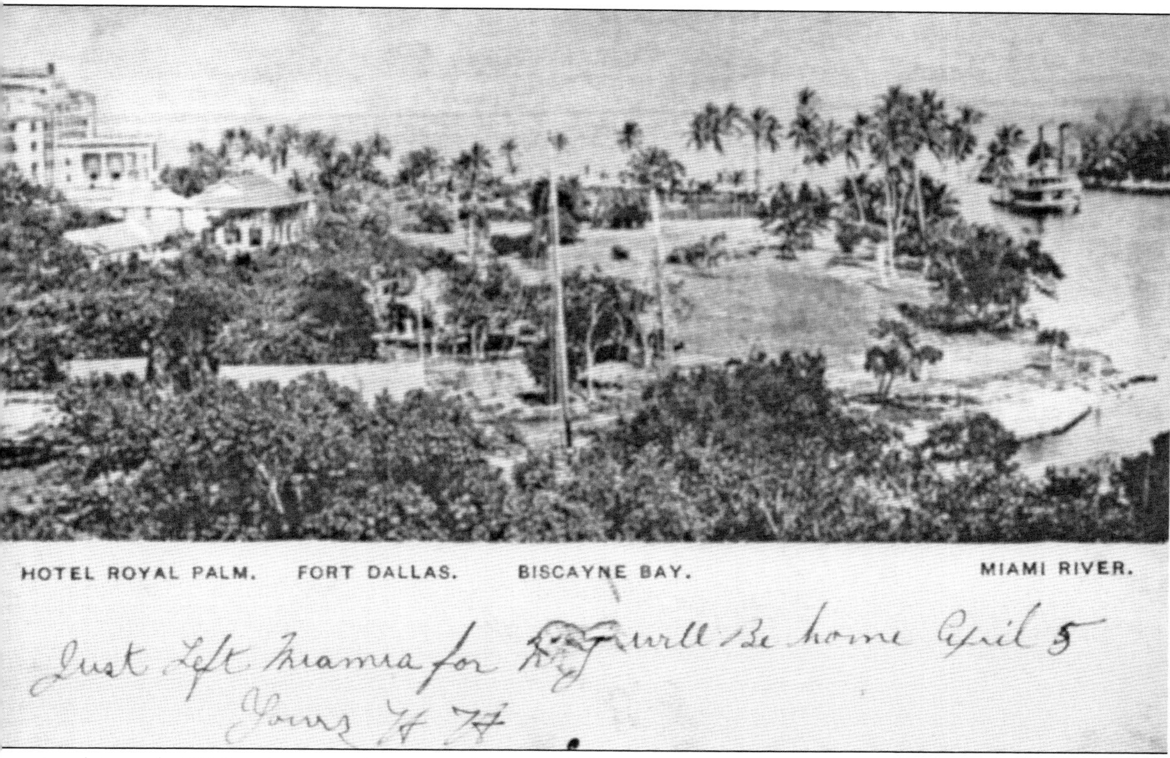

As this early-1900s photograph attests, Henry M. Flagler's magnificent Royal Palm Hotel, at five stories in height, loomed over everything else in early Miami. Some of the coconut palms behind it were remnants of the stand of trees that lined the north bank of the stream in the years before development commenced in 1896. The tour boat near the upper right-hand portion of the photograph is carrying a large number of visitors upriver to enjoy the splendors of this subtropical slice of paradise. (Courtesy of Scott Silverman.)

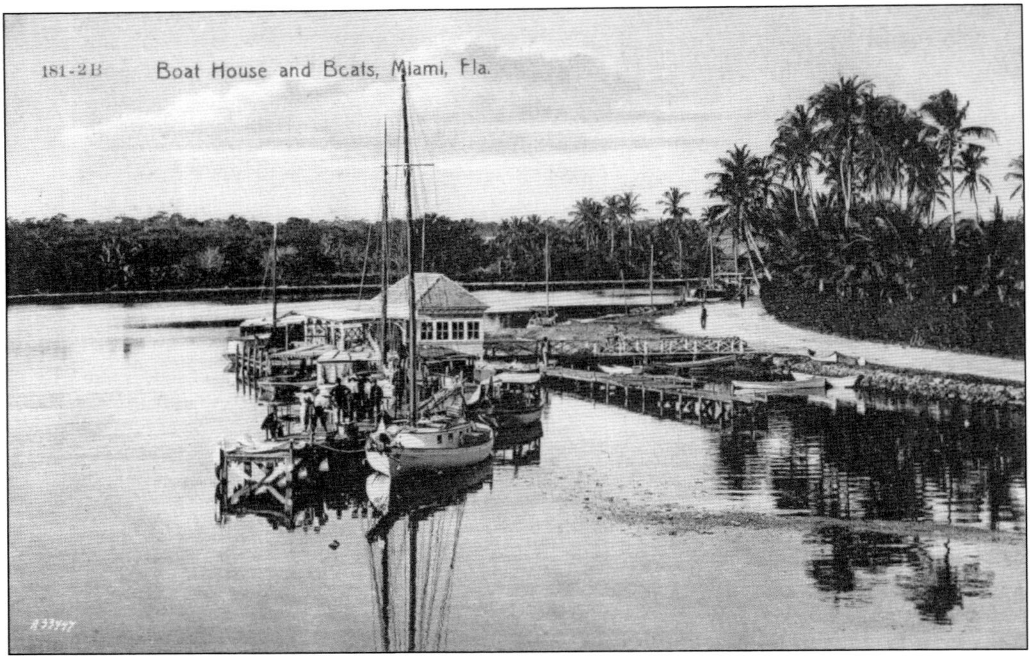

The Royal Palm Hotel's marina, sometimes referred to as the "Dock" or "Docks," traces its beginnings to the years immediately after the great hotel's 1897 opening. Over time, new, larger marinas replaced the original. These photographs, taken in the early 1900s, indicate the brisk business the marina did in wintertime, when the hotel was filled with guests escaping frigid northern climes. (Both, courtesy of Larry Wiggins.)

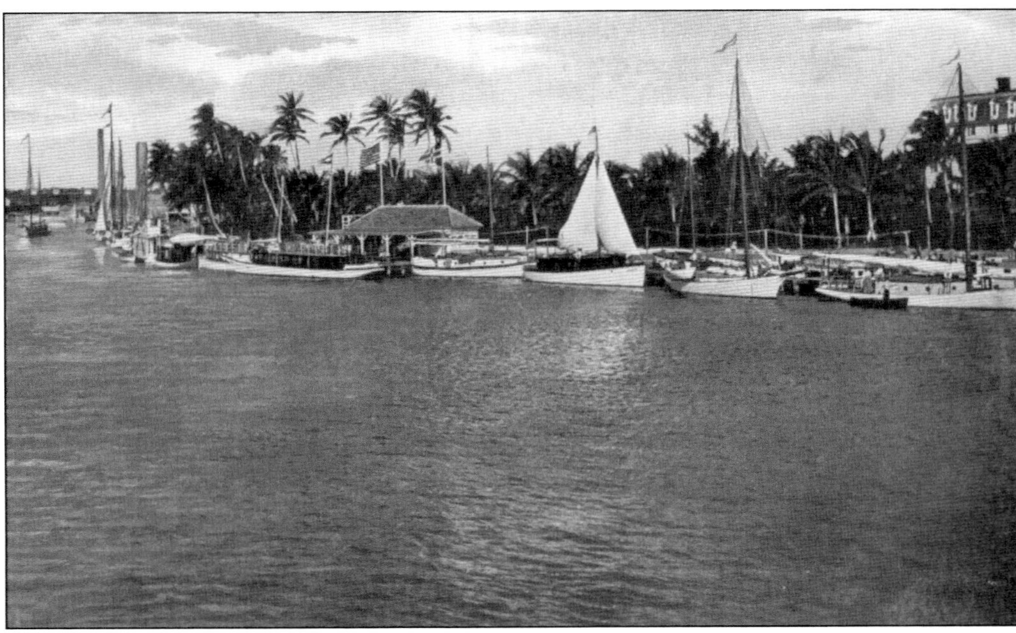

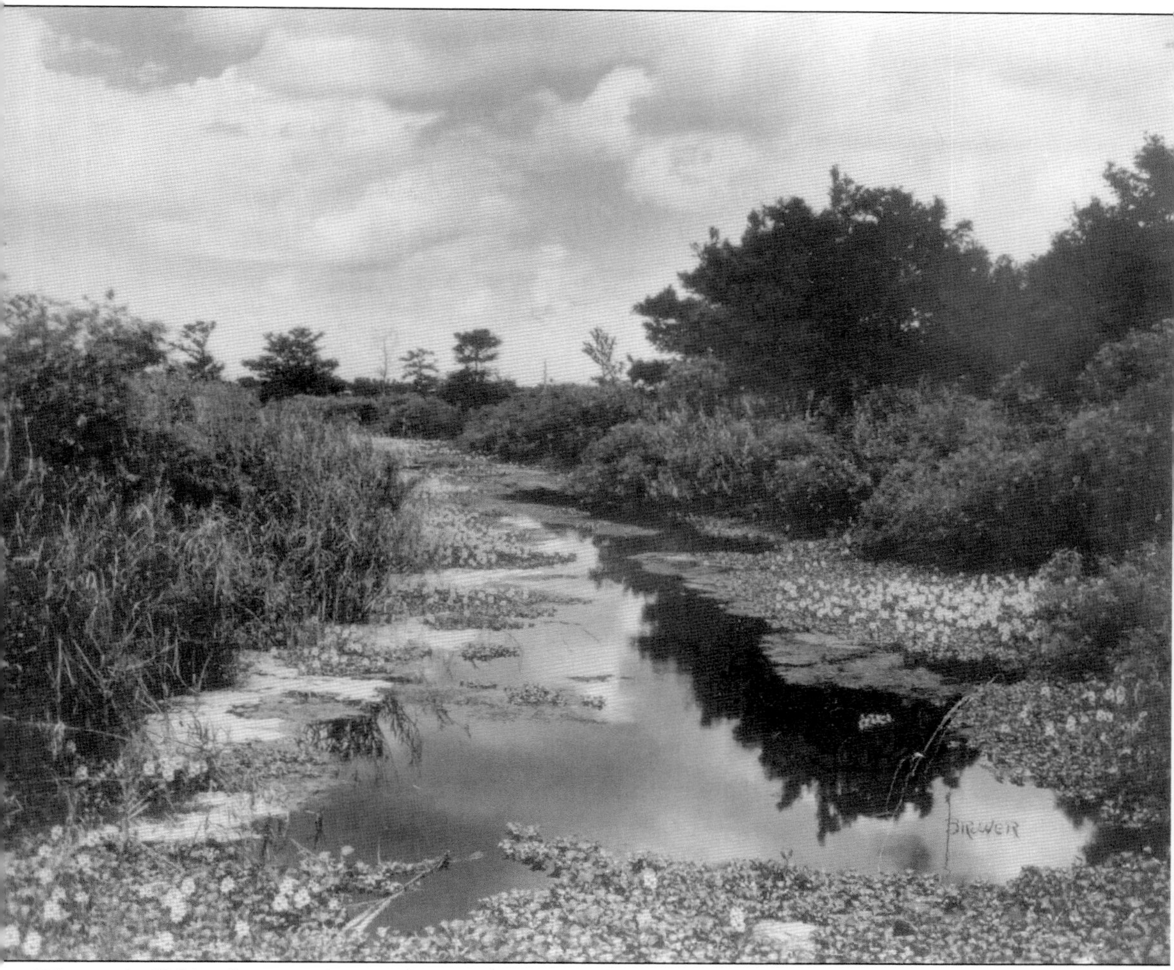

This early-1900s photograph provides another view of the pristine south fork of the Miami River near today's Northwest Twenty-seventh Avenue before the construction of the Huyler-Comfort Canal, just west of this site. Soon after this photograph was taken, Everglades drainage commenced in the Miami area, changing forever the topography and waterways of southeast Florida. (Courtesy of the Arva Moore Parks Photograph Collection.)

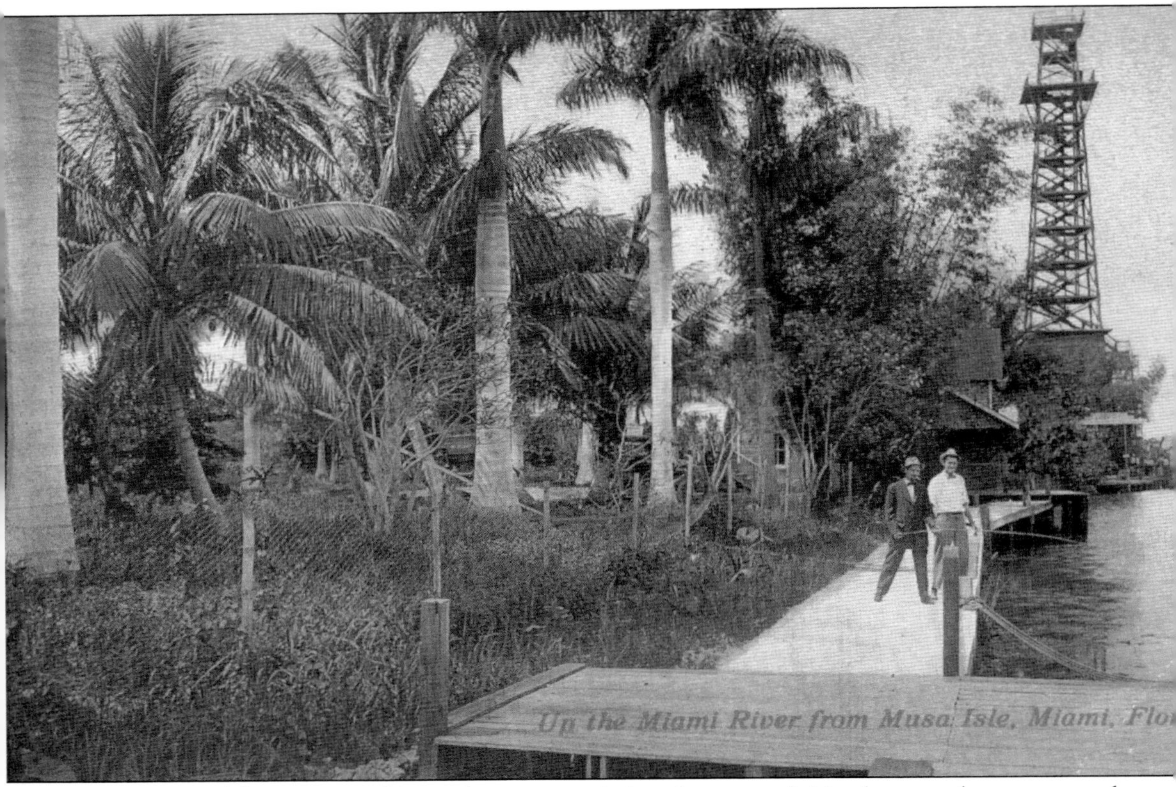

The Cardale Tower, visible in the upper right-hand corner of this photograph, was a popular element of the Cardale Resort on the north fork of the Miami River, just east of today's Northwest Twenty-seventh Avenue in an area known as Musa Isle. Opened in 1912, the resort featured a skating rink and a dance floor in a building shaped like a Quonset hut. The tower, which stood about 90 feet tall at the edge of the river, offered a spectacular view of the nearby Everglades. (Courtesy of Larry Wiggins.)

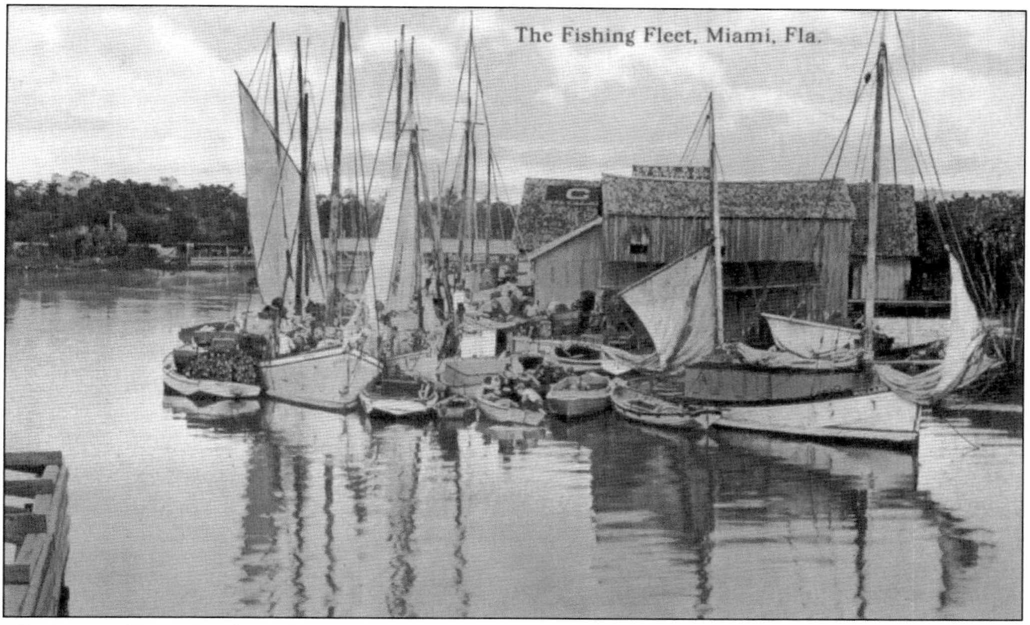

The Miami River has been home to many fishing fleets, which have provided food for restaurants and fresh fish to locals and visitors alike. This photograph dates from the early 1900s. (Courtesy of Larry Wiggins.)

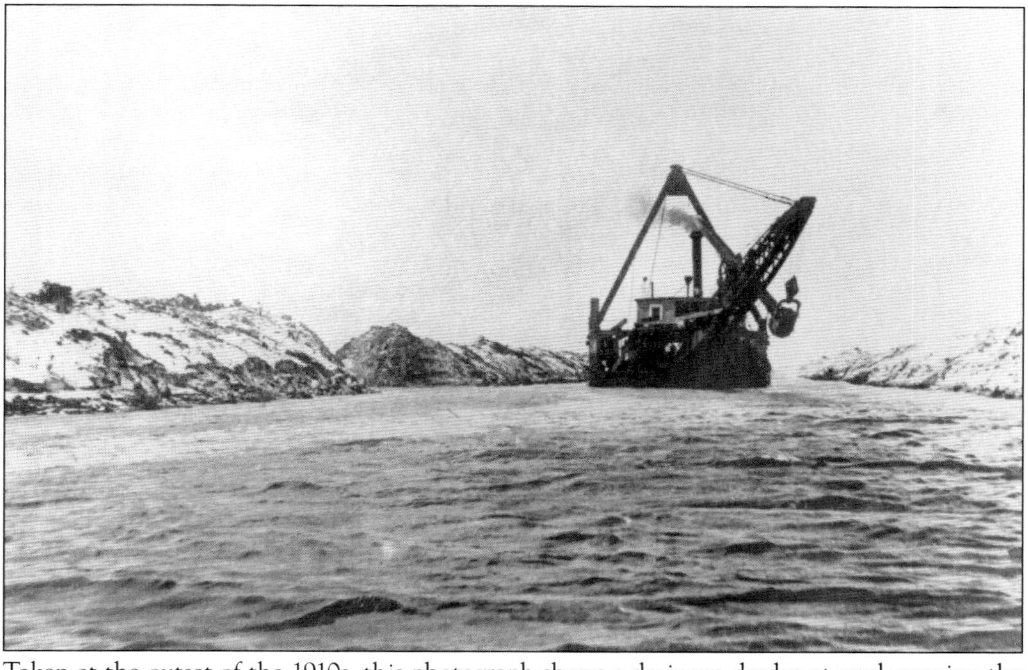

Taken at the outset of the 1910s, this photograph shows a drainage dredge at work carving the Miami Canal out of Everglades swampland. Upon its completion in 1913, the canal stretched north 90 miles to Lake Okeechobee. Champions of drainage could not have known that the extreme eastern portion of the canal would become the bustling Second Port of Miami. (Courtesy of the Florida State Archives.)

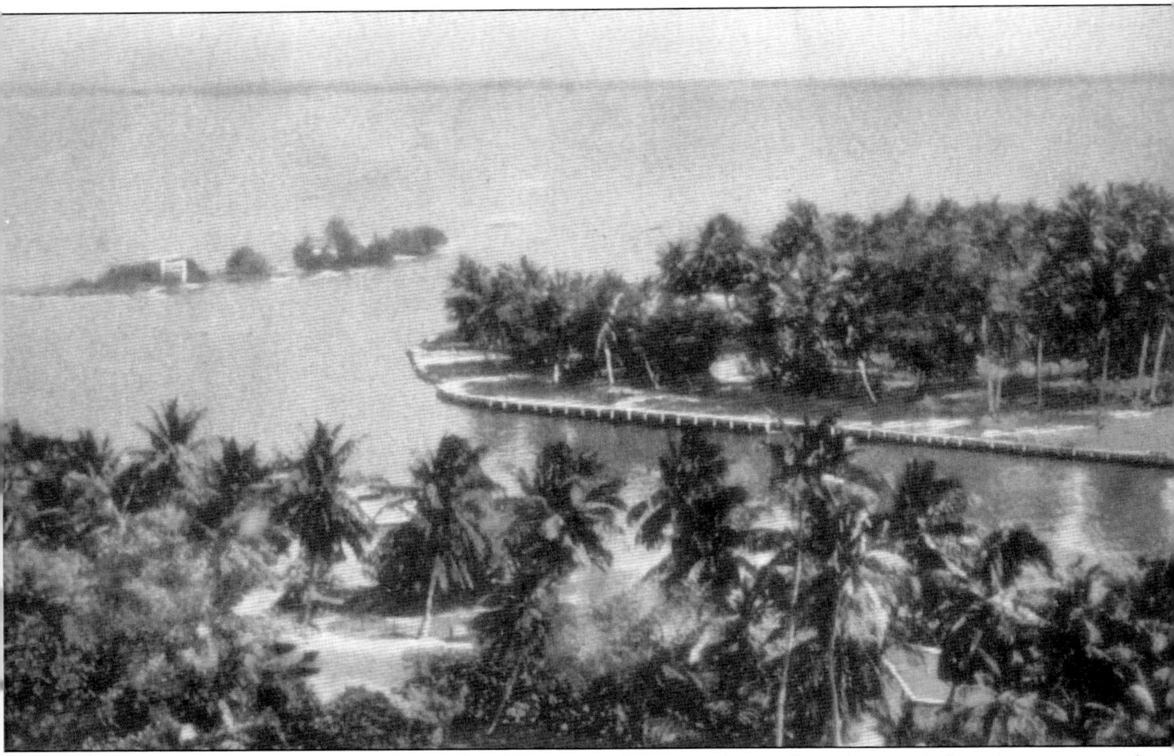

Dredging activities near the mouth of the Miami River in the city's early years led to the creation of a spoil island, seen here near the upper left side of this photograph, known initially as Burlingame, for its owners Margaret and John Burlingame. In the early 1940s, Atlanta businessman Ed Claughton purchased the undeveloped island with a plan to develop it. In conjunction with the Army Corps of Engineers, Claughton enhanced its size significantly, but it remained undeveloped. Finally, in 1979, the Hong Kong–based firm Swire Ltd. began developing the island. Known today as Brickell Key on Claughton Island, the island is almost totally built out and serves as a home or workplace for thousands of people. (Courtesy of Larry Wiggins.)

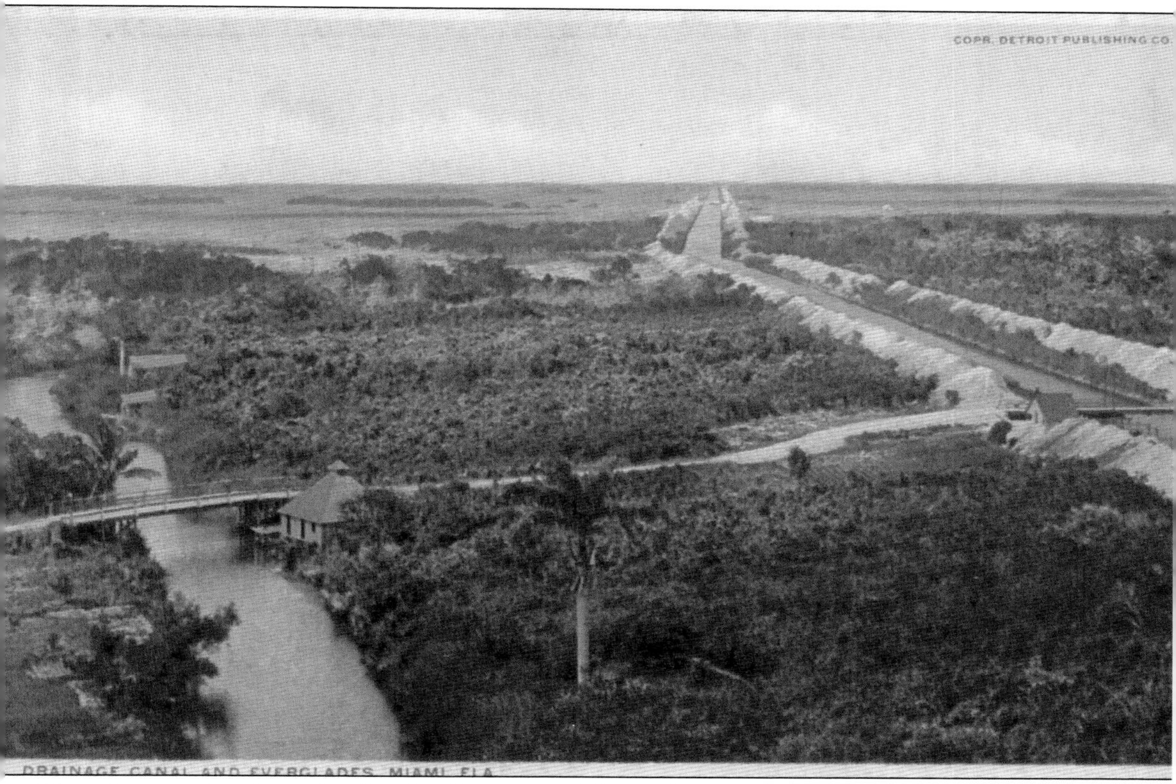

This picture, taken from the Cardale Tower, which loomed above the north fork of the Miami River (left) near today's Northwest Twenty-seventh Avenue, offers one of the most stunning views of man's transformation of the Everglades. Note the topographical differences between the high ground in the bottom two-thirds of the photograph and the Everglades in its upper portions. On the right is the Miami Canal, built between 1909 and 1913. As noted, this drainage canal reached as far north as Lake Okeechobee. By taking surface water away from the swamp and delivering it to large bodies of water far from the Everglades, it forever changed the wetlands. (Courtesy of Larry Wiggins.)

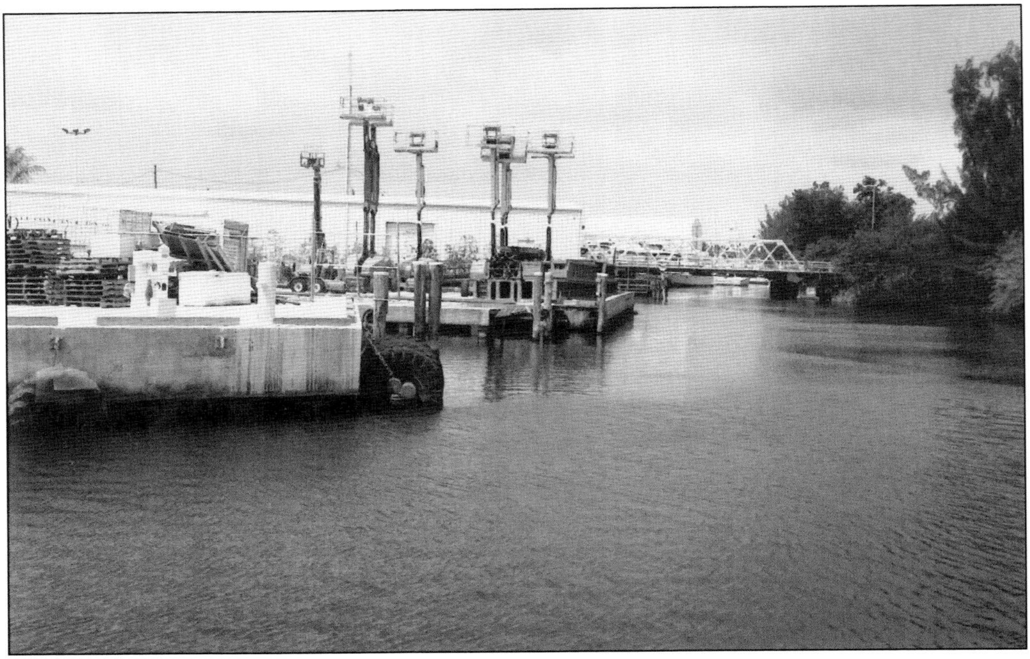

Here are contemporary looks at a portion of the same area depicted in the photograph on the previous page. (Both, courtesy of Elliot Salloway.)

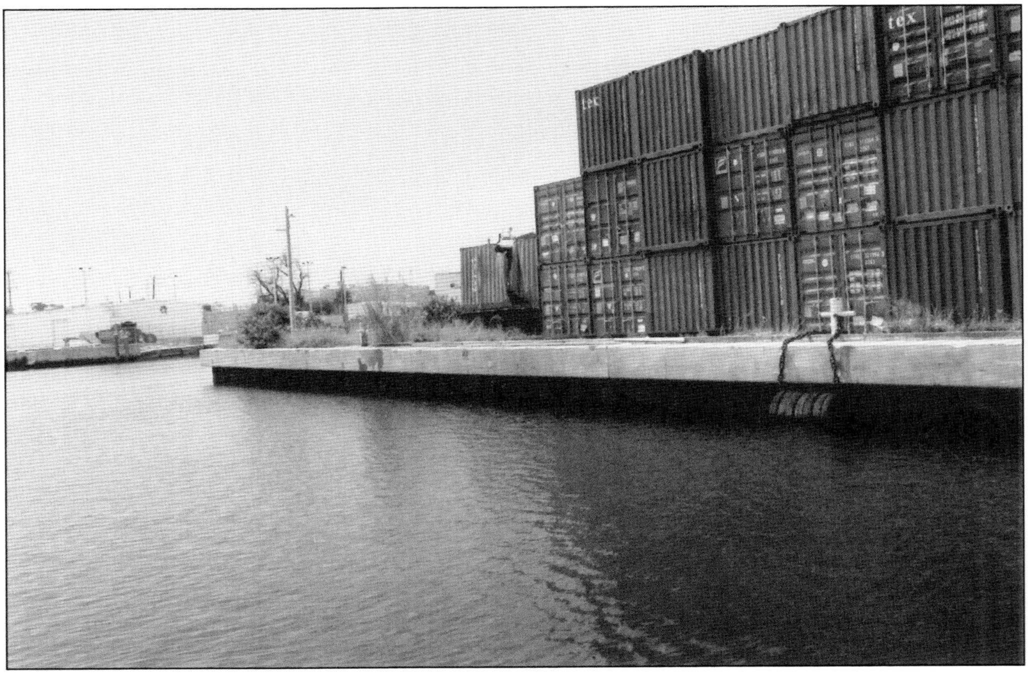

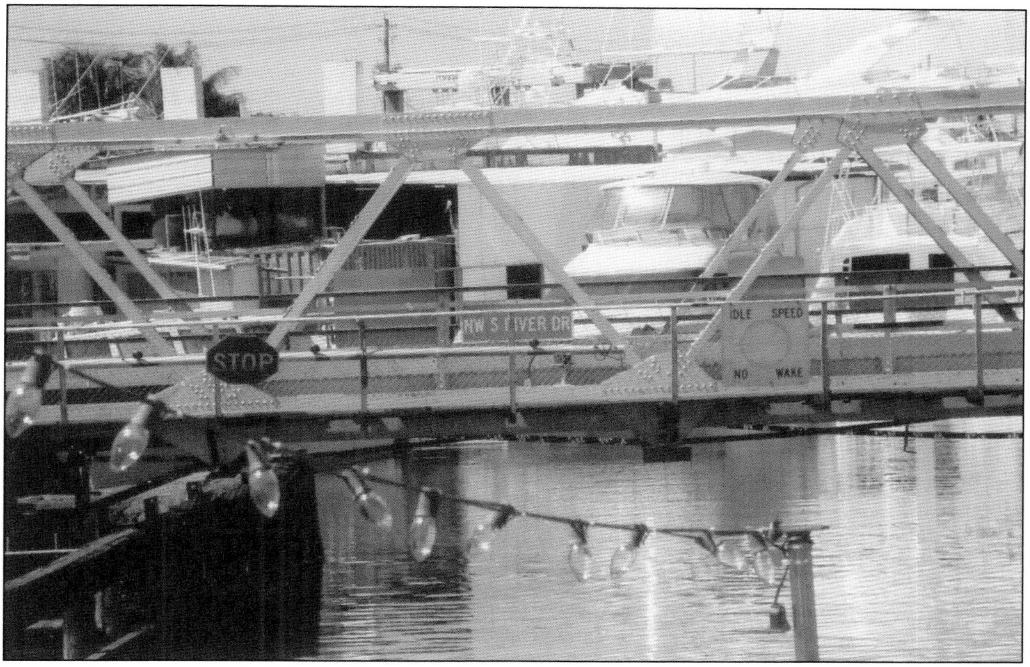

A rare example of recycling in Miami, this turn bridge resting over the Tamiami Canal (another drainage canal, flowing into the Miami Canal near Northwest Thirty-second Avenue) initially operated as a span over the former waterway at Northwest Twenty-seventh Avenue. Built in 1910, the bridge turns on one axis to allow for the movement of vessels between the two waterways. (Courtesy of Elliot Salloway.)

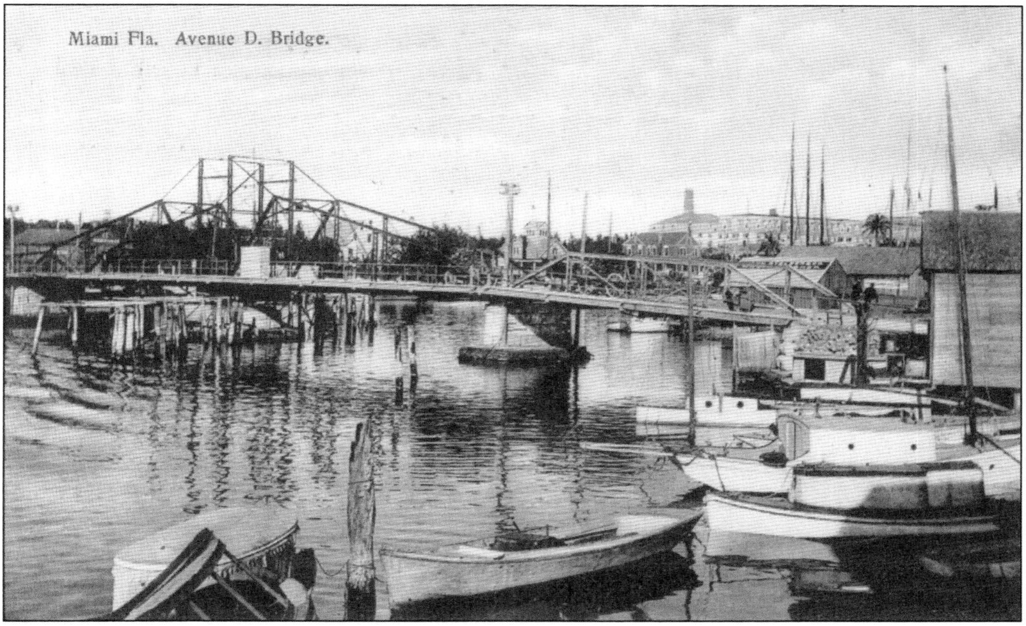

By the time this c. 1910 photograph was taken from the Avenue D Bridge, a city was already developing quickly along both banks of the Miami River. (Courtesy of Larry Wiggins.)

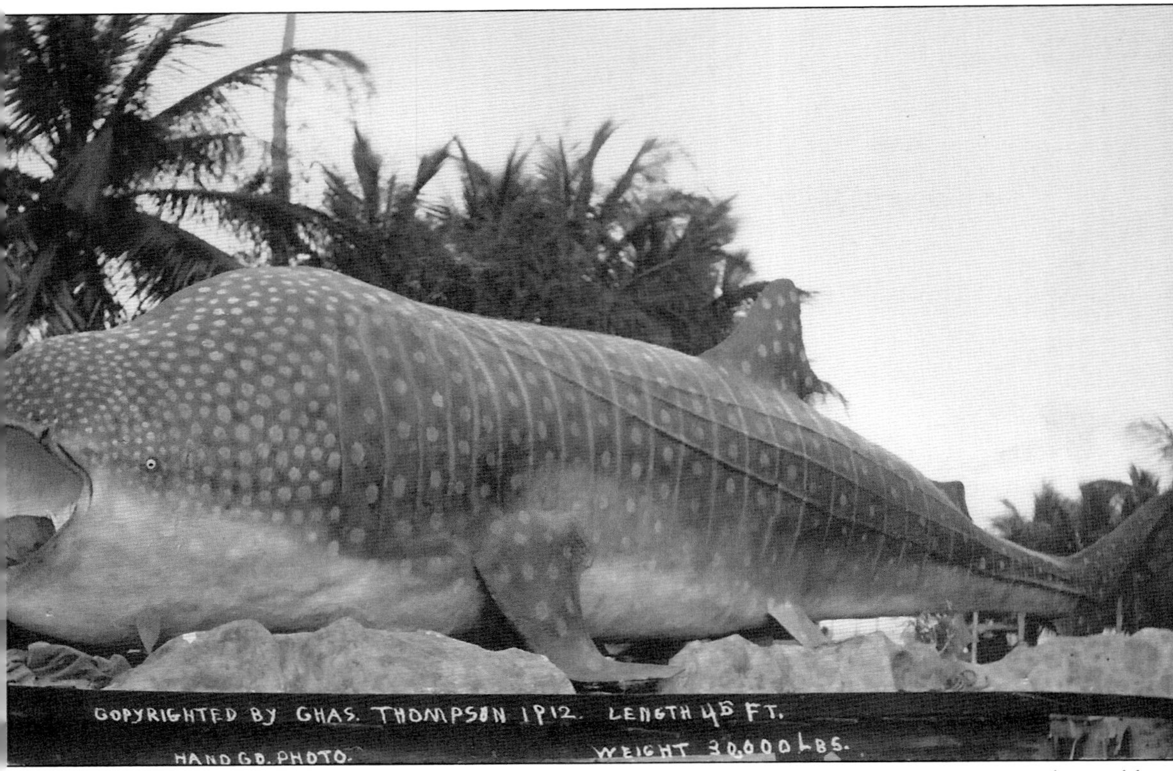

Like any community, Miami has experienced its share of the bizarre. One prime example would be the appearance of a 30,000-pound whale shark on the north bank of the Miami River in 1912. Harpooned and shot off of Knights Key (an island in the middle Florida Keys) by a fishing party led by noted guide Charlie Thompson, the monster was dragged to the Miami River and later reposed east of the downtown Burdine's store, early Miami's premier emporium. Later, the carcass was taken on tour to other parts of the United States. (Courtesy of Larry Wiggins.)

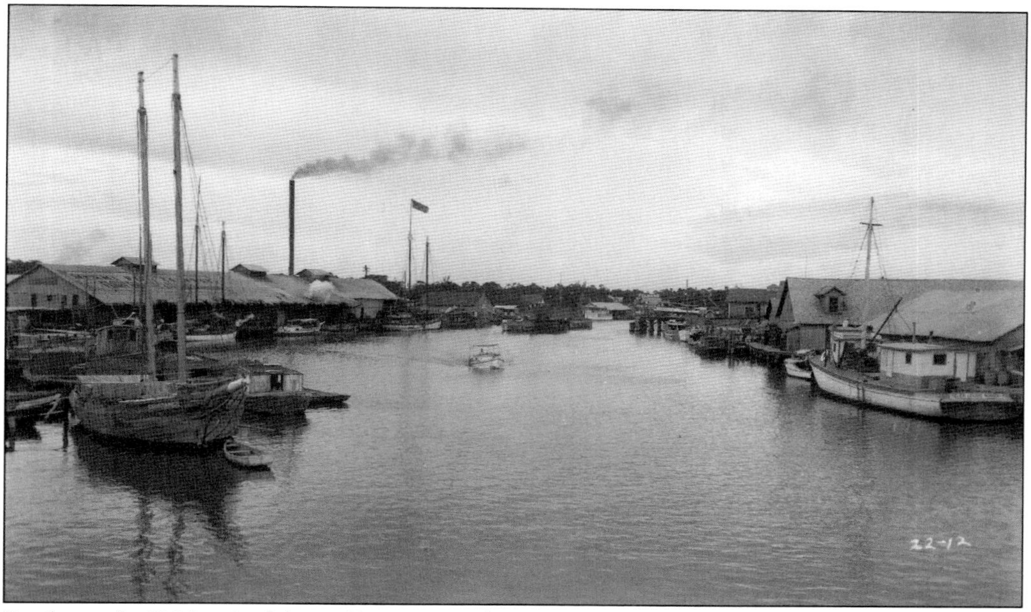

By the early 1900s, the Miami River was a busy stream, already assuming the character of a working river. Businesses included shipping, boat repair, and storage. Miami's hinterland was rich in produce, much of which was shipped to market via the Miami River. Although mostly concentrated near the mouth, the activity along the river at this stage extended as far as today's West Flagler Street. (Courtesy of HistoryMiami).

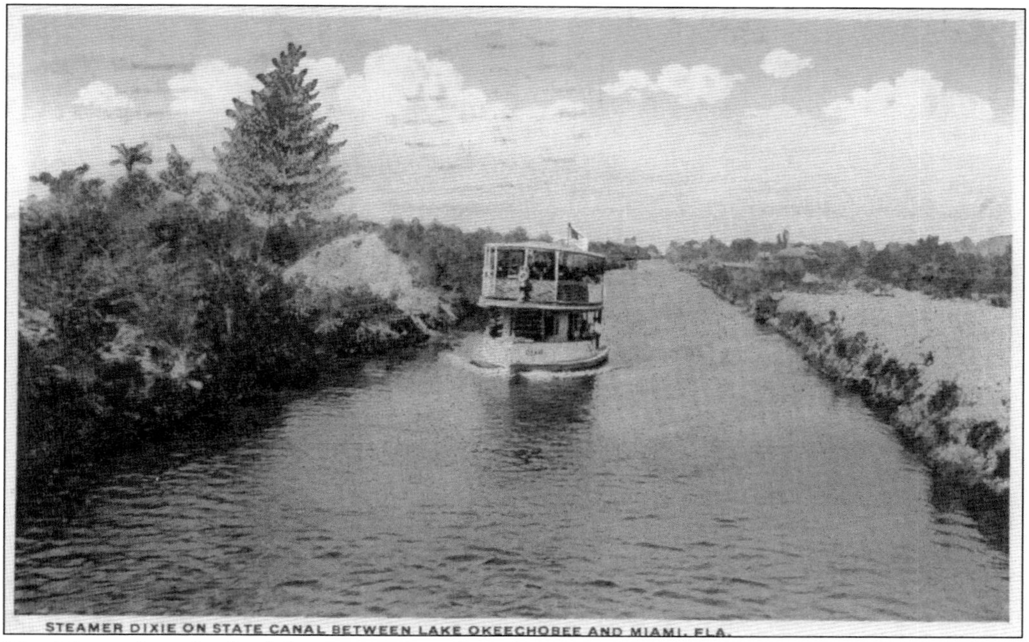

The Miami Canal, which begins at about Northwest Twenty-fourth Avenue on the north fork of the Miami River and extends north to Lake Okeechobee, was one of several drainage canals designed to transform the Everglades into farmland. This photograph shows the *Dixie* on a portion of the canal west of Miami. (Courtesy of Larry Wiggins.)

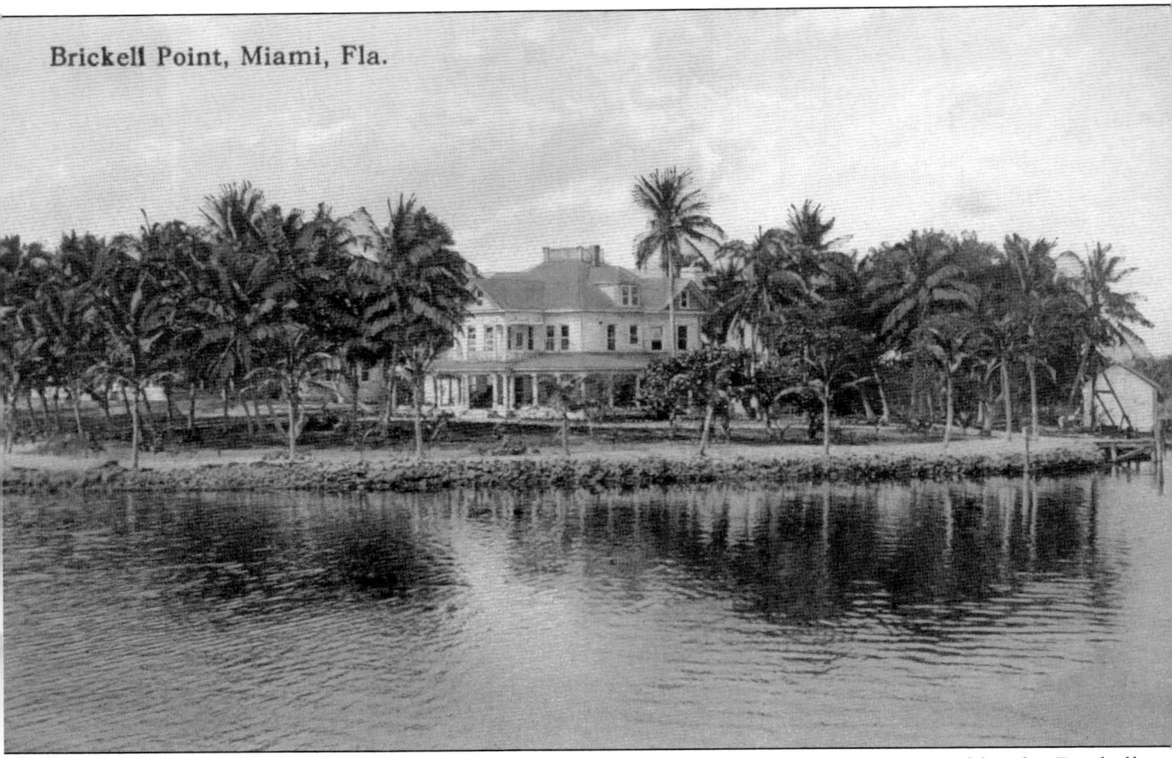

Brickell Point, which stands on the site of the old Indian trading post operated by the Brickell family, began transforming itself in the early years of the 20th century as the trading post gave way to a small number of capacious wood-frame homes erected by the Brickells amid a profusion of coconut palm trees and other subtropical foliage. (Courtesy of Larry Wiggins.)

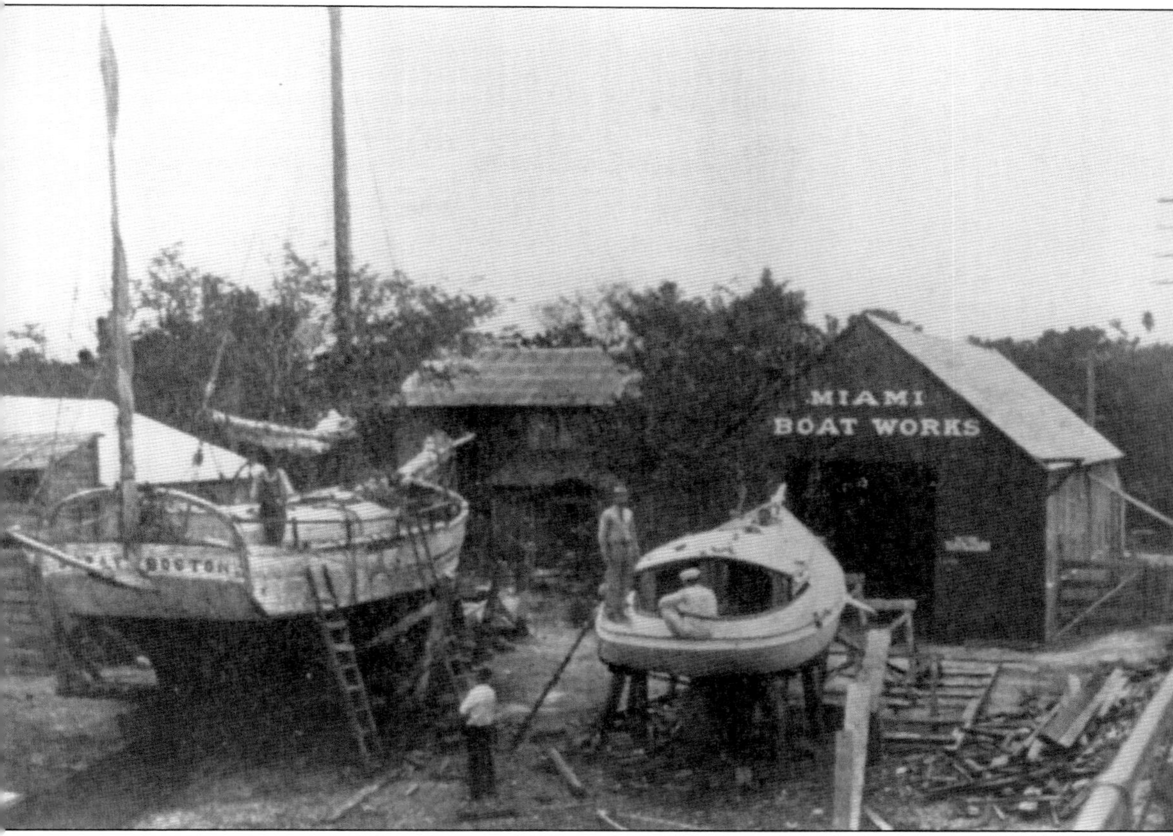

Standing on the south bank of the Miami River, just east of Avenue D/Miami Avenue, the Miami Boat Works (pictured here in 1908) was one of the stream's oldest boatyards. Established around 1903, it was involved in the construction of a wide variety of vessels. Its most famous customer, seen here in his 40-foot yacht, *Spray* (the vessel on the right), is Capt. Joshua Slocum, who took this vessel around the world solo in the 1890s. Soon after this picture was taken, the Miami Boat Works became the Miami Yacht & Machine Company, ushering in an era of expansion and increased business for the boatyard. (Courtesy of HistoryMiami.)

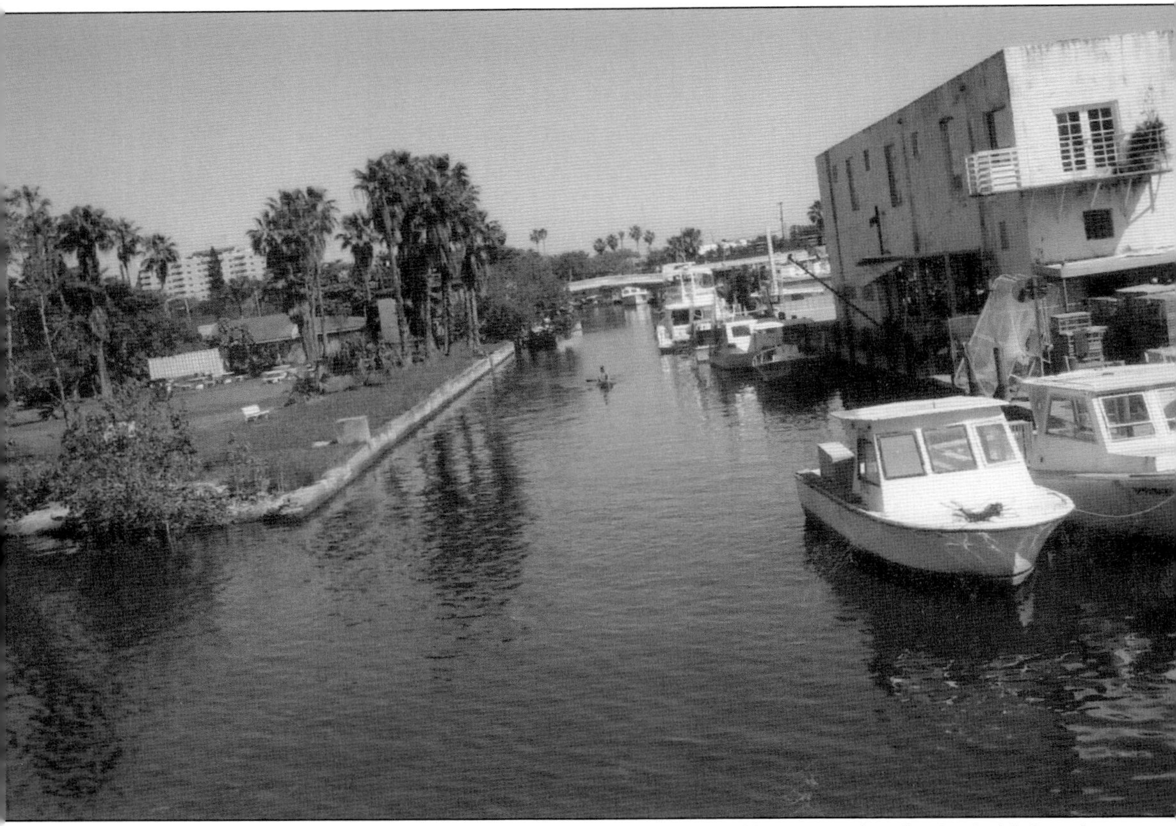

Initially known as Wagner Creek for William Wagner, a local homesteader, the Seybold Canal runs along the eastern edge of beautiful Spring Garden, an early-20th-century Miami neighborhood. The canal, which flows off of the Miami River just northwest of downtown, was widened and deepened in the early 1900s, when John Seybold, Miami's premier banker, carved Spring Garden out of a subtropical hammock. Note the Seybold (or "Humpback") Bridge in the distant center of the photograph. In the left-hand portion of the picture is Spring Garden Point Park, a city park that provides striking views of the busy river as well as of the towers of the downtown and Brickell Avenue neighborhoods to the southeast. (Courtesy of Elliot Salloway.)

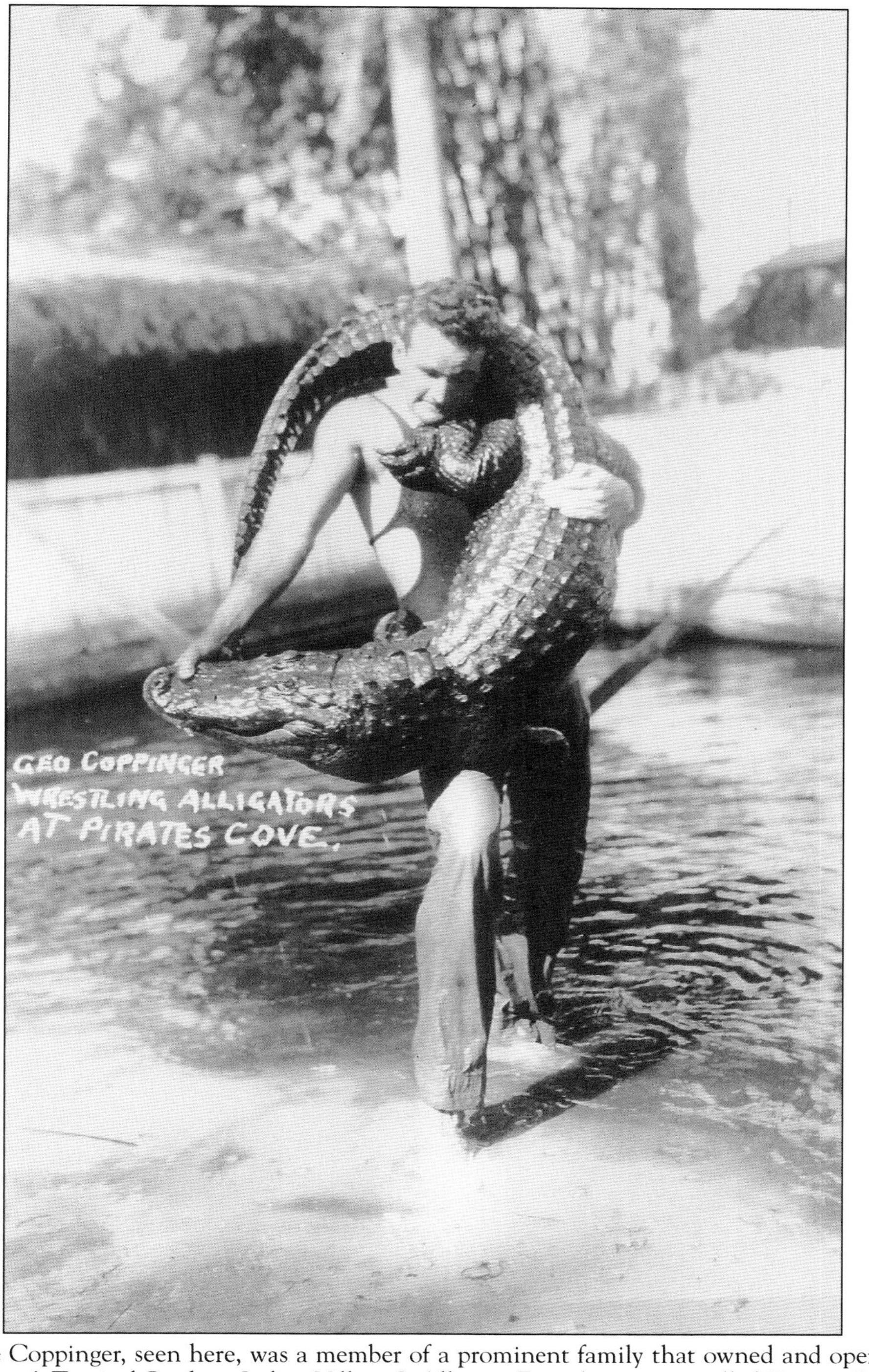

George Coppinger, seen here, was a member of a prominent family that owned and operated Coppinger's Tropical Gardens, Indian Village & Alligator Farm (sometimes called "Pirates Cove") on the south bank of the Miami River at Northwest Nineteenth Avenue. George, his father, Henry Sr., and brother Henry Jr. thrilled thousands of visitors over the course of many years with their alligator wrestling feats. (Courtesy of Larry Wiggins.)

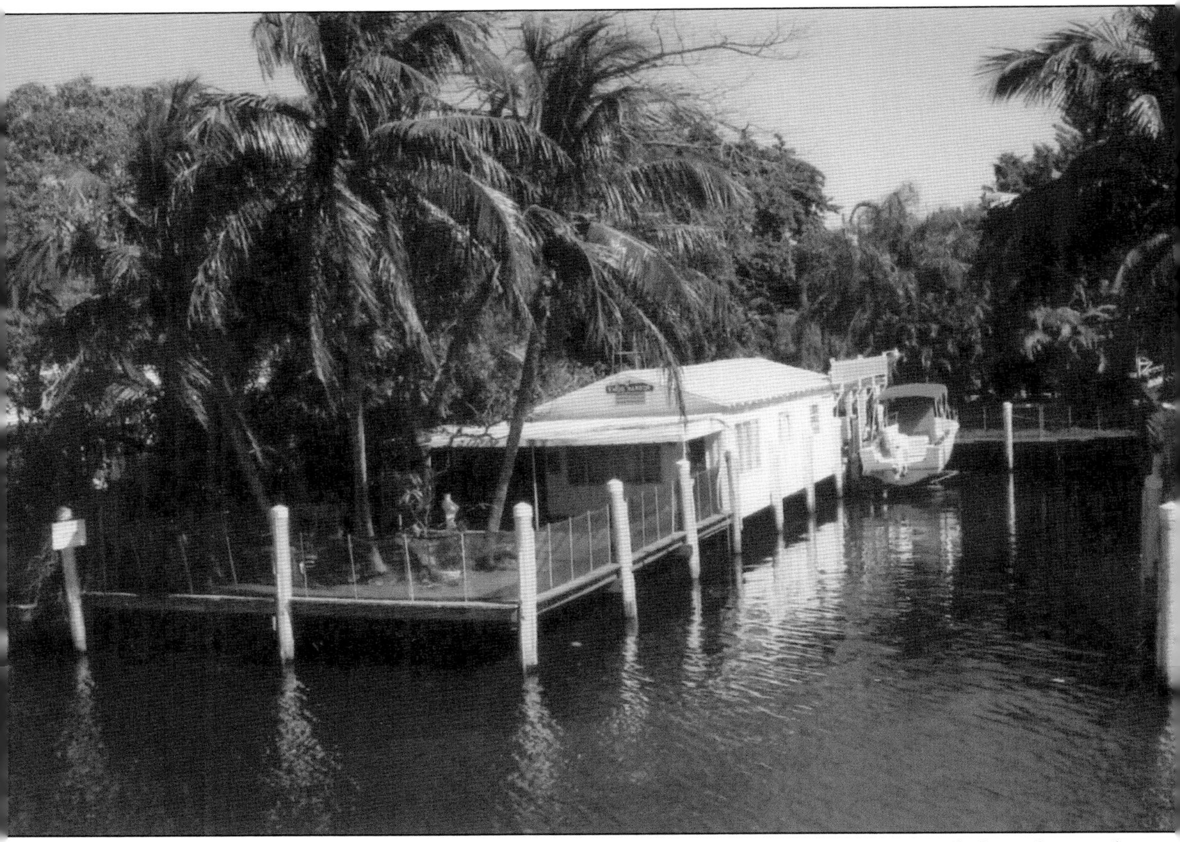

This idyllic view of Spring Garden shows one of its earliest structures surrounded on three sides by water. A subtropical hammock before its development nearly 100 years ago, Spring Garden remains a verdant village. (Courtesy of Elliot Salloway.)

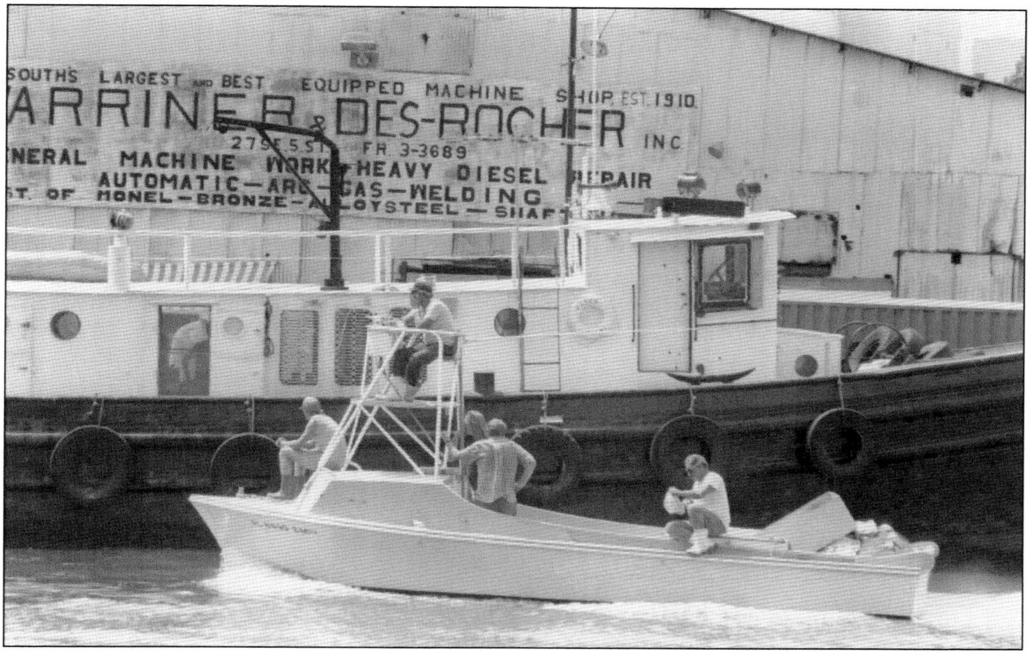

Warriner & Des-Rocher, Inc. was an early machine shop on the Miami River that developed into one of the area's largest marine-engine-repair businesses. Located east of South Miami Avenue, it began operating in 1910 and continued in business for more than a half century. (Courtesy of the author.)

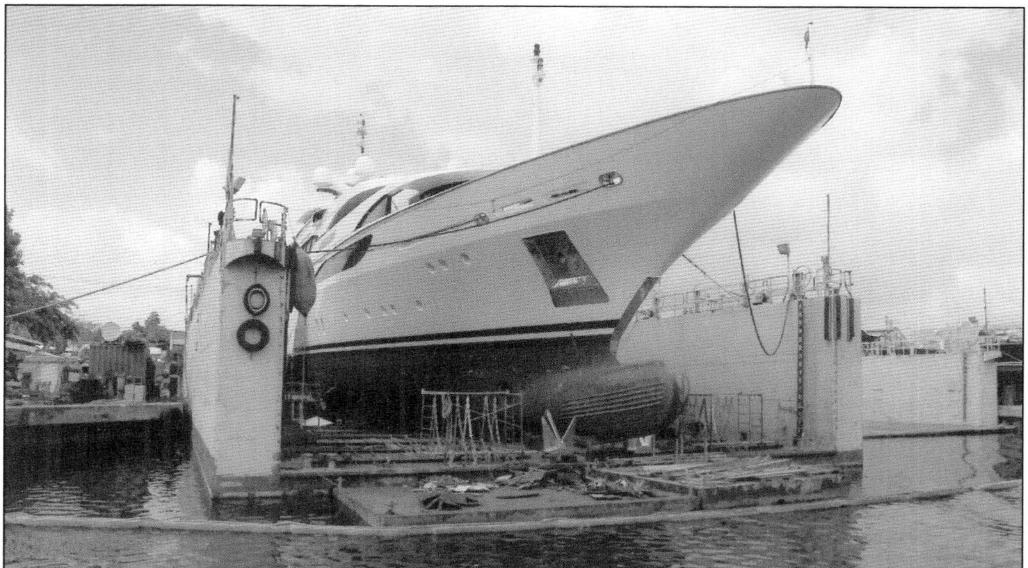

Founded nearly 100 years ago, Jones Boatyard is the oldest extant business on the Miami River and the largest boatyard in southeast Florida. Located at 3399 Northwest South River Drive, Jones Boatyard was operated by its namesake family until recent years; its present owner is Jose Bared. The boatyard features three dry docks and is capable of working on vessels of 300 feet in length. (Courtesy of Elliot Salloway.)

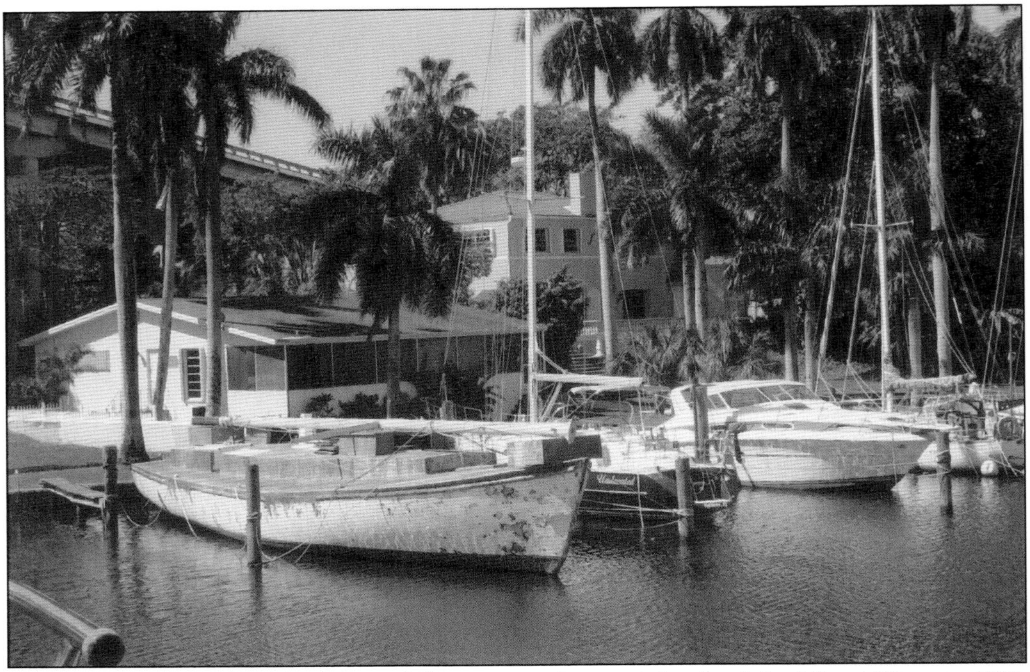

Beautiful Grove Park opened as a subdivision on the south bank of the Miami River in 1921. Situated between Northwest Seventeenth and Fourteenth Avenues, with Northwest Seventh Street as its southern border, the subdivision was another development of the Tatum brothers—Smiley, B.B., J.H., and R.F.—who were among early Miami's most important developers. To sell lots in this new subdivision, the brothers employed full-page advertisements in local newspapers, exhorting readers: "Don't Be A Bolshevist, Buy a Lot." (Courtesy of Elliot Salloway.)

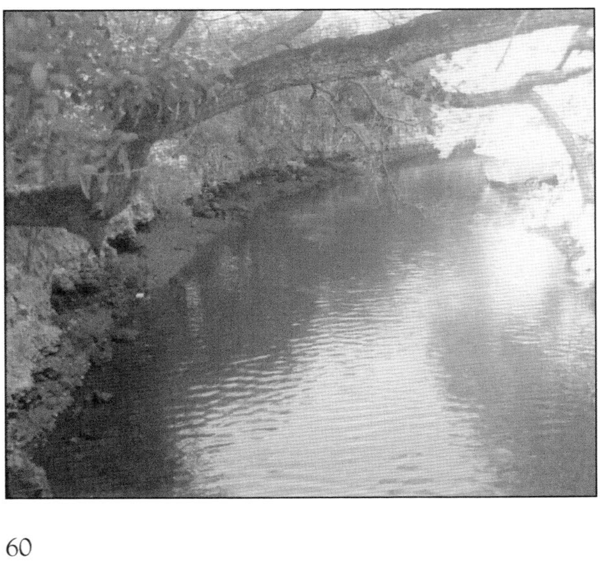

Built by developer W.A. Williams as part of his Lawrence Park subdivision in the early 1920s, the shallow Lawrence Canal cut through the oolitic limestone ridge running along the south bank of the river in the Northwest Seventeenth Avenue area. Named for Gen. Samuel Lawrence, the onetime property owner, the canal flows past "Indian Caves" and under the Dolphin Expressway en route to its southern terminus at Northwest Seventh Street. Williams envisioned the stream as a "grand inland waterway" for his subdivision. (Courtesy of the author.)

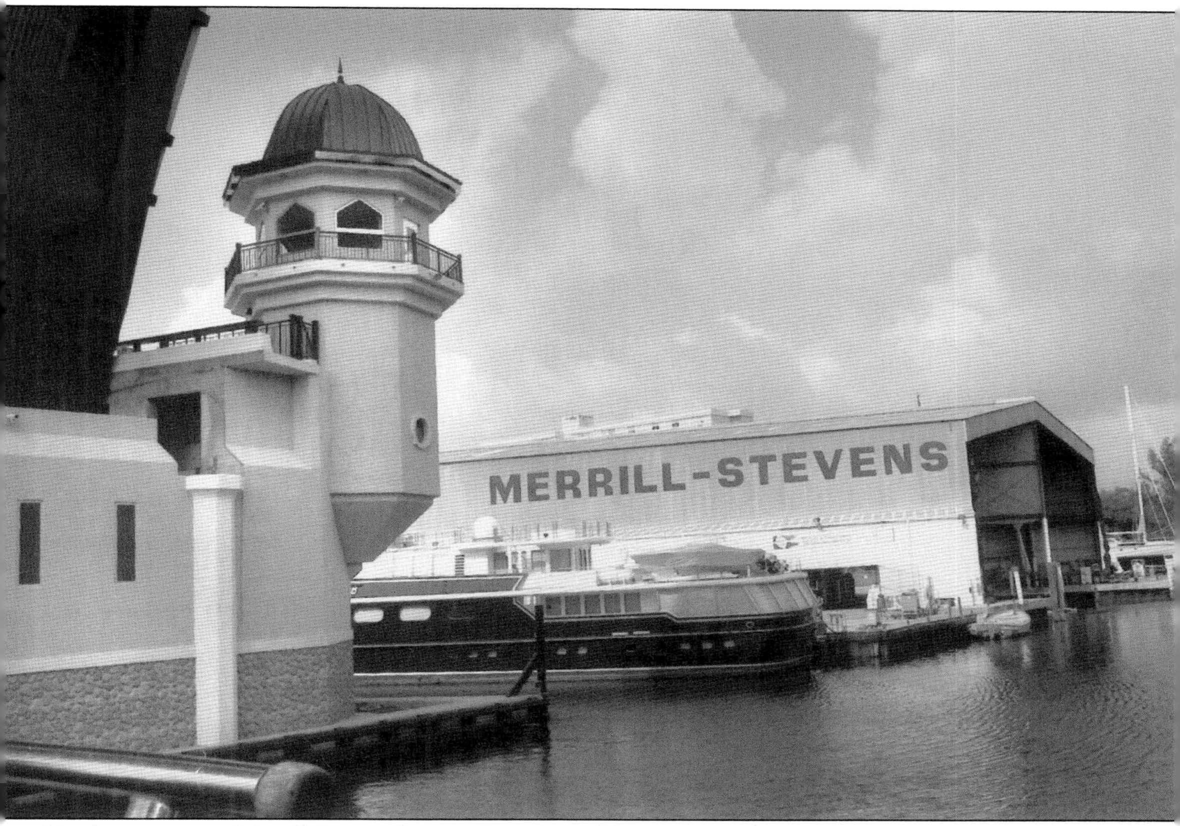

Until recent years, Merrill-Stevens boatyard was one of the most venerable and important businesses on the Miami River. Founded in the 1860s in Jacksonville, the company opened a Miami boatyard in 1923, servicing many of the finest yachts in the region. Beset by financial problems, it closed in 2009. Today, one of its former principals has opened a yacht business on the premises, which lie on both banks of the Miami River just west of the Northwest Twelfth Avenue Bridge. This photograph highlights the shed located on the south bank of the stream. The turreted bridge tender's office, seen here on the recently completed span, replicates the same element on the Hindu Temple home standing in Spring Garden. (Courtesy of Elliot Salloway.)

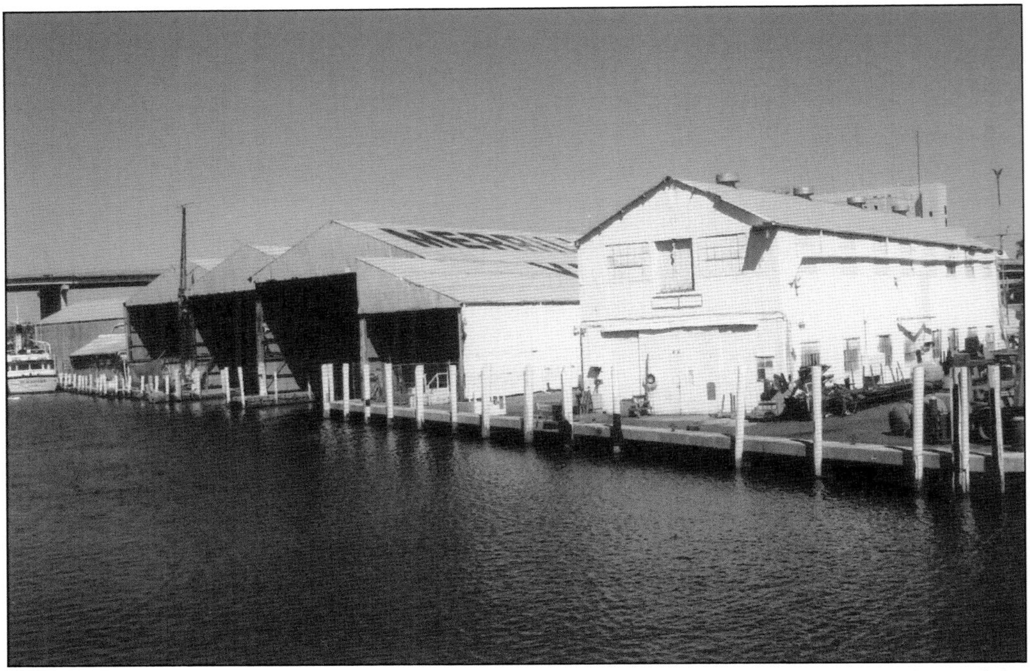

The original location of Merrill-Stevens on the Miami River was on the north bank, just beyond the Northwest Twelfth Avenue Bridge. The sheds seen here were built in the aftermath of the mighty hurricane of 1926, which destroyed the original 1923 facility. (Courtesy of Elliot Salloway.)

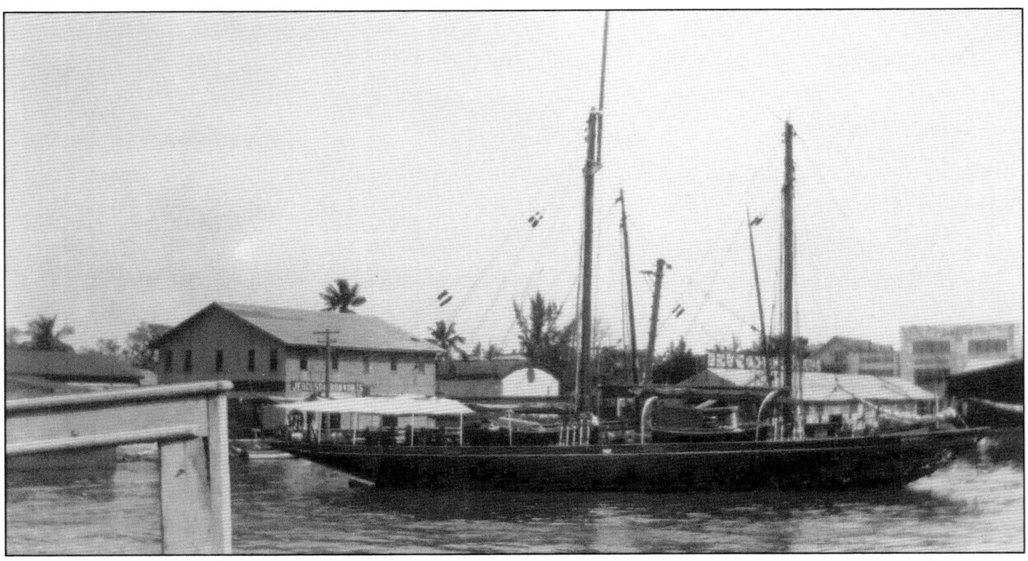

The English vessel the *Mystery*, pictured on the Miami River in 1924, presages the arrival of many more recycled freighters from that country that would be employed in moving cargo in and out of the Second Port of Miami, the state's fifth-busiest port. (Courtesy of the Arva Moore Parks Photograph Collection.)

Three

The Emerging Metropolis

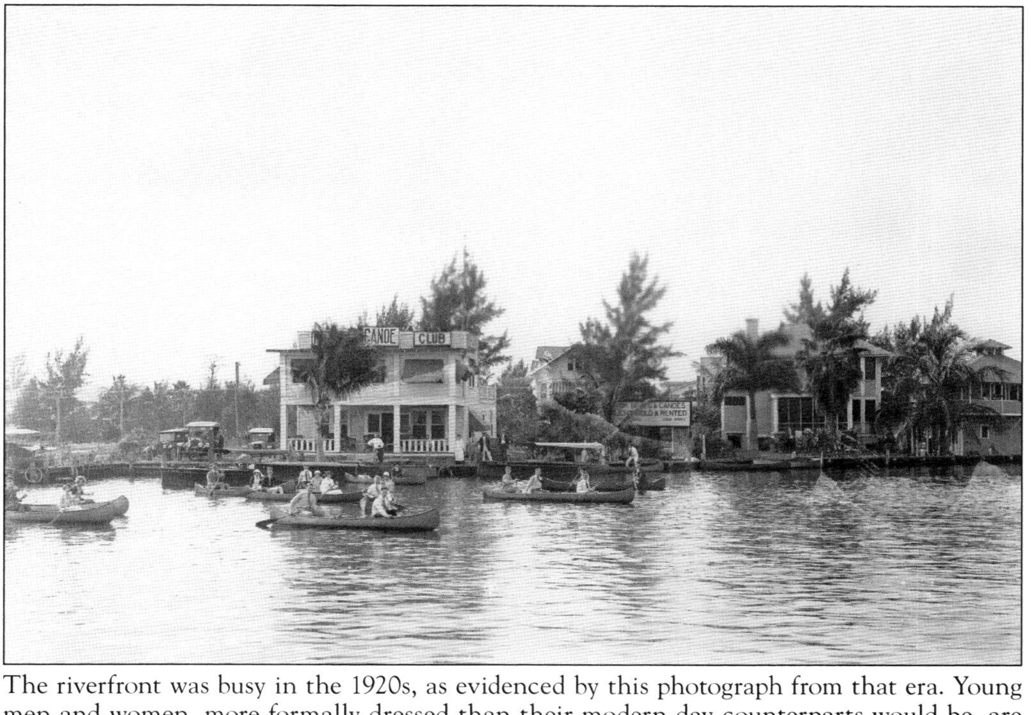

The riverfront was busy in the 1920s, as evidenced by this photograph from that era. Young men and women, more formally dressed than their modern-day counterparts would be, are seen rowing in front of the clubhouse for the Miami Canoe Club. To the right of the building, located on the south bank of the stream near Southwest Fourth Avenue and Second Street, are several handsome wood-frame buildings that date to the beginnings of the beautiful subdivision of Riverside in 1904. Today's splendid Miami River Inn incorporates some of these structures. (Courtesy of the author.)

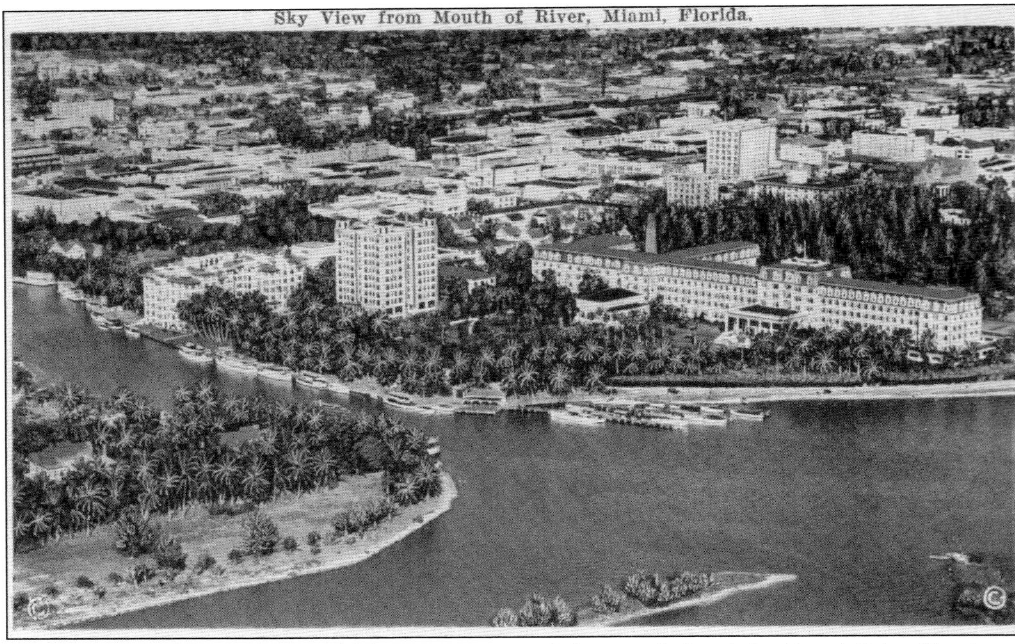

As Miami developed, the junglelike appearance of the area behind the Royal Palm Hotel was replaced by trees arranged in a more symmetrical fashion. Across the river from the Royal Palm, the Brickell property remained sparsely developed and even more verdant. At the bottom center of this mid-1920s photograph sits Burlingame Island, still small and undeveloped. (Courtesy of Larry Wiggins.)

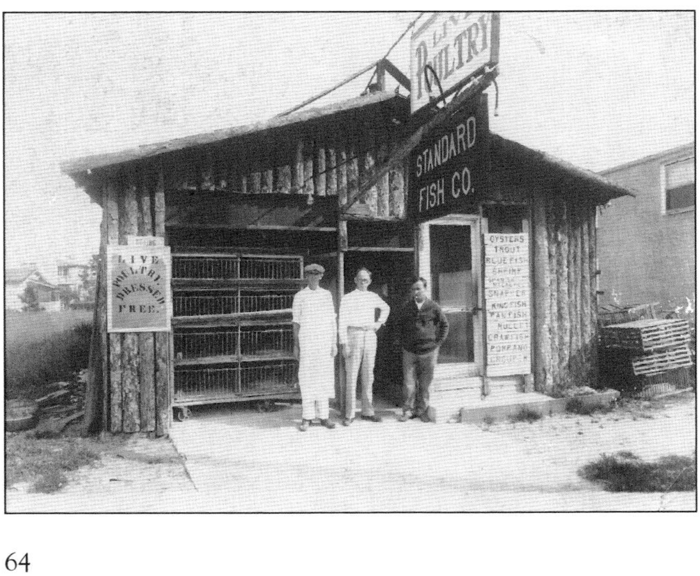

Early Miami contained a large Bahamian population, and many Bahamians were involved in maritime endeavors. Pictured in the 1920s, William "Tweedy" Sawyer (center), arrived in Miami from the Bahamas in the early 1900s and established the Standard Fish Company on West Flagler Street, near the Miami River. Fishing boats on the river brought fresh catches to Sawyer's business. (Courtesy of the author.)

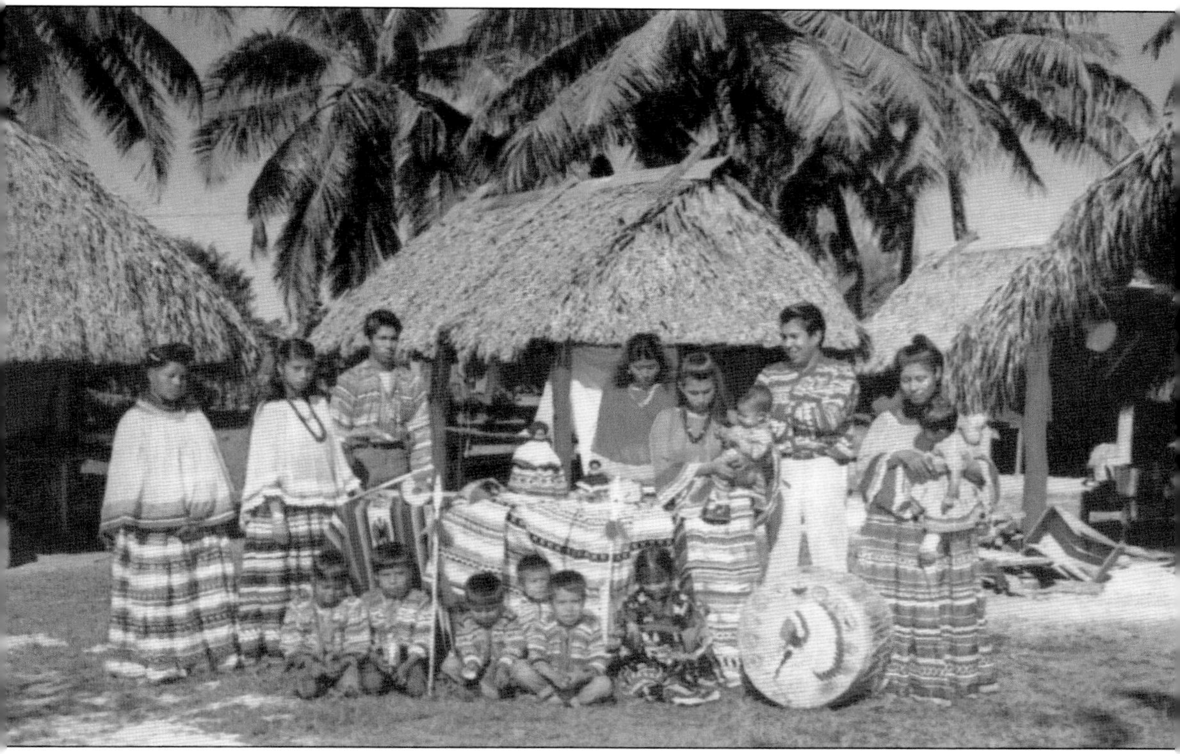

Henry Coppinger opened Coppinger's Tropical Gardens on the south bank of the Miami River, near Northwest Nineteenth Avenue, in 1914. This popular tourist attraction offered alligator wrestling and beautiful gardens. Miccosukees lived here at Coppinger's and were objects of curiosity for the many tourists who visited the attraction. Coppinger's underwent many changes in name and appearance during its lengthy period of operation; it closed in the 1960s. (Courtesy of Larry Wiggins.)

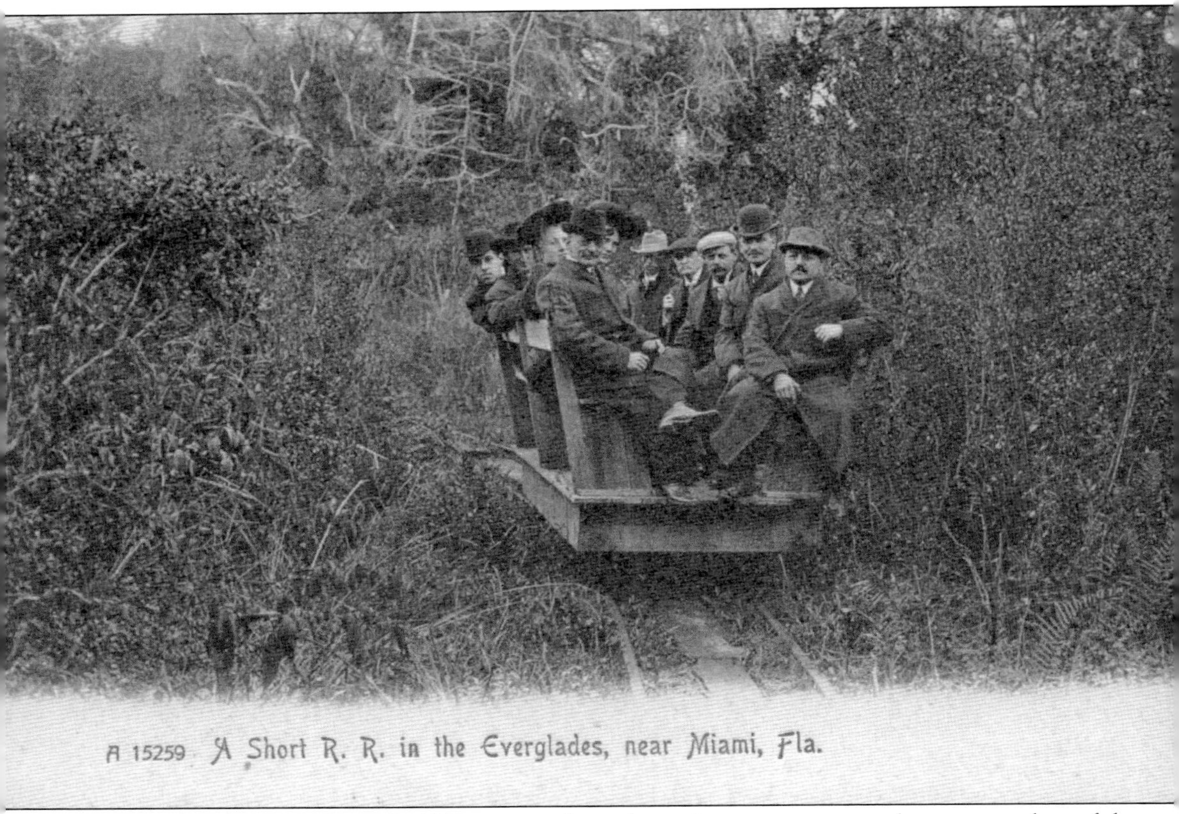

For a brief time in the early 1900s, a train brought curious passengers to the eastern edges of the Everglades, just west of the north fork of the Miami River. The vehicle, known as the *Everglades*, consisted initially of three railcars pulled by a powerful African American man known simply as George. Later, the system was reduced to one car pulled by a mule. The railway took guests to a large house with an observatory room from which to view the mysterious Everglades lying to the west. (Courtesy of Larry Wiggins.)

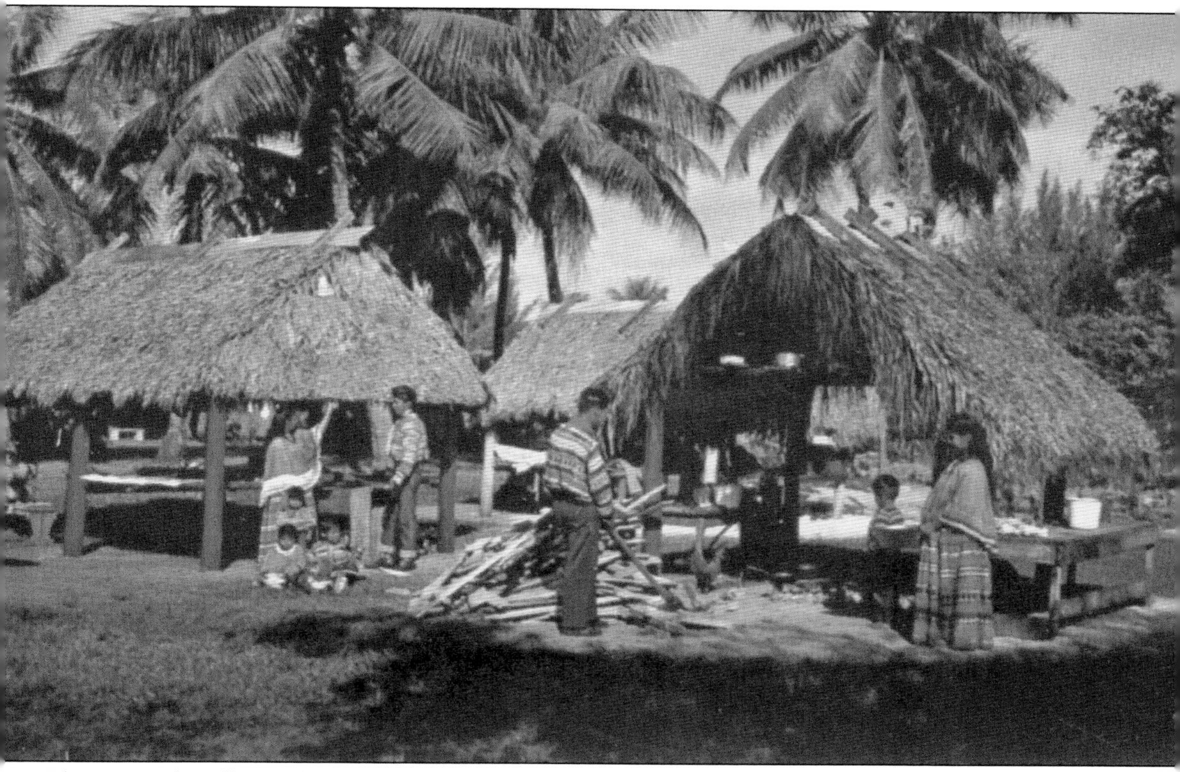

The Musa Isle Village, which opened in 1919, was the most famous of the numerous "villages" that attracted large numbers of tourists during the first half of the 20th century. Located on the south bank of the north fork of the Miami River, near Northwest Twenty-seventh Avenue, the attraction operated until the 1960s. Its most popular offerings involved Miccosukees and Seminoles who lived and performed at the attraction. To add authenticity to the village, chickee huts provided cover and shelter for the denizens of Musa Isle. (Courtesy of Larry Wiggins.)

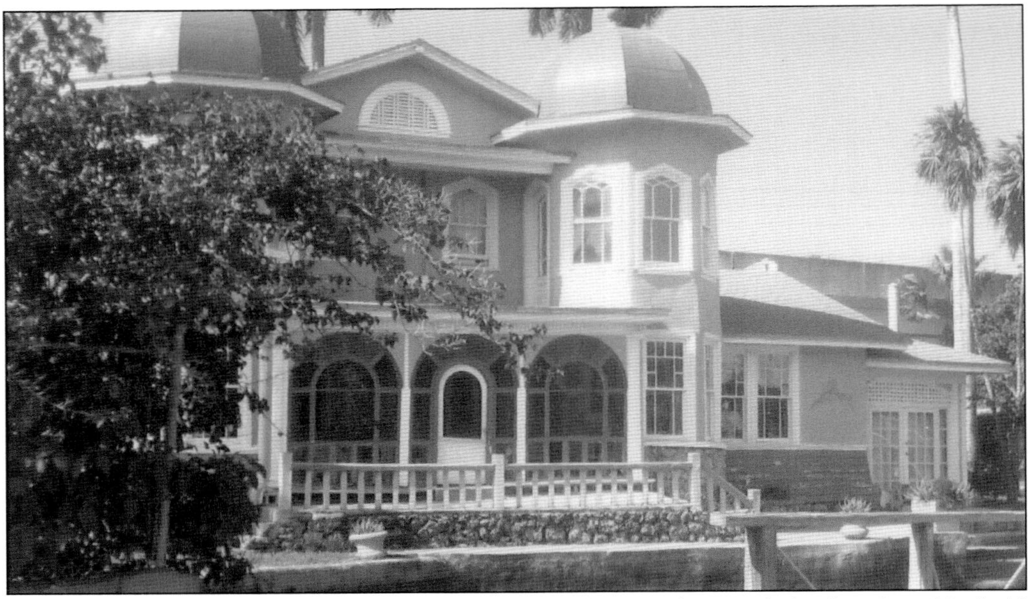

The most stunning home in Spring Garden, the legendary Hindu Temple (at the edge of Seybold Canal) was designed by famed architect August Geiger and built in the mid-1920s for John Seybold. Seybold was inspired by the props for *The Jungle Trail*, a silent movie filmed in Spring Garden in 1919, and the home he had constructed bore something of a resemblance to the movie set. For many years, it was the home of actor Charles O. Richardson; it was also used in filming of the 1994 Sylvester Stallone movie *The Specialist*. (Courtesy of the author.)

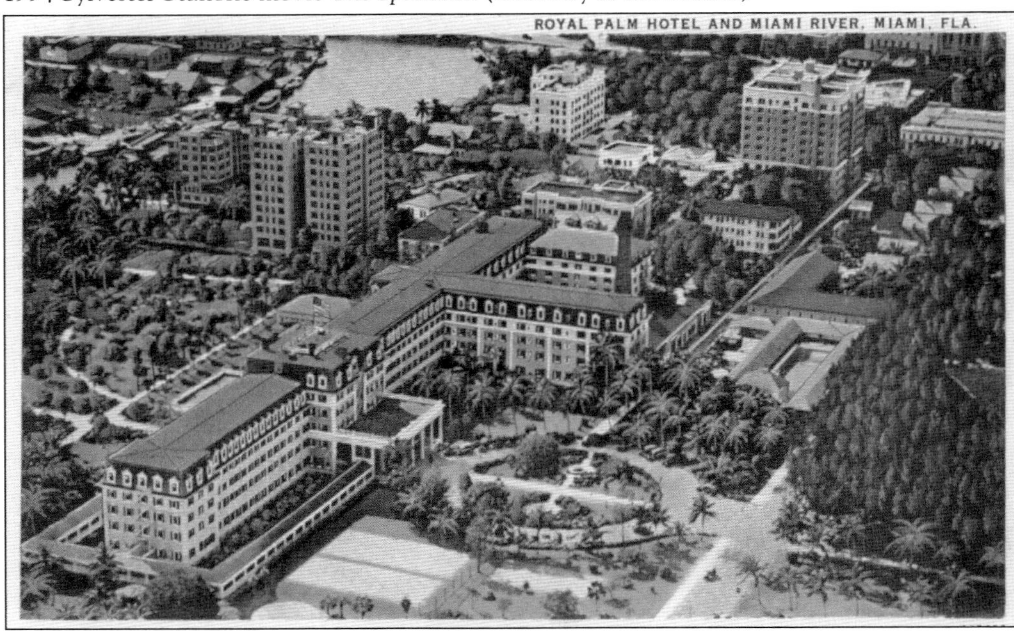

This 1920s aerial view of the Royal Palm Hotel captures it in its full splendor. The gardens behind the hotel extend to the north bank of the Miami River. By this time, a hotel district had arisen to its west, in the Fort Dallas Park neighborhood. The Royal Palm was then entering its final stages and would be unceremoniously razed in 1930. (Courtesy of Larry Wiggins.)

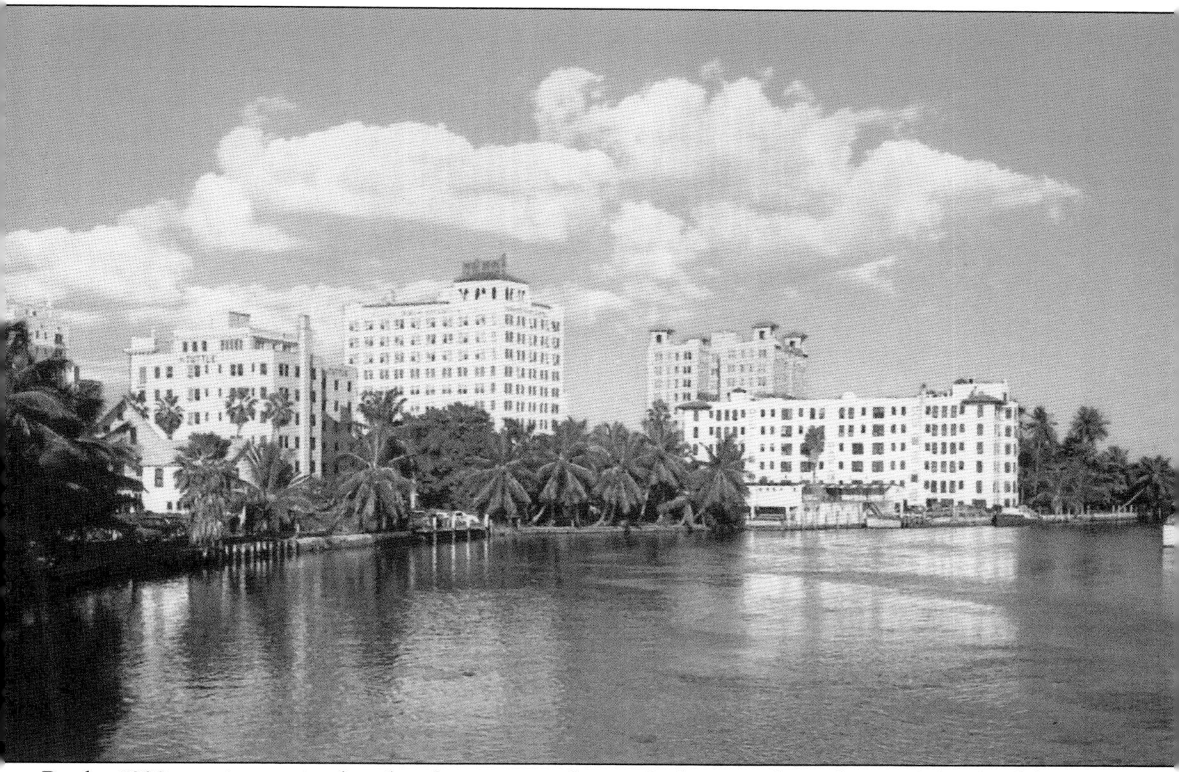

By the 1920s, an impressive hotel and apartment district had arisen along the north bank of the Miami River in the Fort Dallas Park neighborhood (pictured here around the 1930s). The hotels and apartments included the Julia Tuttle, the Henrietta Arms (sometimes known as the "Henrietta Towers"), the Robert Clay, the Dallas Park, and the Granada. The Fort Dallas neighborhood also included an ample amount of green space. (Courtesy of Larry Wiggins.)

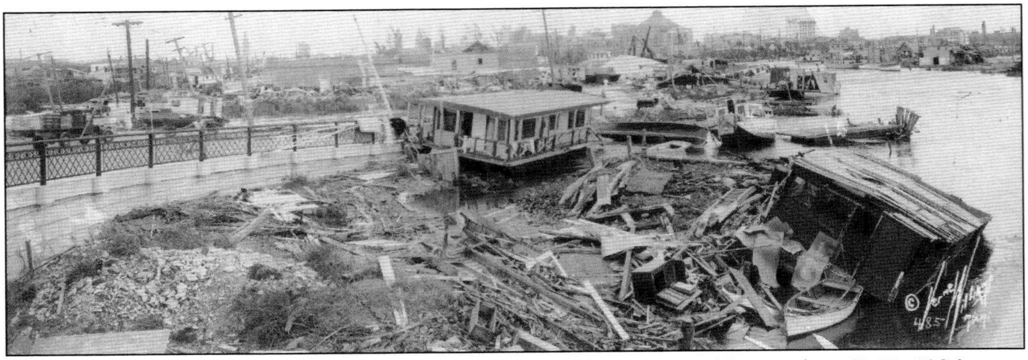

With winds in excess of 130 miles per hour, the mighty hurricane of September 17–18, 1926, cut a wide swath of destruction through Greater Miami. The Miami River felt the storm's fury as a water surge from the stream damaged many properties, and numerous vessels were lifted onto land and damaged. In this photograph, a houseboat is seen sitting next to the Northwest Fifth Street Bridge amid a vast zone of destruction, including the wreckages of other boats. Near the top right-hand corner of the photograph is the majestic Scottish Rite Temple. (Courtesy of Larry Wiggins.)

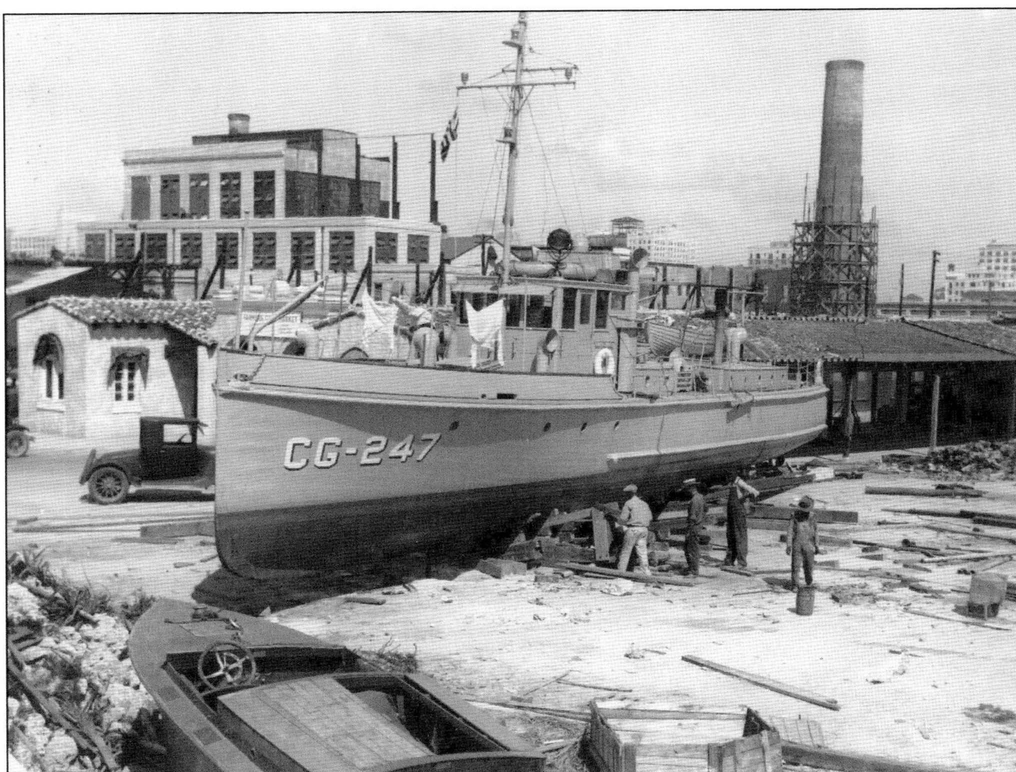

As noted, the mighty hurricane of September 17–18, 1926 sent a water surge over the river's banks in the downtown area and elsewhere, lifting vessels like this US Coast Guard cutter onto the land. This boat is positioned near the Southwest Second Avenue Bridge and the city's Farmer's Market, which stood on the north bank of the River till the 1930s. (Courtesy of Florida State Photographic Archives.)

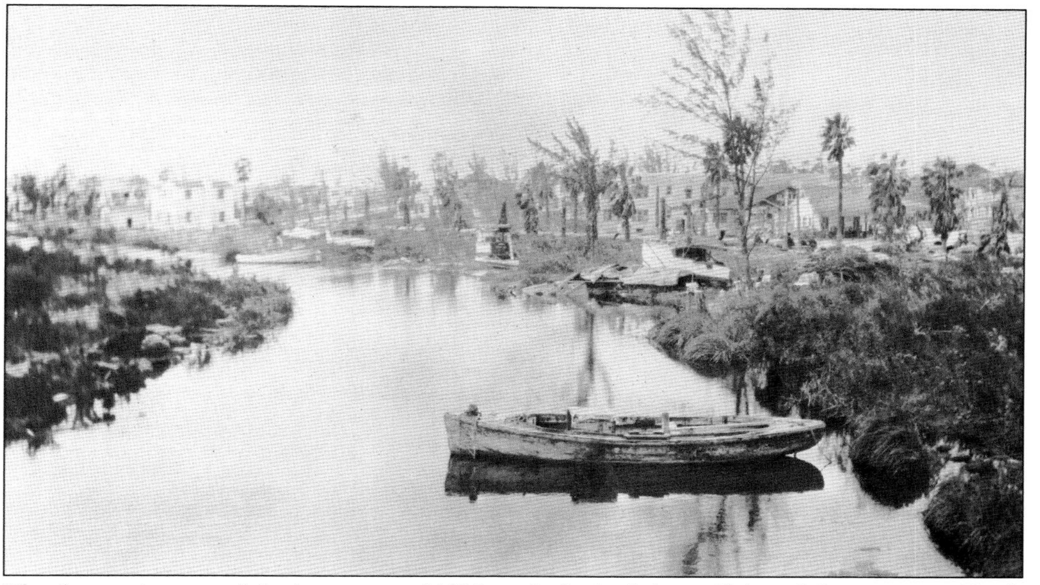

The destructiveness of the hurricane of 1926, with the high loss of life and devastation of both the built and natural environments, is evident in this photograph of the Miami River just beyond the city's downtown sector. (Courtesy of Florida State Photographic Archives.)

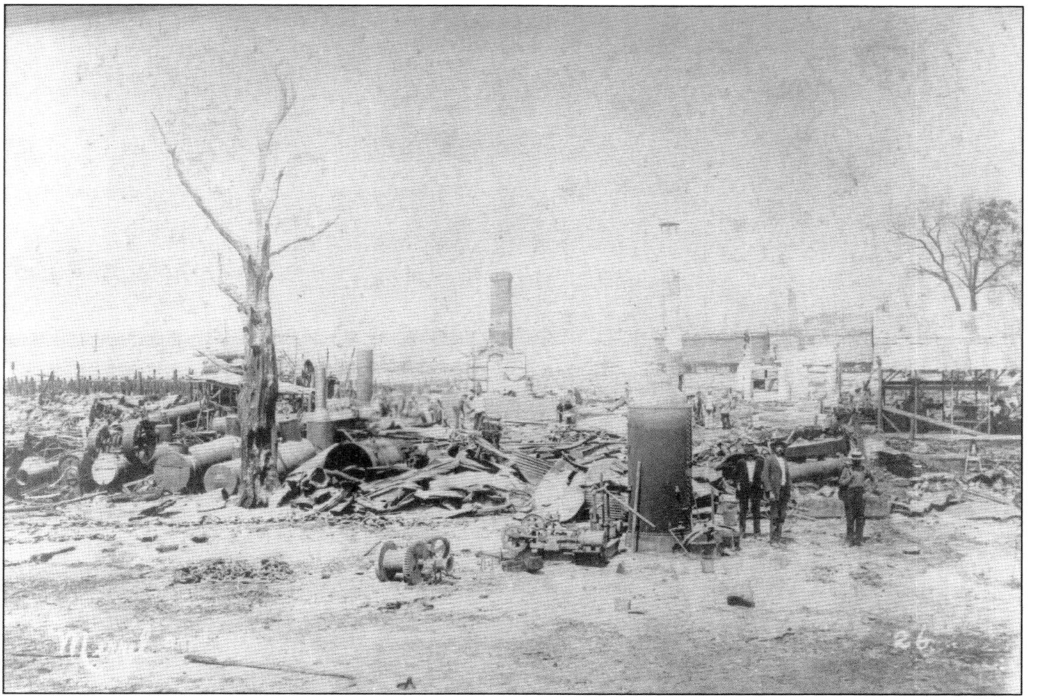

This same hurricane wreaked widespread damage on the Merrill-Stevens boatyard, and the original sheds that constituted the facility were destroyed by the storm. They were quickly replaced by those that are standing today. (Courtesy of the author.)

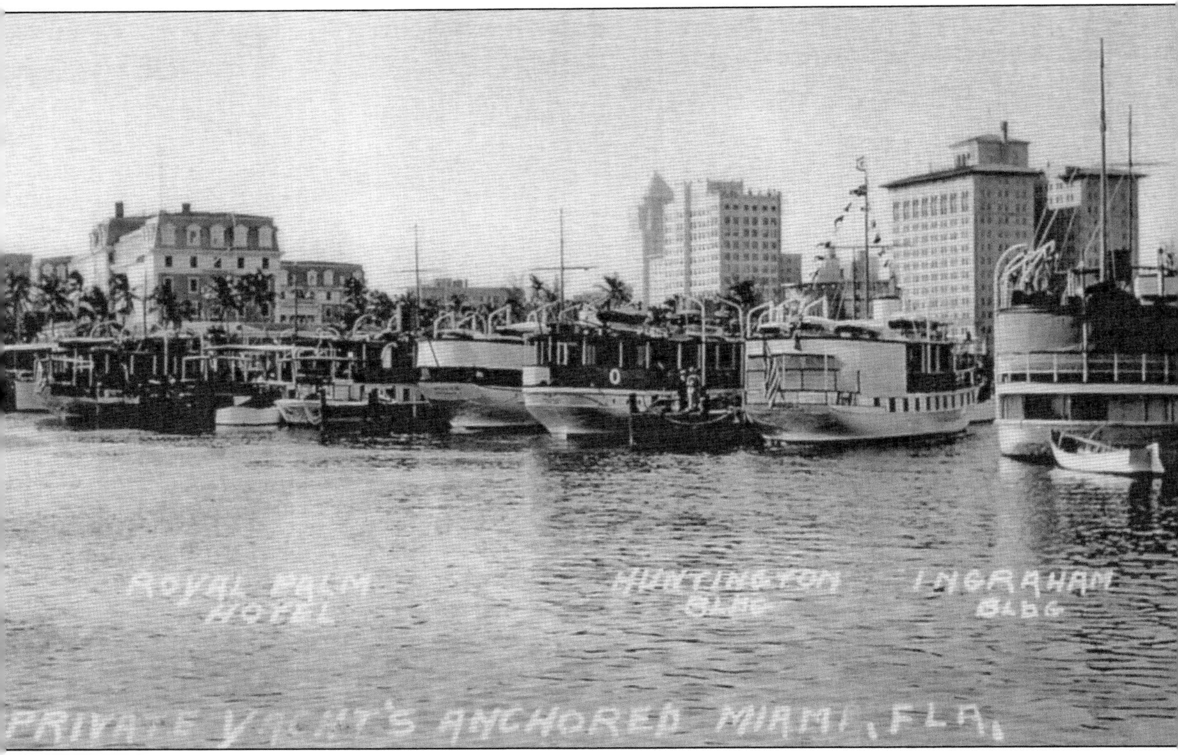

This rare, late-1920s photograph of downtown Miami was taken from Brickell Point on the south bank of the Miami River, near its mouth. The busy Royal Palm Hotel docks are pictured in the center. The venerable Royal Palm Hotel stands in the left-hand corner of the photograph. The three other tall buildings, all products of that era's real estate boom, are, from left to right, the Dade County Courthouse (with its signature ziggurat stepped roof), the Huntington Building, and the Ingraham Building. (Courtesy of Larry Wiggins.)

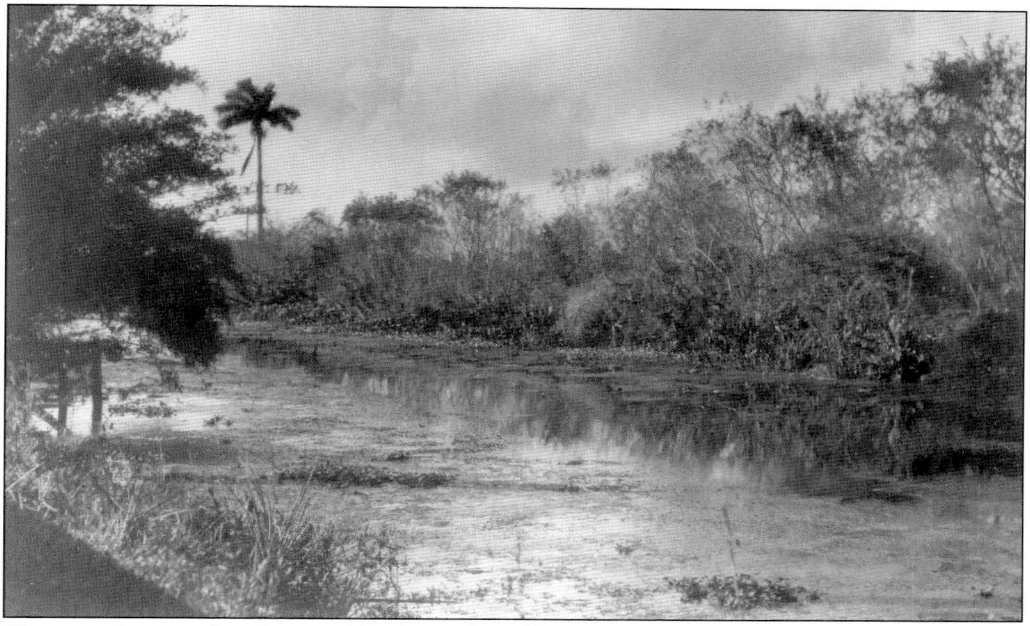

This rare photograph, taken in 1932, shows the still pristine south fork of the Miami River near its headwaters at today's Northwest Twenty-seventh Avenue and Eleventh Street. In the early 1900s, the construction of the Huyler-Comfort Canal (known today as the Comfort Canal) extended the south fork westward where it joined other waterways. (Photograph by Gleason Romer, courtesy of the Arva Moore Parks Photograph Collection.)

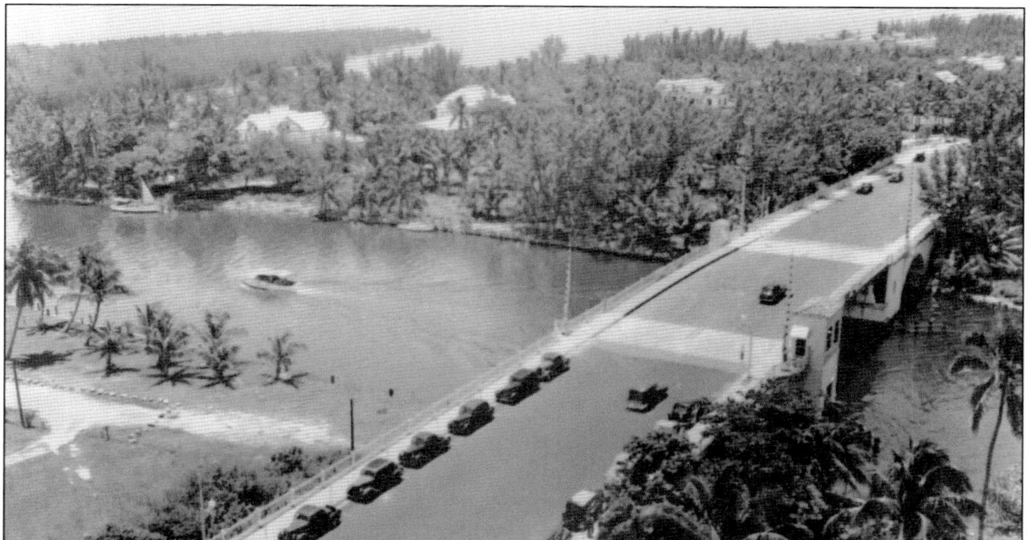

The Brickell Avenue neighborhood, seen in the upper portion of this photograph, was a quaint area at the time of this 1930s picture. It remained a residential neighborhood into the post–World War II era. Today, Brickell Avenue, the neighborhood's signature street, is a forest of high-rise office buildings, hotels, and residential towers. This beautiful thoroughfare, which begins on the south bank of the Miami River, is one of the most pulsating streets in the South. The Brickell Avenue Bridge, seen here, opened in 1930. (Courtesy of the author.)

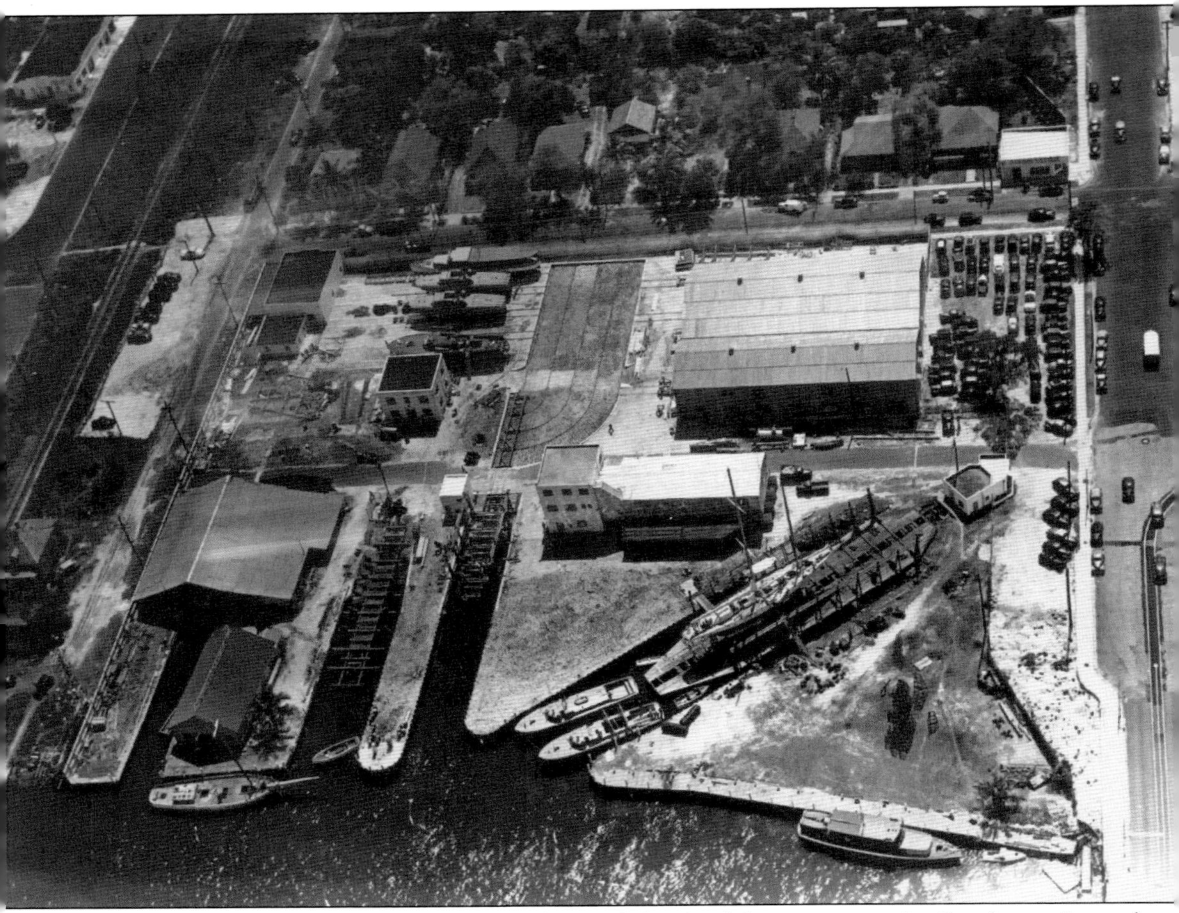

From the outset of the 20th century, the south bank of the river near the Southwest Second Avenue Bridge was the venue for shipbuilding and servicing, as seen in this aerial image taken around the early 1940s. During World War II, the shipyards crafted military vessels, including PT boats. In the lower right-hand corner of the photograph, the trolley tracks host the train that had earlier ambled from downtown Miami across the Southwest Second Avenue Bridge before turning west into the picturesque Riverside neighborhood. Miami in the 1920s and 1930s possessed one of the most extensive streetcar networks in the country. (Courtesy of HistoryMiami.)

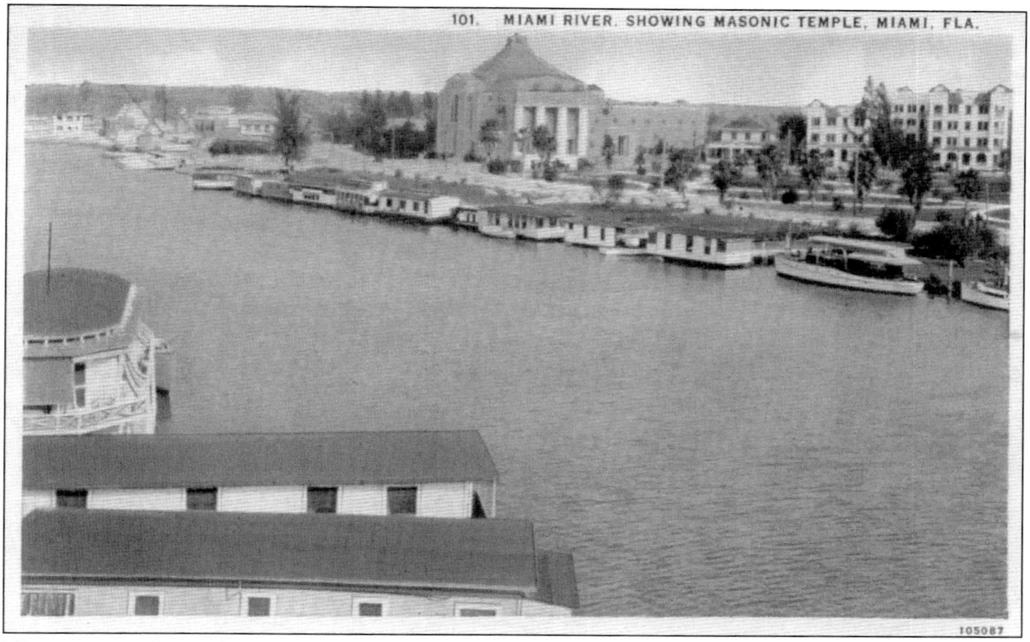

The majestic Scottish Rite Temple, completed in 1924, overlooks the Miami River from its perch at the corner of Northwest Fourth Avenue and Third Street. At the time of this 1930s photograph, the area of the river near the building hosted a large number of houseboats. Between the river and the temple is the northwest edge of historic Lummus Park, one of the county's oldest parks. (Courtesy of Larry Wiggins.)

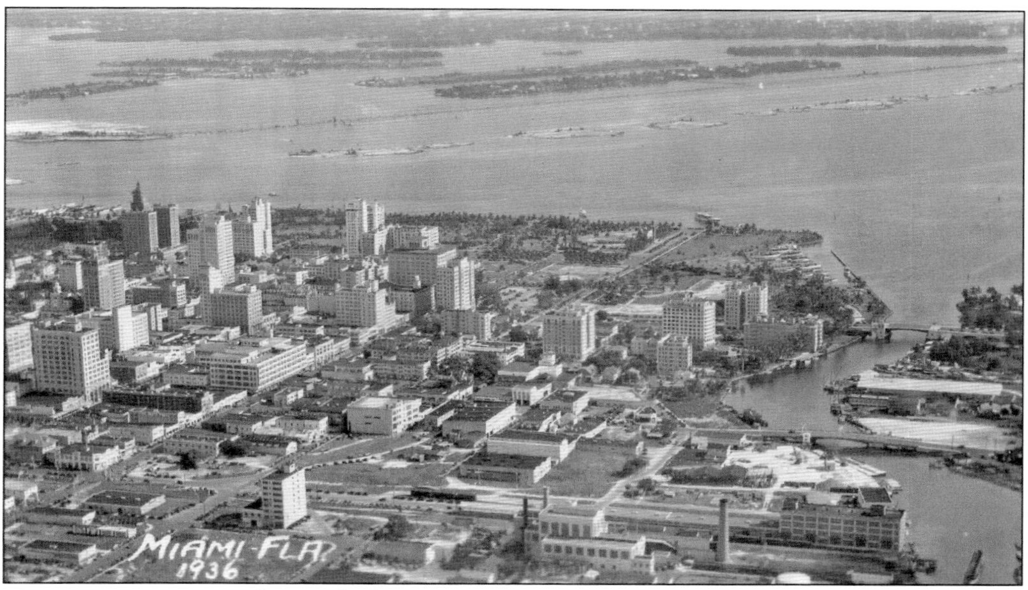

Miami is a watery paradise, with the Miami River spilling into wondrous Biscayne Bay. East of the bay, separated by a onetime barrier peninsula (now the fabled island of Miami Beach), are the warm waters of the Atlantic Ocean. In this 1936 photograph, the serpentine Miami River is flanked on its northern edges by a downtown radically transformed by the great real estate boom of the previous decade. (Courtesy of Larry Wiggins.)

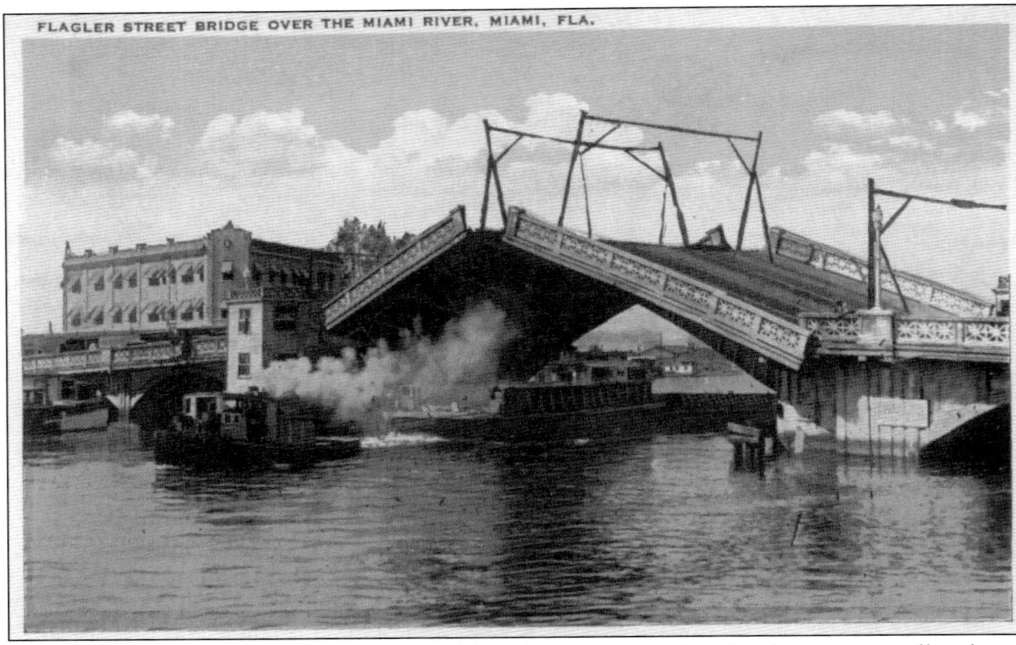

This c. 1930s photograph shows a powerful tugboat spewing diesel exhaust as it pulls a barge upriver while passing under the Flagler Street Bridge. Prior to 1896, the river was a clear, pristine stream, but it quickly became a working river after Miami was incorporated. Conversely, the New River, its deepwater counterpart 25 miles north, which courses through the historic heart of Fort Lauderdale, has remained essentially a pleasure-boat stream. (Courtesy of Larry Wiggins.)

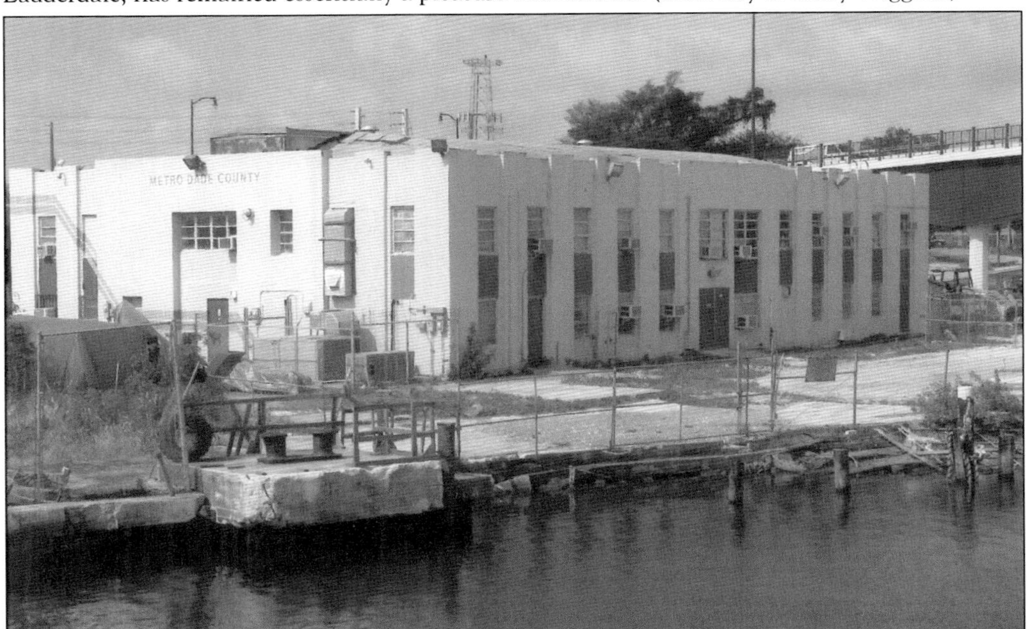

This Art Deco–styled building served as a Naval armory during and after World War II. Later, the county housing authority used the building. Today, it is all but abandoned. (Courtesy of Elliot Salloway.)

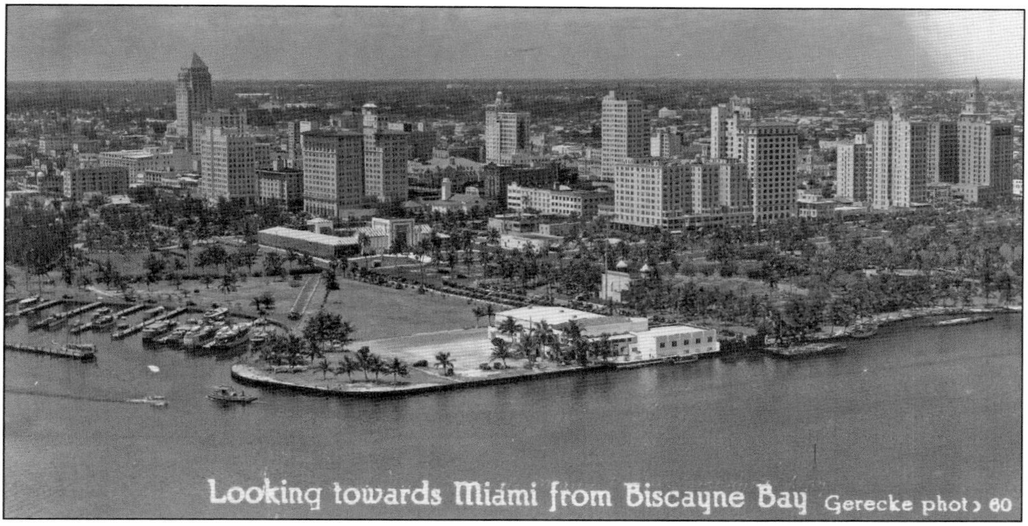

Like the rest of nation, Miami in the 1930s was mired in the Great Depression. The tall buildings seen here in the downtown sector were the result of the great real estate boom of the mid-1920s, whose collapse in 1926 caused an economic downturn in Miami and many other parts of Florida three years before that of the rest of the nation. In the left-hand portion of the photograph, the Royal Palm docks, which once sat behind the great hotel by the same name, reach into the murky waters of the Miami River. In the 1940s, the docks were removed, and the area of the river they once occupied was filled in, narrowing its mouth. (Courtesy of Larry Wiggins.)

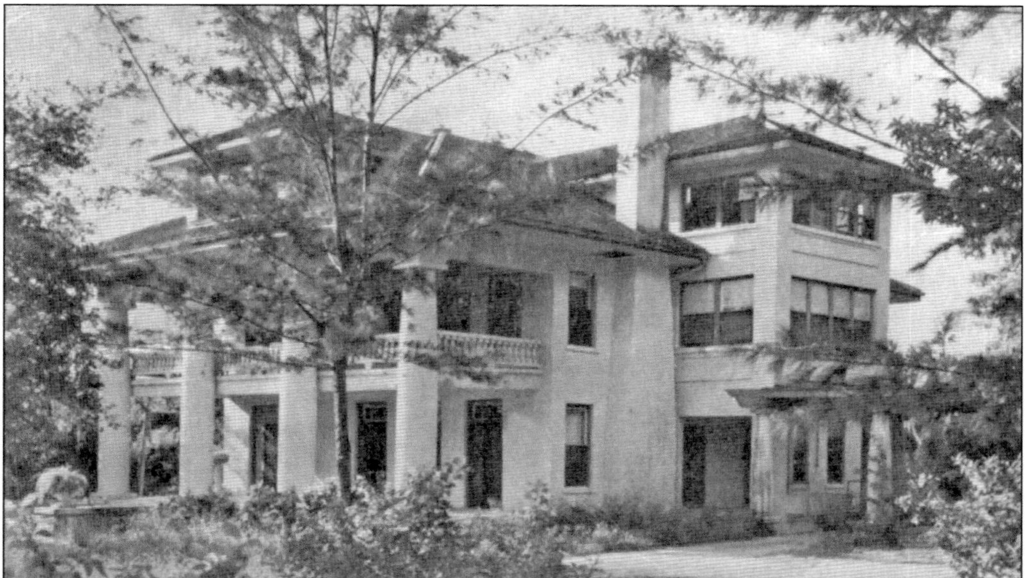

Standing a few blocks northeast of the new Miami Marlins ballpark (the former Orange Bowl site), on six acres of ridge land overlooking the Miami River, Rivermont Park consisted of 30 rooms for patients desirous of "rest, convalescence and treatment." Operated by two physicians, this 1930s-era facility was part of a medical complex that included offices in New York. Today, the Robert King High Tower and the Haley Sofge Towers, both subsidized housing facilities for the elderly, rest on a large portion of this site. (Courtesy of Larry Wiggins.)

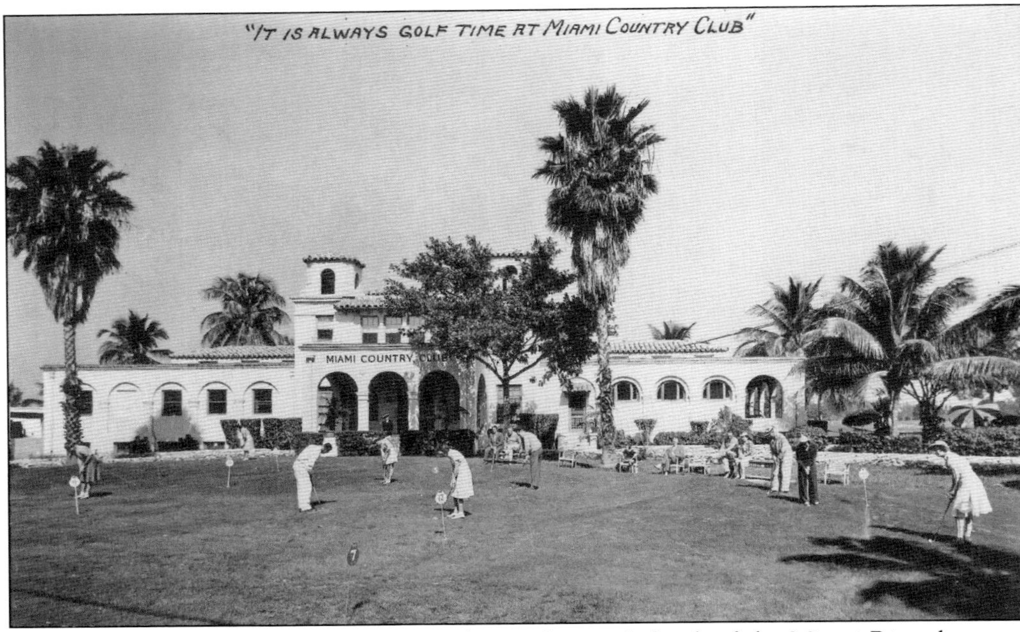

The beautiful Miami Country Club stood near the north bank of the Miami River between Northwest Twelfth and Fourteenth Avenues. Opened in the mid-1920s, the club thrived until the land hosting it was condemned through eminent domain in the mid-1950s. Thereafter, a massive civic center and hospital complex arose on the site of the clubhouse and the old 18-hole golf course that had hosted major golf tournaments, and even, on occasion, initiations for a Miami chapter of the Ku Klux Klan. (Courtesy of Larry Wiggins.)

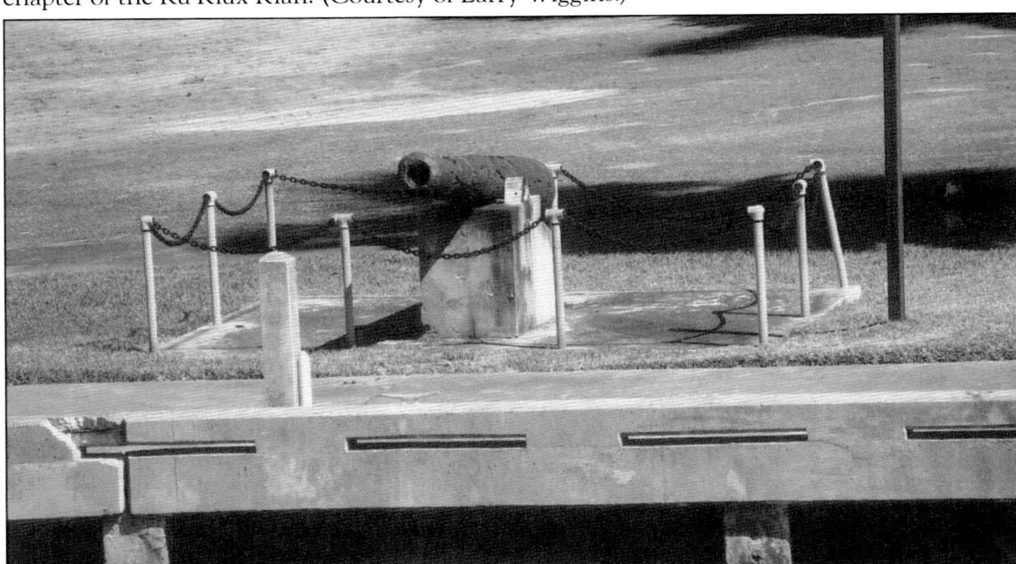

The oldest artifact on the Miami River, this cannon was retrieved from the waters off of Elliot Key in the southern sector of Biscayne Bay. Originally, it sat aboard the HMS *Winchester*, a British war frigate, which went down in stormy seas in 1695. This cannon, along with others, was retrieved more than 70 years ago and brought to this location on the north bank of the river, near Northwest Seventeenth Avenue. (Courtesy of Elliot Salloway.)

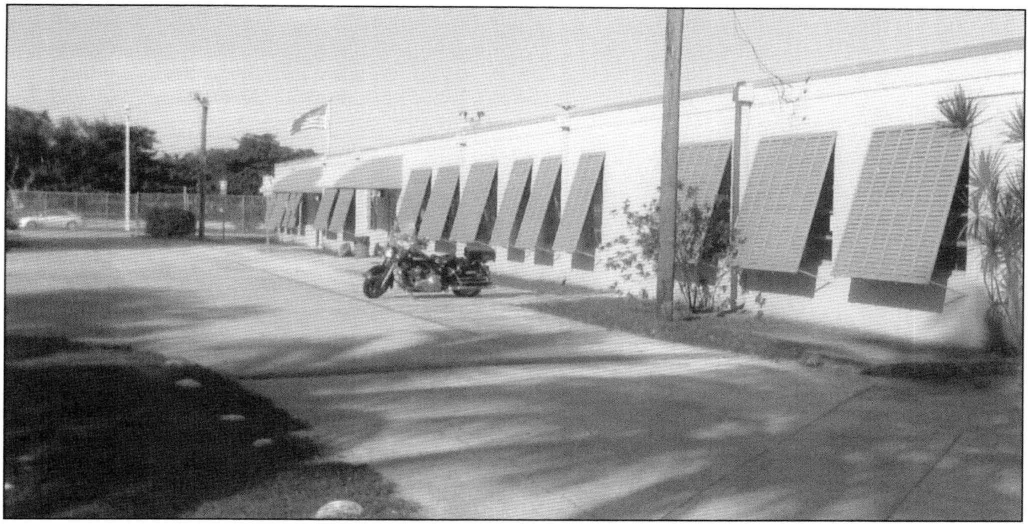

The long, low-lying building located near the south bank of the Miami Canal at 2929 Northwest Seventeenth Street was the home of Fleischer Motion Picture Studios between the late 1930s and the early 1940s. The Fleischer brothers, Max and Dave, produced the highly successful *Superman*, *Betty Boop*, and *Popeye* cartoons in New York City before moving to Miami, where they continued their work. In 1942, Paramount Pictures purchased Fleischer Studios and, soon after, moved production back to New York City. Today, the old movie studio is a Miami Police Department facility. (Courtesy of the author.)

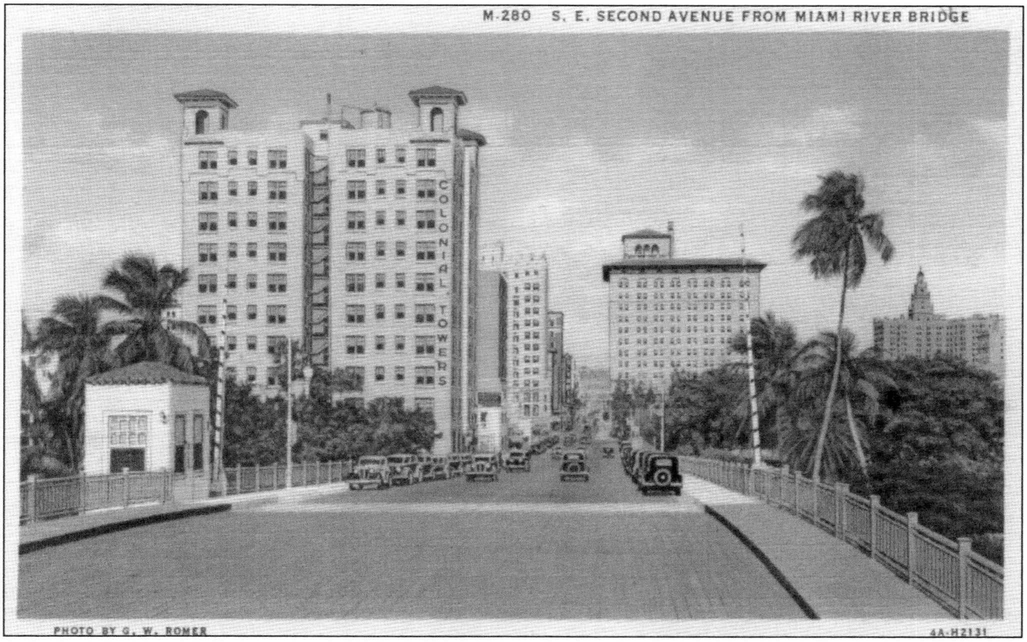

The Brickell Avenue Bridge opened over the mouth of the river in 1930, transforming a quiet neighborhood south of the stream by granting it better access to downtown Miami. Its opening was made possible by the razing of the Royal Palm Hotel, a portion of which, till the late 1920s, stood across the future downtown access to the span. The bridge stood until 1993; two years later, a new span was completed over the river at this critical location. (Courtesy of Larry Wiggins.)

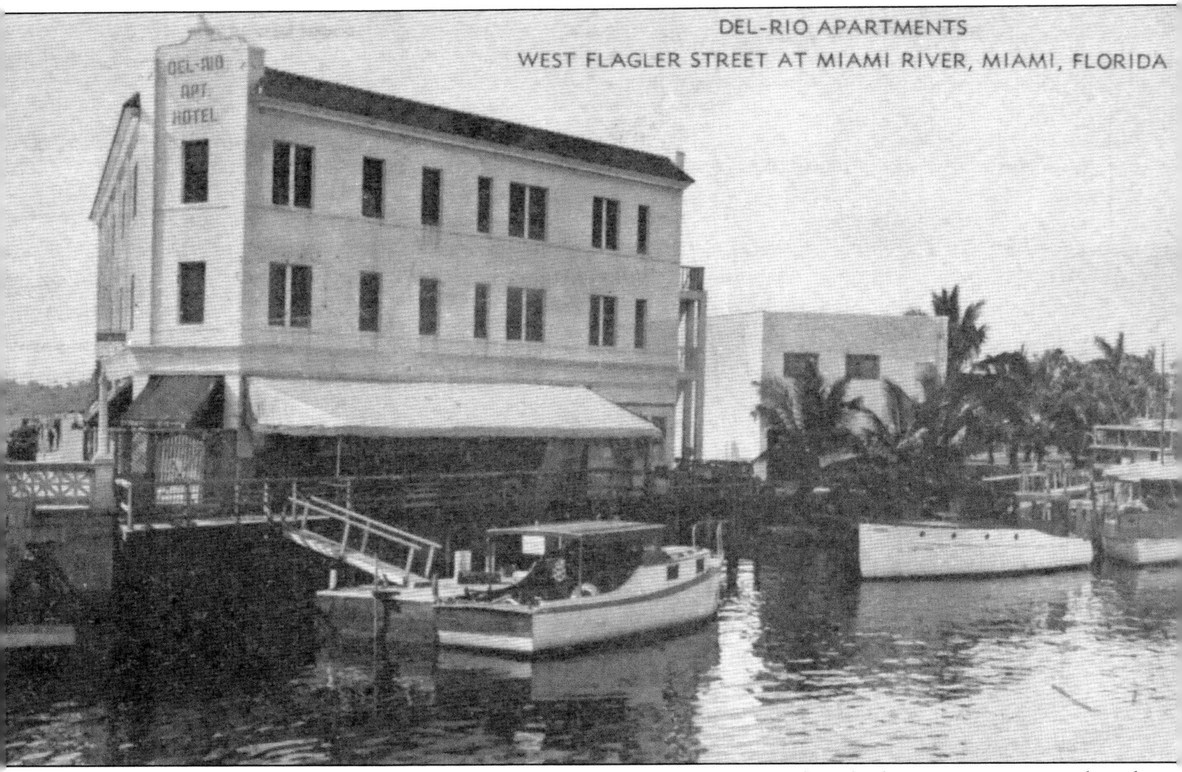

In the mid-20th century, the west bank of the Miami River in the Flagler Street area was lined with apartments, maritime businesses, and even restaurants. The Del-Rio Apartments were among the most prominent of these accommodations. (Courtesy of Ronnie Hurwitz.)

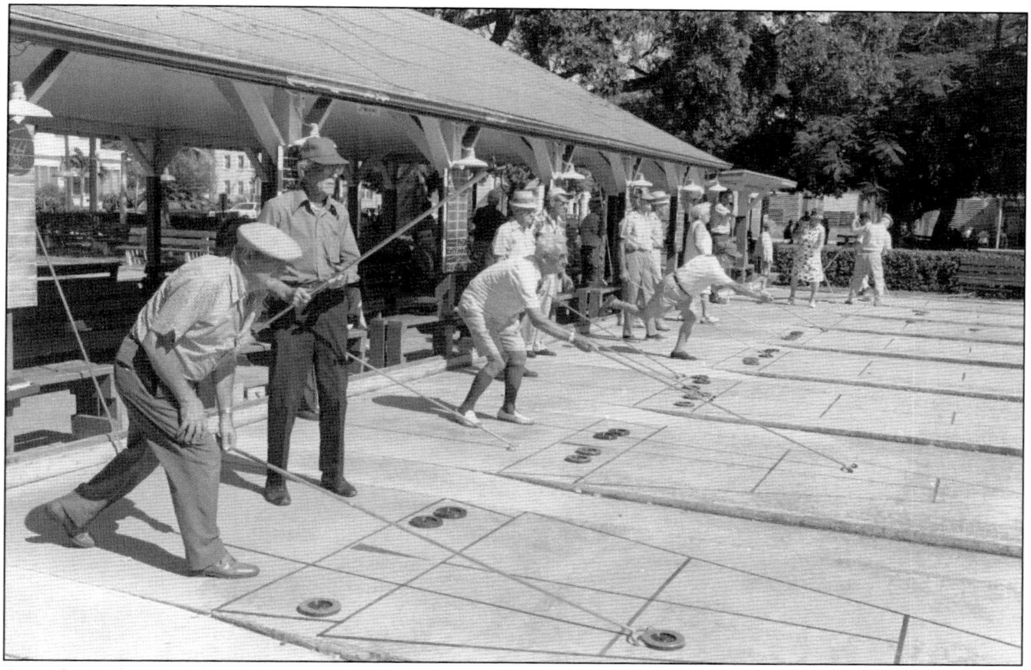

Standing close to the east shore of the Miami River, just northwest of downtown Miami, Lummus Park was the venue for shuffleboard, a sport much loved by tourists. Shuffleboard has left the park, but this greensward remains the home of two of south Florida's most historically important buildings: the William English Slave Plantation House/Fort Dallas and the William Wagner Homestead House. (Courtesy of the author.)

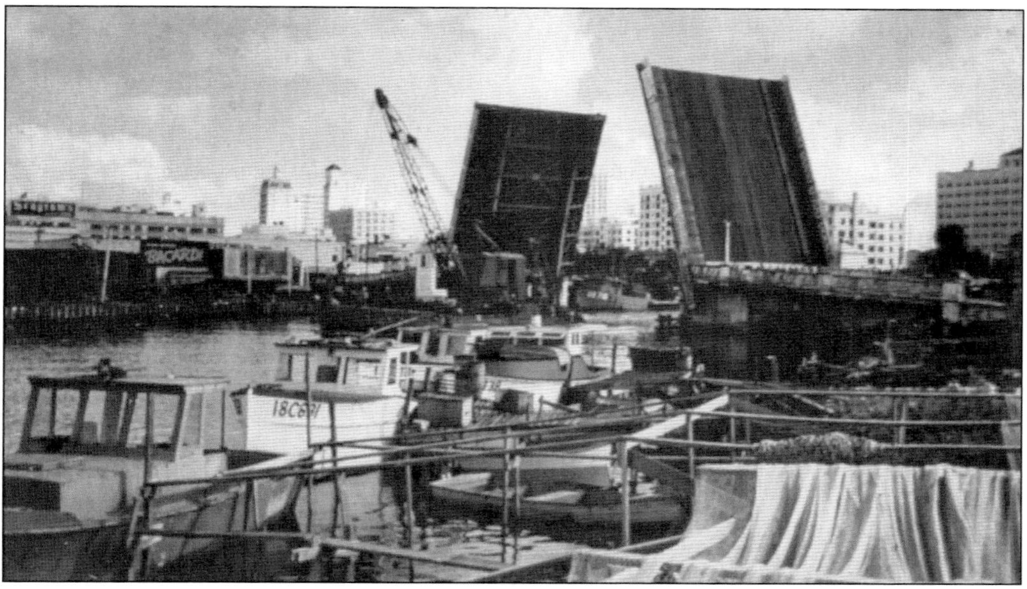

The busy Southwest Second Avenue Bridge, which operated from 1924 till 2001, was quaint in comparison to its high-tech successor. It was, however, busy, as seen in this mid-century photograph. More so in those days than today, boats used to line the shoreline on the south side of the river. (Courtesy of Larry Wiggins.)

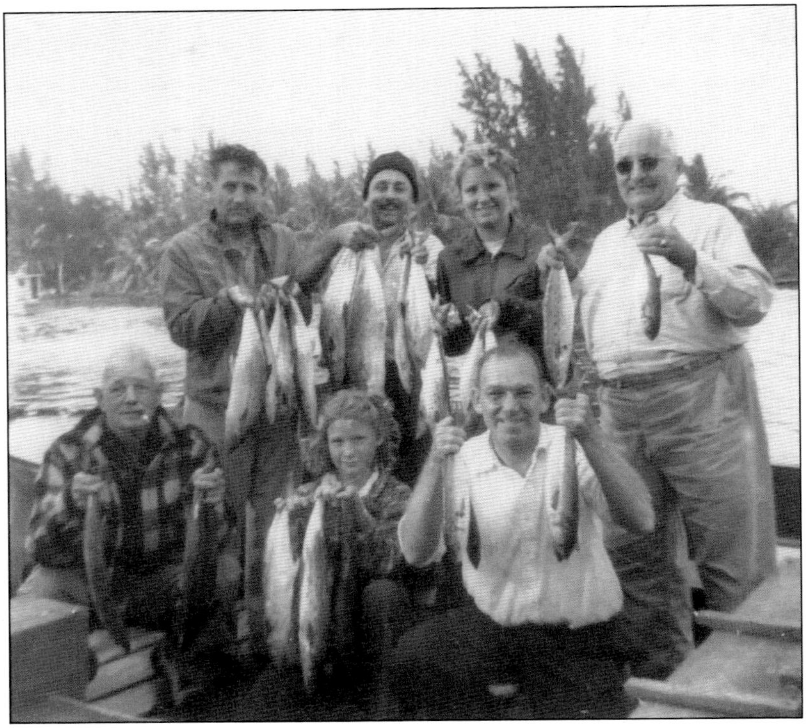

The gleeful Stebbins family, denizens of beautiful Grove Park on the south bank of the Miami River, proudly show off their catches from the nearby waters of Biscayne Bay. The river is the backdrop for this photograph, taken in the late 1940s. (Courtesy of Fred Stebbins.)

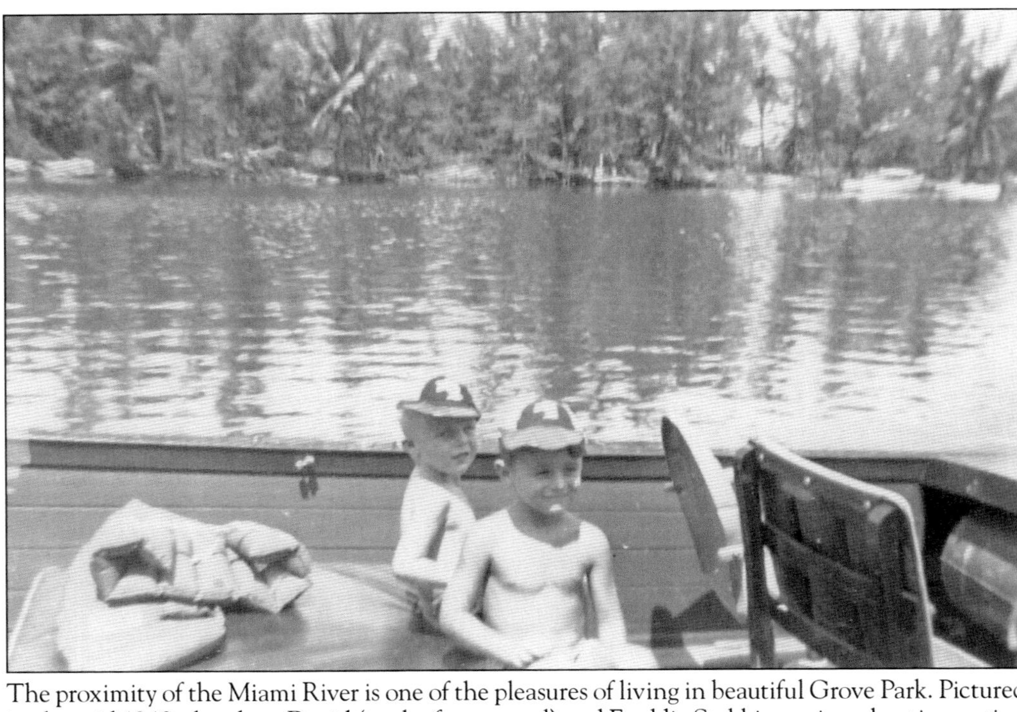

The proximity of the Miami River is one of the pleasures of living in beautiful Grove Park. Pictured in the mid-1940s, brothers David (in the foreground) and Freddie Stebbins enjoy a boating outing on the stream near Northwest Sixteenth Street. (Courtesy of Fred Stebbins.)

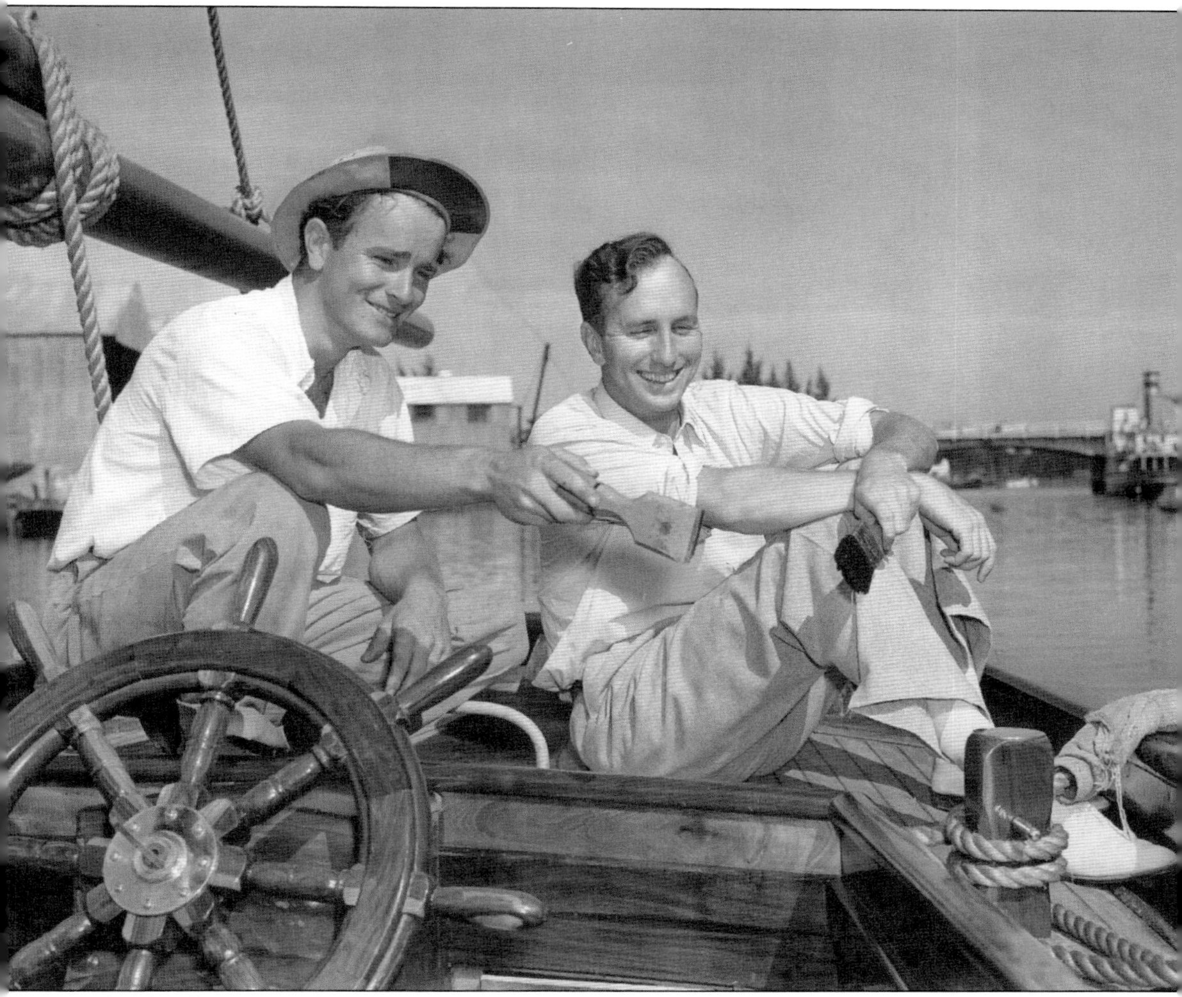

Founded by the sons of famed Dade County sheriff Dan Hardie, the Hardie Yacht Basin was engaged in many maritime tasks, maintaining a significant presence on the river for 60 years with five generations of Hardie family members (including the legendary lawman) employed there until its closing in 2004. Richard (left) and William Hardie, pictured here, were two of the sons of Dan Hardie and were instrumental in the founding and operation of the yacht basin, which encompassed a marina, marine-supply store, fueling dock, pleasure-craft showroom, and a television set for *Miami Vice* and other shows. William Hardie built a schooner called the *Dan Hardie*, which was docked at the Hardie Yacht Basin and retrofitted in World War II as a Nazi-submarine hunter. The versatile yacht basin stood at 2100 Northwest North River Drive. (Courtesy of HistoryMiami.)

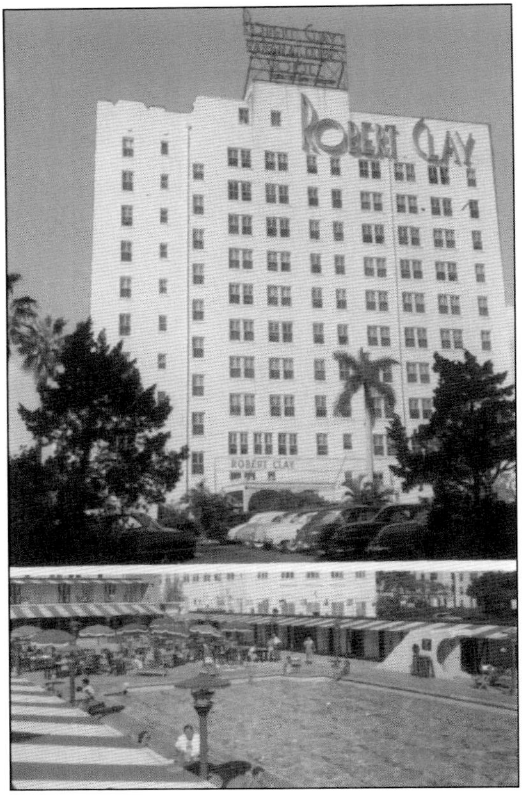

Standing on the site of Julia Tuttle's historic home, the Robert Clay Hotel (named for owner Dr. Robert Clay Hogue) opened for business in the boom era of the mid-1920s. In the immediate aftermath of World War II, as indicated in this photograph, the hotel added a swimming pool and cabana in what had been a tree-laden area abutting the Miami River. (Courtesy of Larry Wiggins.)

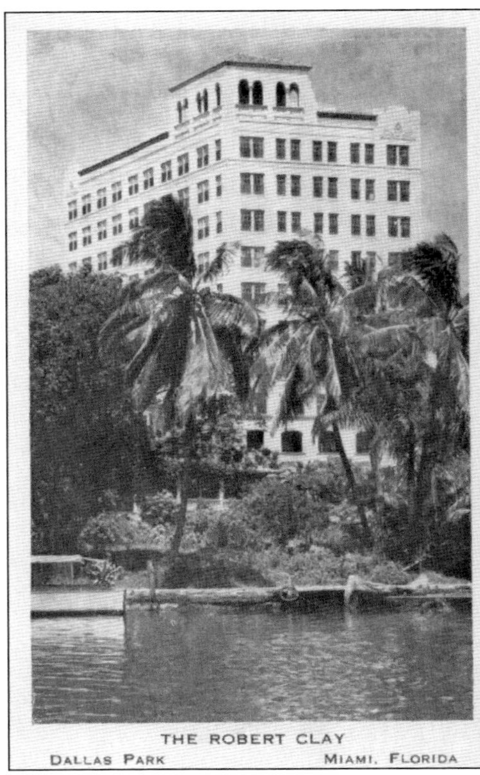

One of the city's premier hostelries in its early decades, the Robert Clay succumbed to the wrecking ball in 1979. Today, the Hyatt Regency Miami and the Knight Center rest on its footprint. (Courtesy of Larry Wiggins.)

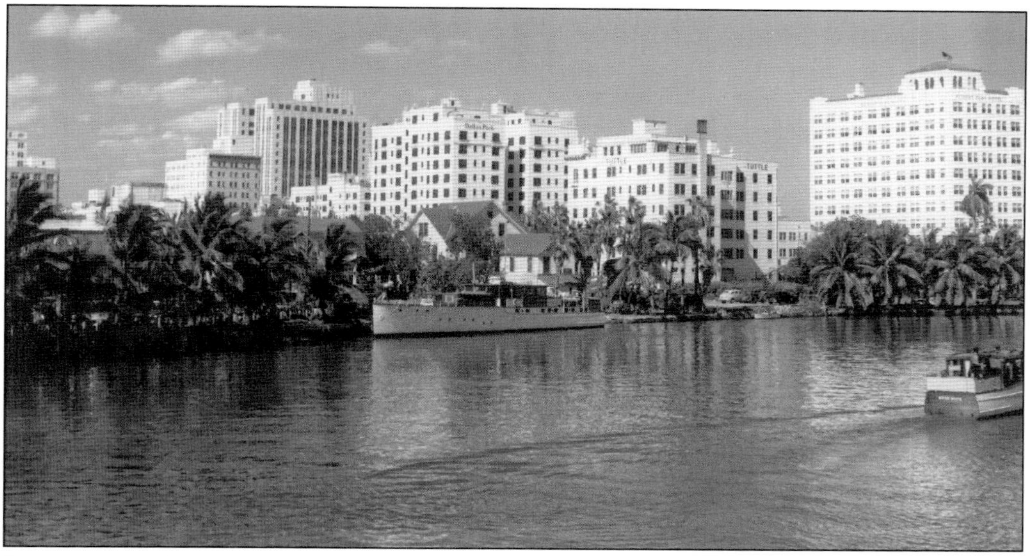

Does it get any better than this? This mid-20th–century image captures a glistening Miami River with light boat traffic. The north bank of the river was still studded with coconut palms, while the old downtown Miami hotel and apartment district, now but a distant memory, remained intact. (Courtesy of the author.)

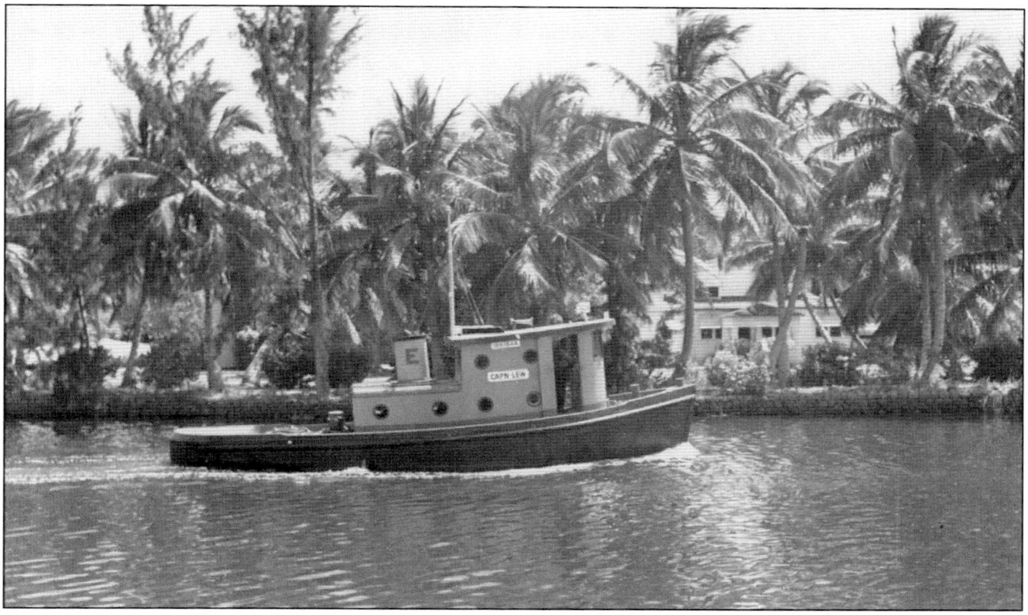

One of Miami Dade County's most venerable businesses, the Ebsary Foundation Company has been building foundations, bulkheads, and highway bridges for 90 years. For most of that time, the company has operated from the north bank of the river near Northwest Twenty-second Avenue. In this 1953 photograph, the company's *Cap'n Lew* is returning to the yard from downriver. Across from the vessel on the south bank of the river, surrounded by spreading coconut palm trees, stands a two-story building. This was formerly the home of Gertie Walsh's famed bordello, which catered to a "high-class" and, at times, a not-so-high-class clientele, in the period between the world wars. (Courtesy of Richard Ebsary and the Ebsary Foundation Company.)

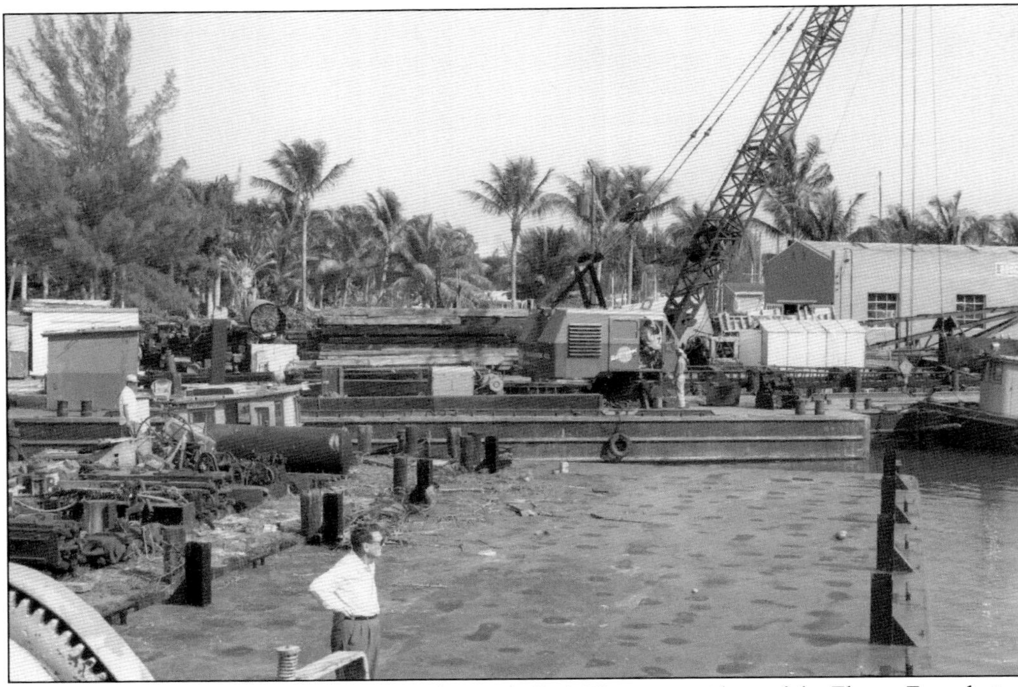

In the foreground of this 1950s photograph stands Dick Ebsary, president of the Ebsary Foundation Company. Some of the company's equipment lies west of him. As the picture indicates, the south bank of the Miami River was rich in coconut palm trees as late as the mid-20th century. (Courtesy of Richard Ebsary and the Ebsary Foundation Company.)

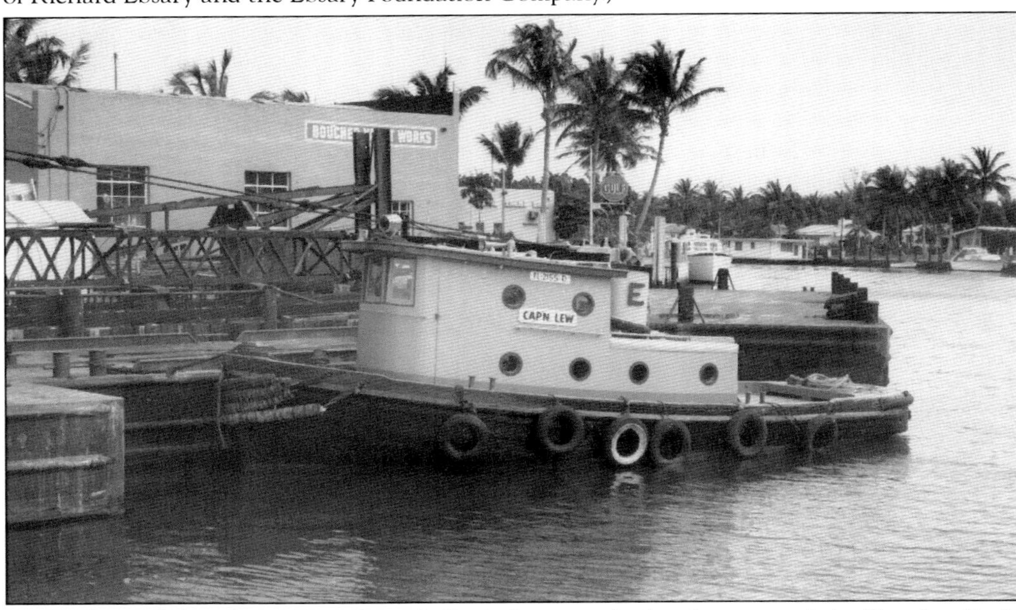

Visible beyond the Ebsary Foundation's *Cap'n Lew* are the headquarters of the Boucher Yacht Works and Hardie's Yacht Basin, which operated at the site for more than 60 years. Across the stream from Hardie's Yacht Basin is beautiful Durham Park. This image dates to around the 1950s. (Courtesy of Richard Ebsary and the Ebsary Foundation Company.)

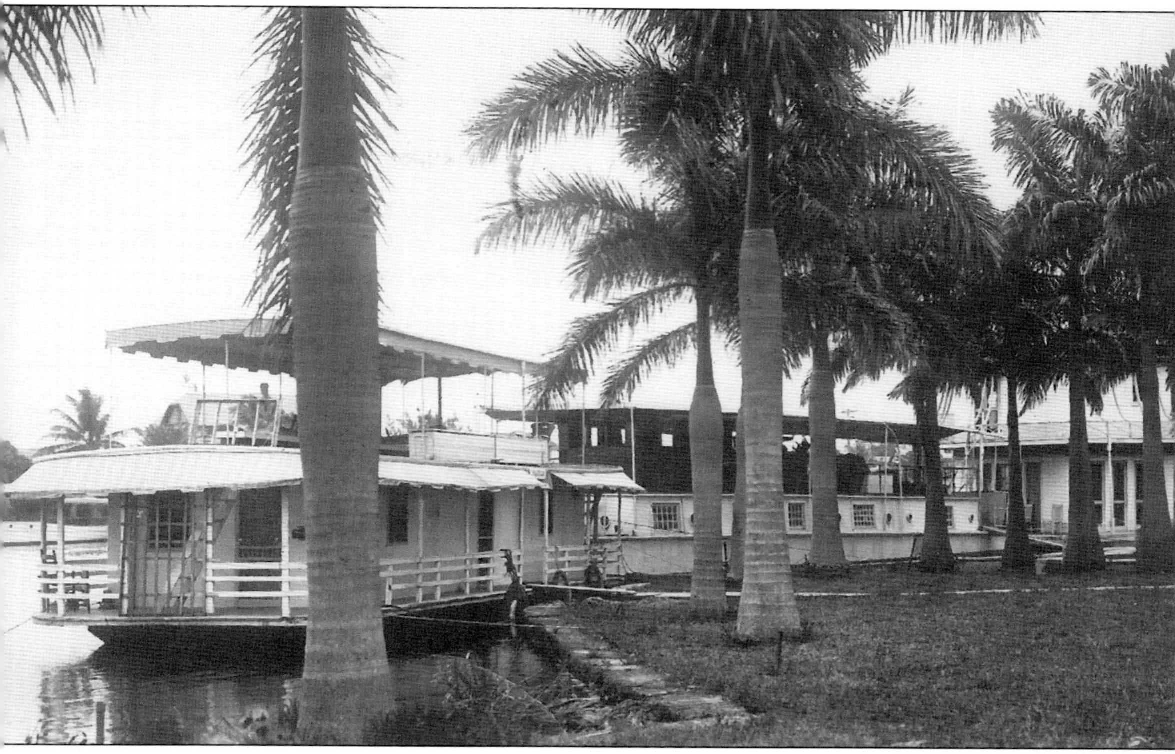
The beautiful Grove Park neighborhood has long been a venue for houseboats like the one seen here. (Courtesy of Larry Wiggins.)

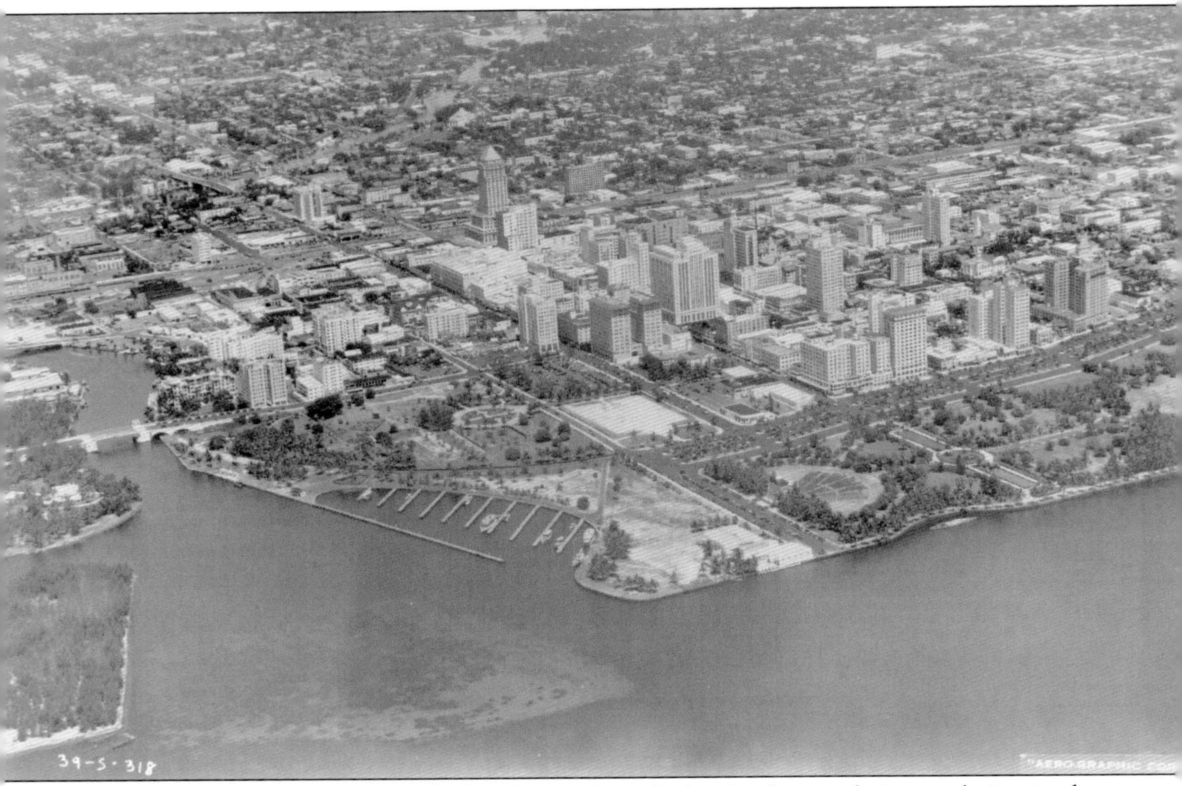

Miami, along with all of south Florida, stood on the brink of a population explosion in the era following World War II. This aerial photograph shows the Magic City poised for the expansive era that followed the conflict. The old Royal Palm Hotel docks are nearly vacant; soon after, their location would be filled in, further constricting the mouth of the Miami River. (Courtesy of Larry Wiggins.)

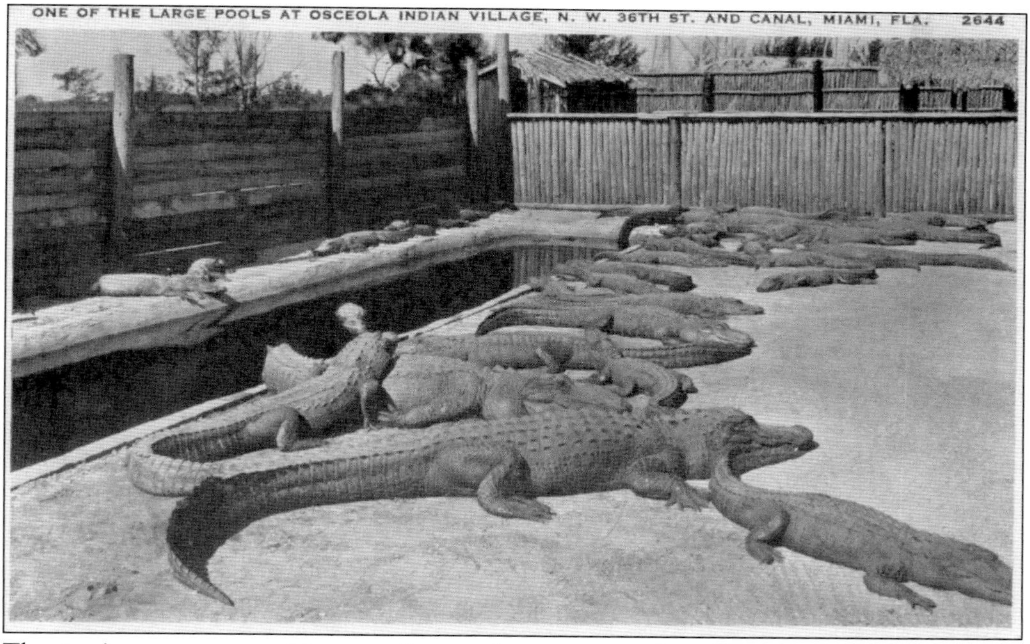

The river's western extremities, as well as nearby areas, were dotted by several "Indian Villages." These popular attractions were owned by white entrepreneurs and featured Seminole and Miccosukee Indians residing and performing therein. Among them were the aforementioned Musa Isle Village and Coppinger's Tropical Gardens, Indian Village & Alligator Farm. Another such site, Osceola Indian Village, stood just west of busy Northwest Twenty-seventh Avenue on the north bank of the Miami Canal, an area that is now part of the Second Port of Miami. (Courtesy of Larry Wiggins.)

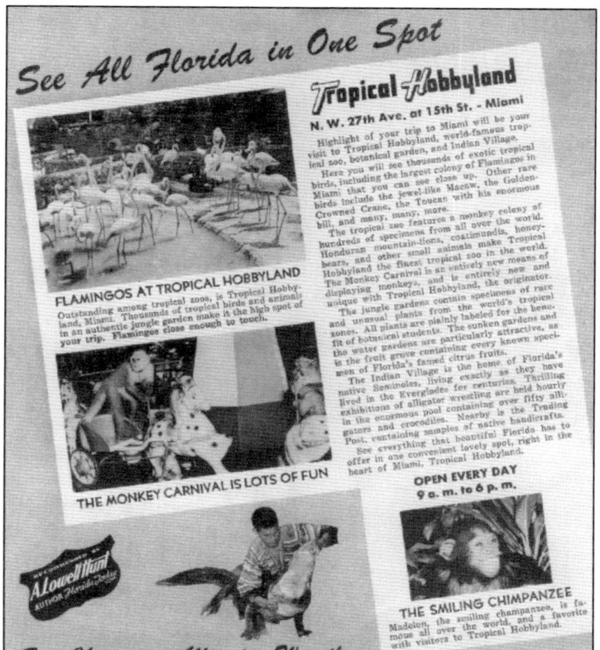

Still another "Indian Village," Tropical Hobbyland, stood south of the Miami Canal on the same thoroughfare and included hourly alligator wrestling, birds, and even such predatory animals as Honduran mountain lions. (Courtesy of Larry Wiggins.)

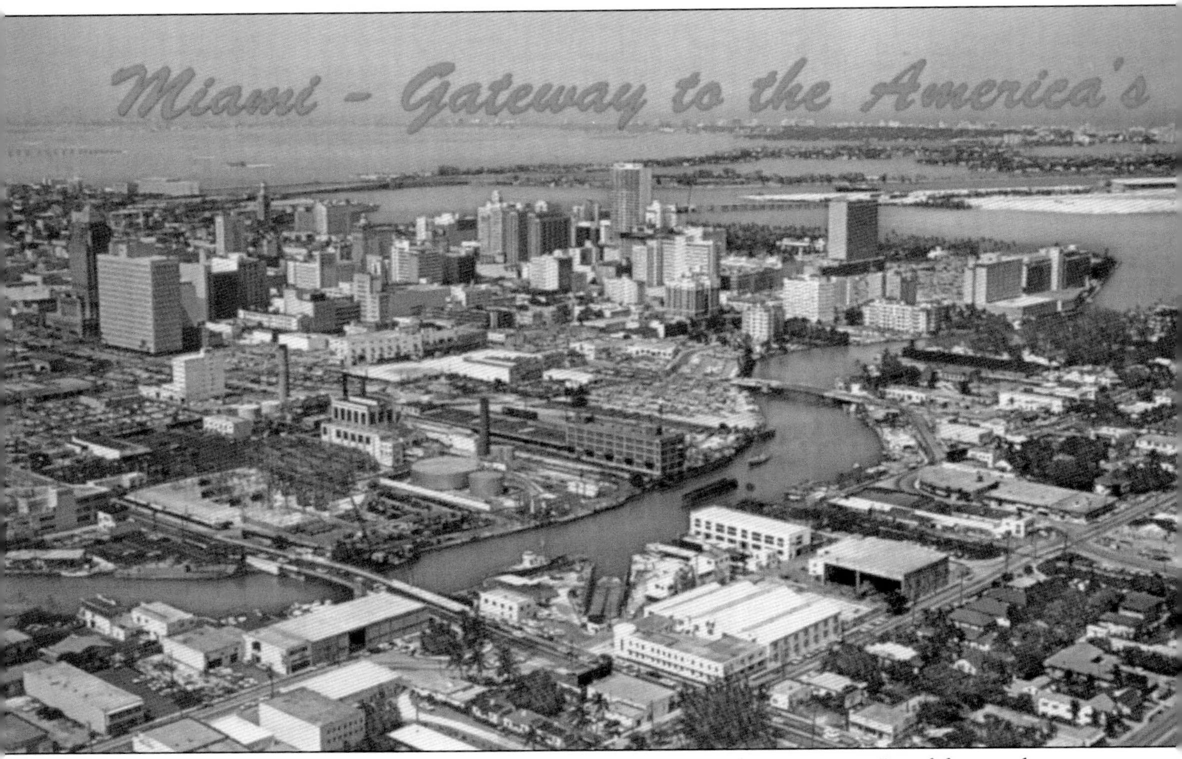

By the 1960s, Miami was billing itself as the "Gateway to the Americas," and for good reason, as the immigrant influx from Castro's Cuba was in full swing, and other groups from the Caribbean and elsewhere in the southern part of the western hemisphere were migrating to the area. This postcard from the 1960s provides a dramatic depiction of the heavy development along both banks of the Miami River in the downtown sector. (Courtesy of Larry Wiggins.)

The *Jungle Queen*, seen in this mid-20th-century photograph, was one of many vessels bringing curious tourists to the Miami River. The banks of the river were still verdant, as indicated here. On the right-hand side of the picture are the Granada Apartments, remnants of the area's 1920s transformation into a hotel and apartment district. (Courtesy of the Arva Moore Parks Photograph Collection.)

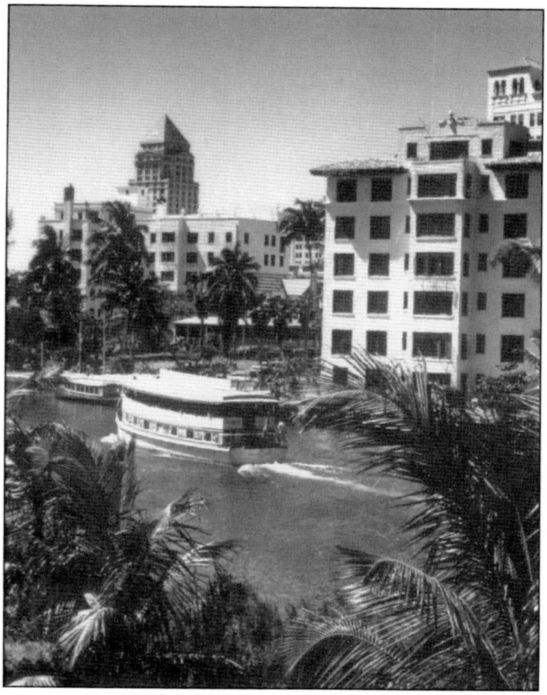

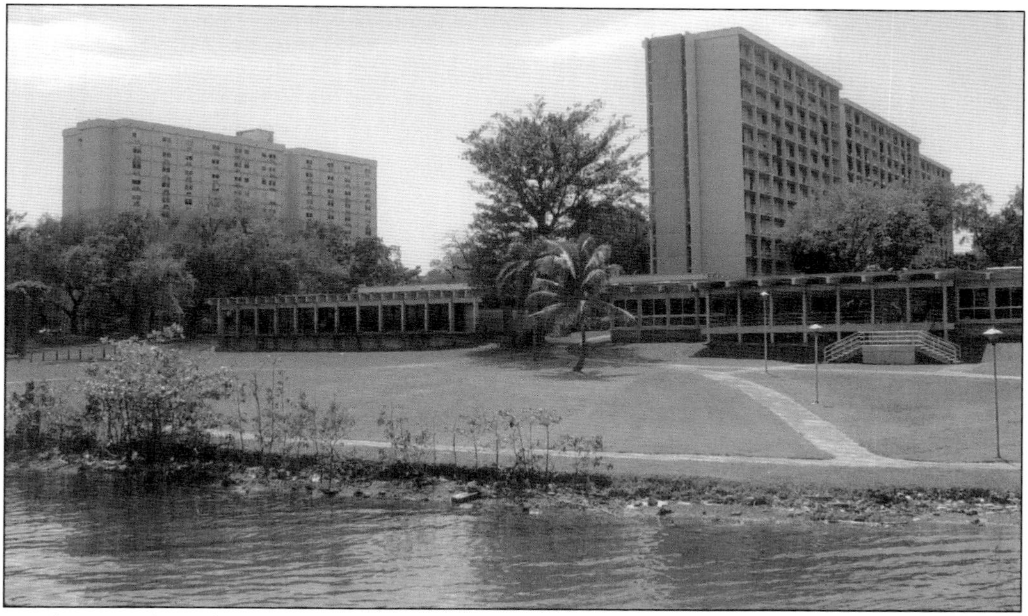

A ridge runs along the Miami River's south bank from Northwest Nineteenth Avenue to Twelfth Avenue. This topographic feature was important to earlier Miamians because of flooding in lower-lying areas during the long rainy season. Today, the Robert King High Towers (on the right) and the Haley Sofge Towers (on the left) rest on the ridge. The retirement facilities, named for a longtime mayor of Miami and a director of the city's housing authority, respectively, opened in the 1960s in this historic area that once encompassed the home and plantation of Civil War Union blockade-runner George Lewis. (Courtesy of Elliot Salloway.)

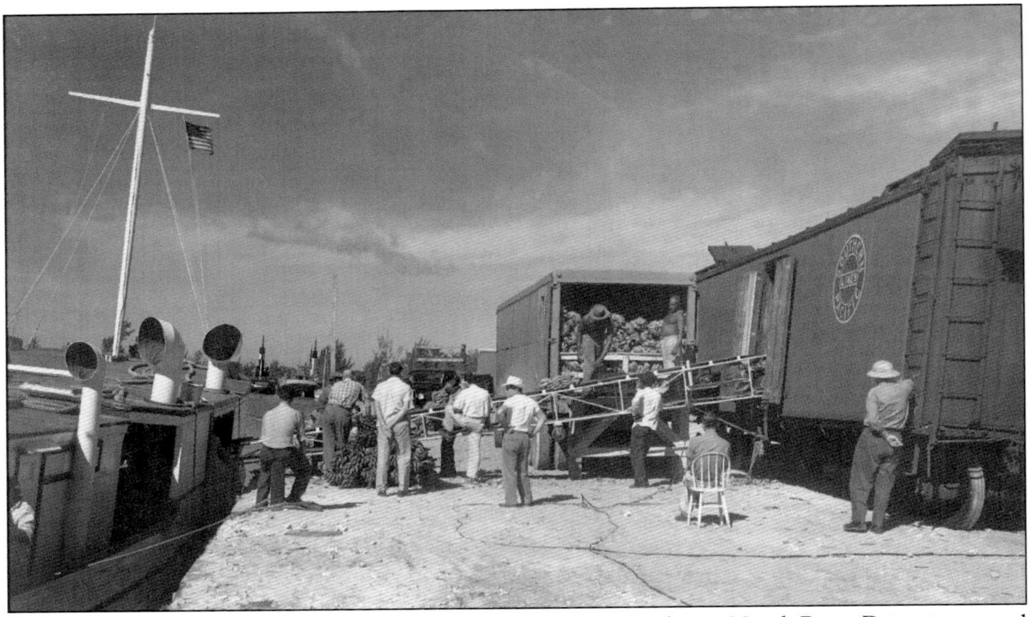

In the 1940s, the Eagle Dotson Warehouse, located at 3226 Northwest North River Drive, imported bananas from the Caribbean for sale in the United States. As this late-1940s photograph indicates, the bananas were transferred from the vessel moored on the north bank of the Miami Canal to trucks (for local sale), and to railcars of the Southern Pacific Railroad (for shipment to other parts of the country). As a rule, the ripe bananas were sold locally, while those of the green variety, with time to ripen, were placed in the railcar. (Courtesy of Bob and Jill Kratish.)

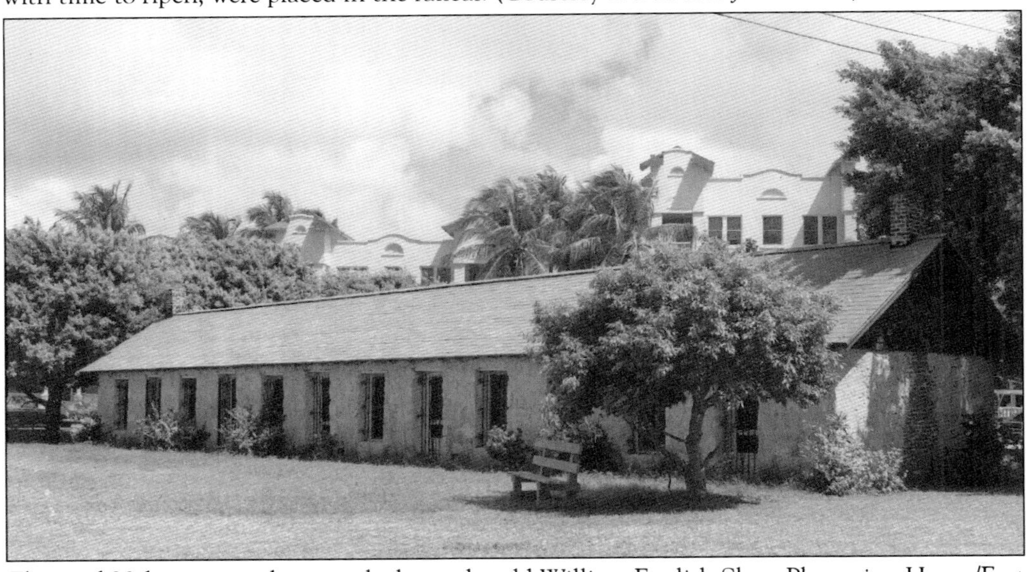

This mid-20th-century photograph shows the old William English Slave Plantation House/Fort Dallas reposing in historic Lummus Park on the Miami River. Built in the 1840s, this structure was saved from destruction in the mid-1920s by the Miami Woman's Club and the Everglades Chapter of the Daughters of the American Revolution, who raised the funds to secure its move from its original site on the north bank of the river near the mouth to the park, located about two thirds of a mile northwest of there. (Courtesy of the author.)

Four

A Working River Amid a City in Flux

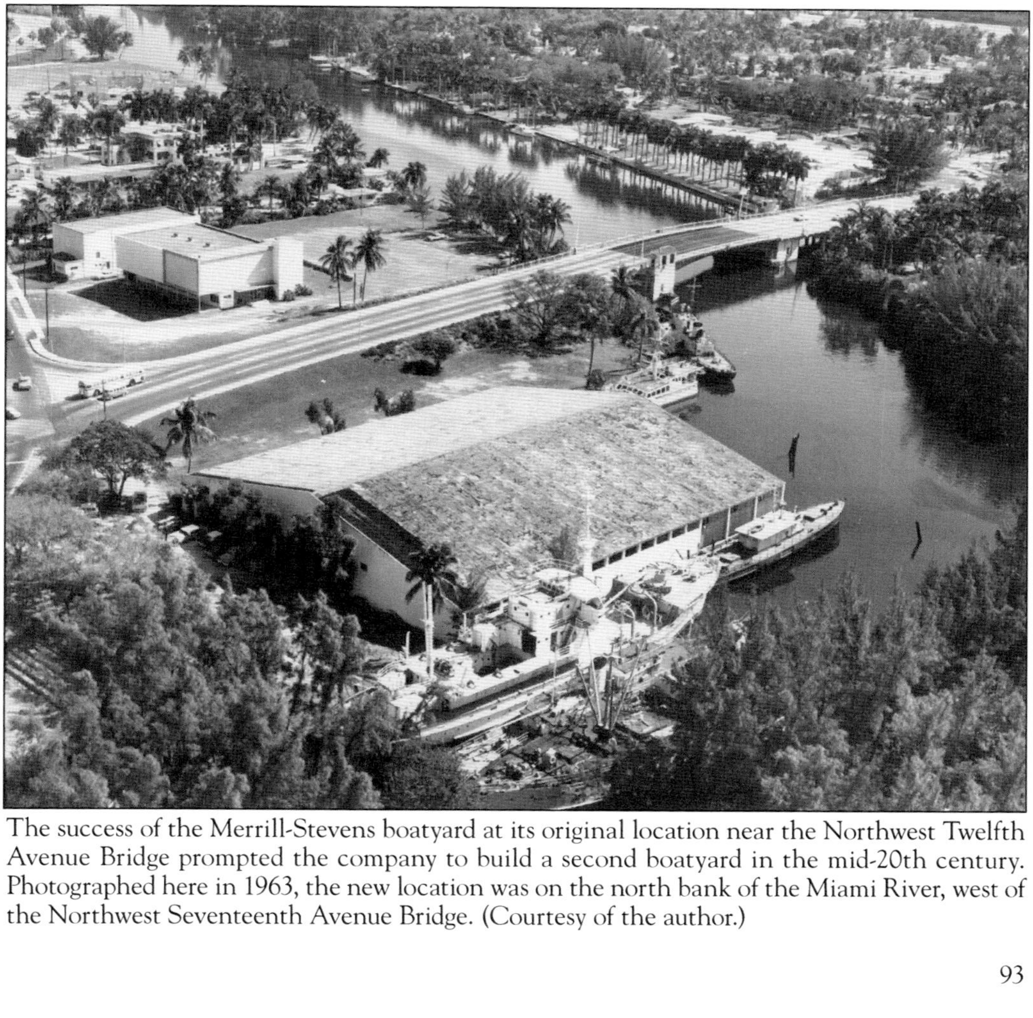

The success of the Merrill-Stevens boatyard at its original location near the Northwest Twelfth Avenue Bridge prompted the company to build a second boatyard in the mid-20th century. Photographed here in 1963, the new location was on the north bank of the Miami River, west of the Northwest Seventeenth Avenue Bridge. (Courtesy of the author.)

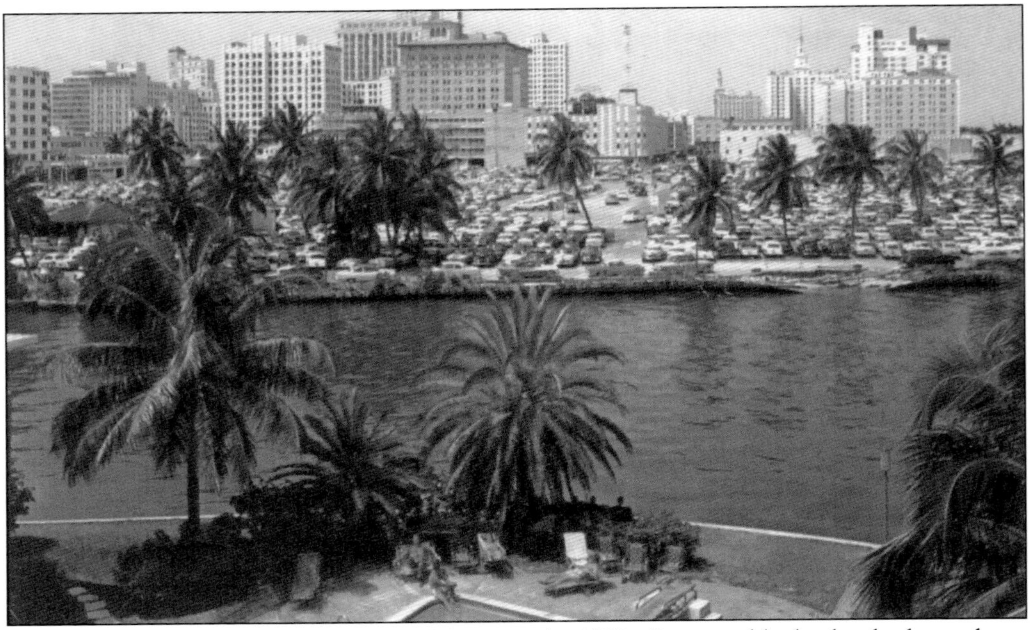

Parking was at a premium in downtown Miami in the 1950s. Four city blocks that had once been the site of the Royal Palm Hotel complex were now functioning as parking lots, as was the area that had once been the location of the hotel's docks. This photograph was taken from the grounds of the newly opened Brickell Point Apartments, which provided residents with a close-up view of the mouth of the river. (Courtesy of Larry Wiggins.)

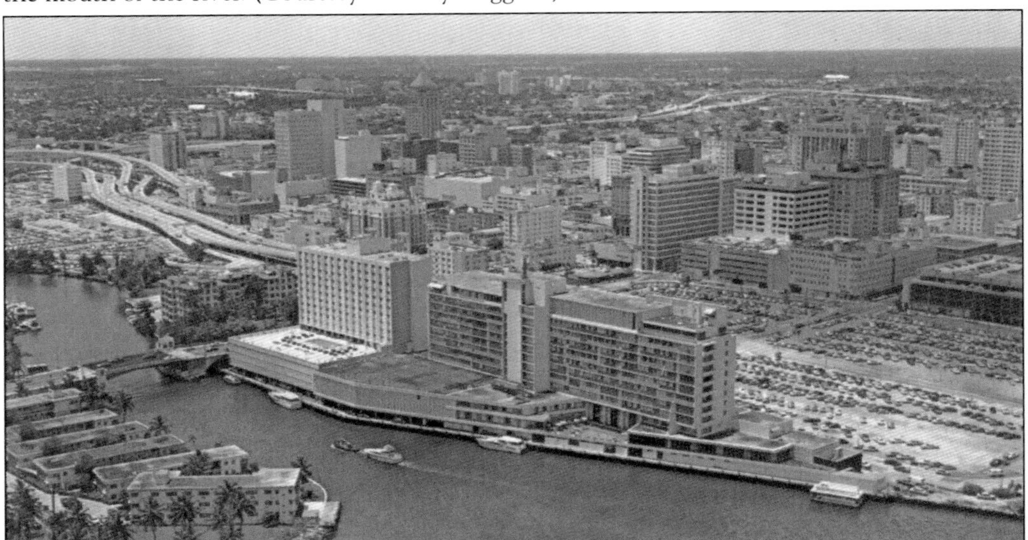

By the late 1950s, a portion of the newly opened DuPont Plaza Hotel rested on the site of the old Royal Palm Hotel marina. Bearing what was later called the Miami Modern/Mid-Century Modern architectural style, known widely as "MiMo," the Dupont Plaza remained open until the early years of the present century. Today, the luxurious Epic Miami, a hotel and condominium complex, stands on its footprint. In the lower left-hand corner of the photograph are the Brickell Point Apartments, built at the outset of the 1950s. (Courtesy of Larry Wiggins.)

This broad aerial view of Miami's bayfront area was taken in 1959. In the bottom half of the photograph stands the earlier Port of Miami, with the large Belcher Oil drums highly visible. There were many links between the Miami River and the Port of Miami, including the presence of Belcher Oil in both venues. By the 1960s, a new Port of Miami would replace this one; the original site would eventually become Bicentennial Park. (Courtesy of Andrew Melick.)

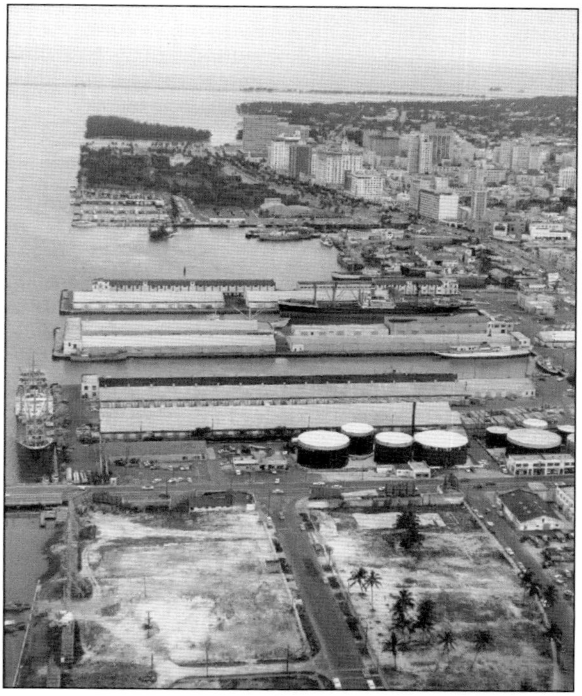

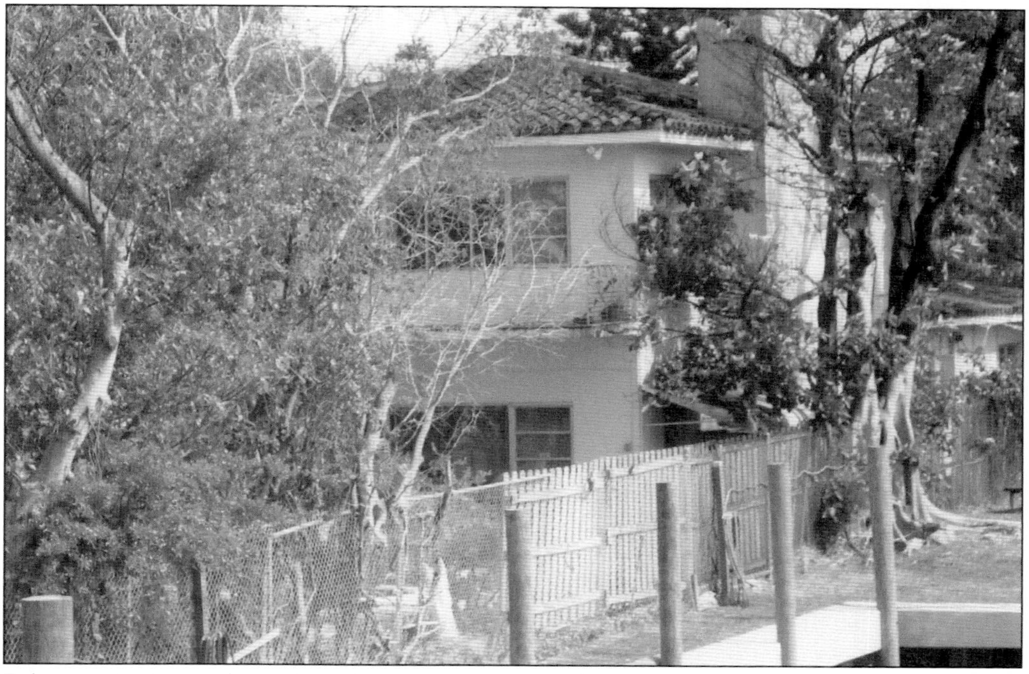

Fulgencio Batista—the Cuban dictator whose flight from Cuba on December 31, 1958, paved the way for Fidel Castro's takeover of the island—owned this home, which he used as a retreat in the 1950s. With reinforced masonry walls; a swimming pool; and, at one time, an impressive bank of telephones, it stands on the southern edge of Spring Garden, abutting the Miami River. (Courtesy of Elliot Salloway.)

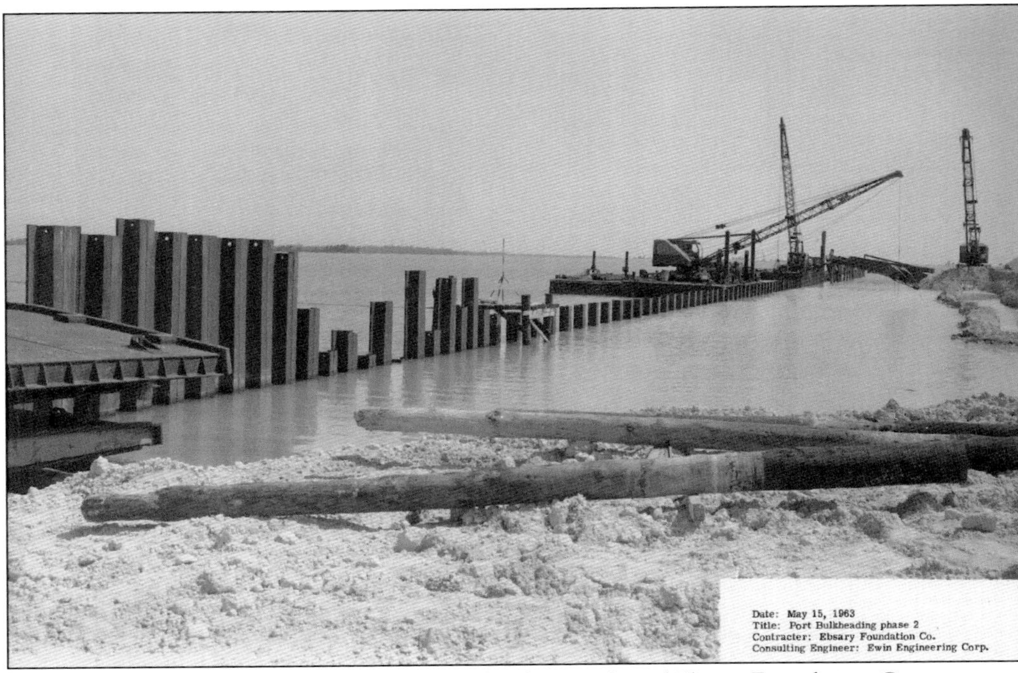

One of the largest mid-20th-century projects for the river-based Ebsary Foundation Company was the creation of the bulkhead for the new Port of Miami, which arose in Biscayne Bay in the 1960s (pictured here in 1963). Today, the Port of Miami is the busiest cruise-ship port in the world; the south side of the facility hosts the premier container port in Florida. (Courtesy of Richard Ebsary and the Ebsary Foundation Company.)

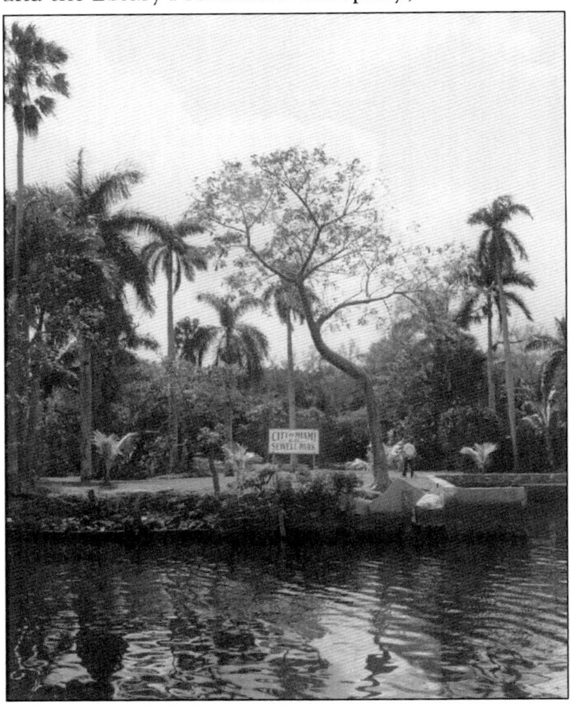

Everest G. Sewell Memorial Park (named for a three-term mayor who was also a Miami pioneer and publicist par excellence for the young city) is one of Miami's best-kept secrets. Located on the south bank of the Miami River just west of Northwest Seventeenth Avenue, in an area that had previously been occupied by private residences, the park opened in 1965 after the city acquired the property. The land had been owned by former Union general Samuel Lawrence at the beginning of the 20th century. (Courtesy of Elliot Salloway.)

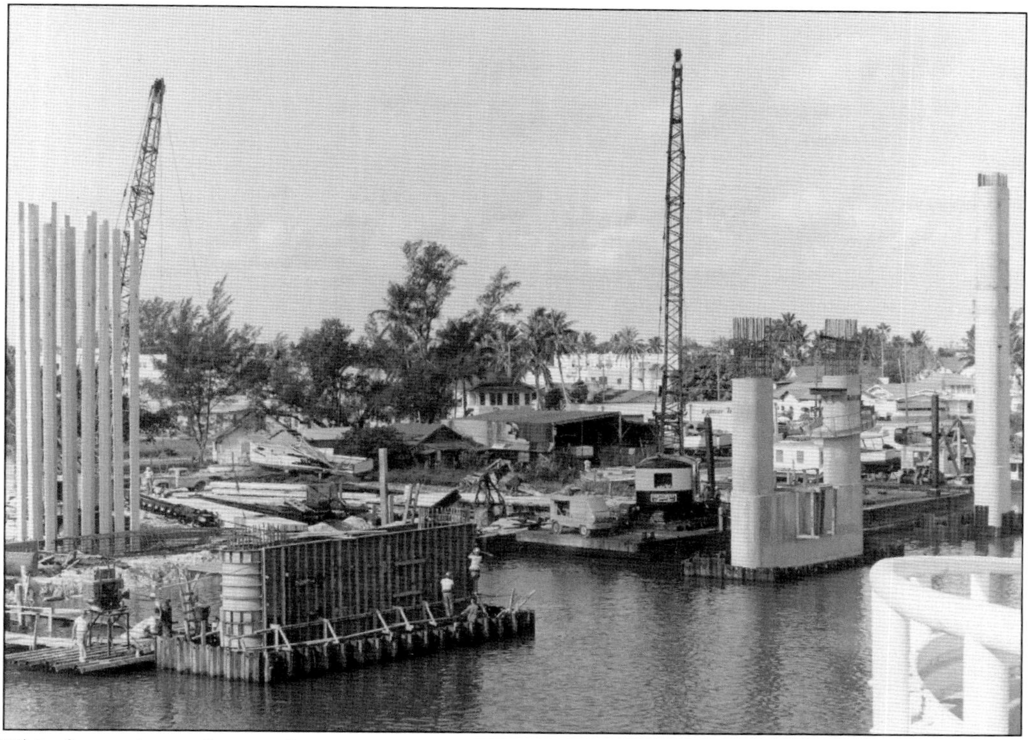

This dramatic northwesterly view from December 1966 shows Interstate 95 pushing in the direction of the Miami River. By the following year, the bridges over the river had been completed. On the left side of the photograph is the historic Riverside neighborhood, today's East Little Havana, which lost a significant amount of housing stock as the expressway was built through its eastern sector. (Courtesy of the Florida State Photographic Archives.)

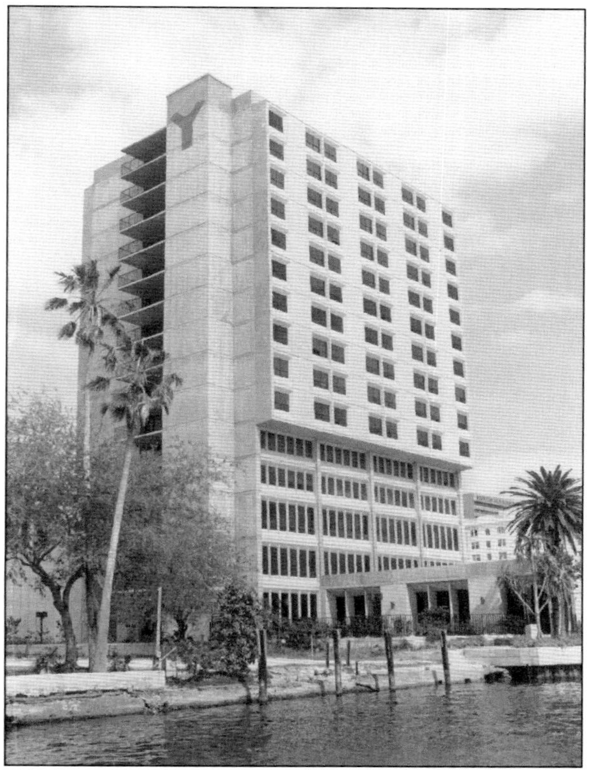

Even before the destruction of the Patricia and Dallas Park Hotels, another tall, new building, housing the Young Women's Christian Association (YWCA), opened on the river in a portion of Fort Dallas Park. Built in the late 1960s, this poured-concrete pile was a far cry from the quaint wood-frame homes from the Fort Dallas Park days. Later, the Bauder Fashion College and several boutique hotels occupied the building. (Courtesy of the author.)

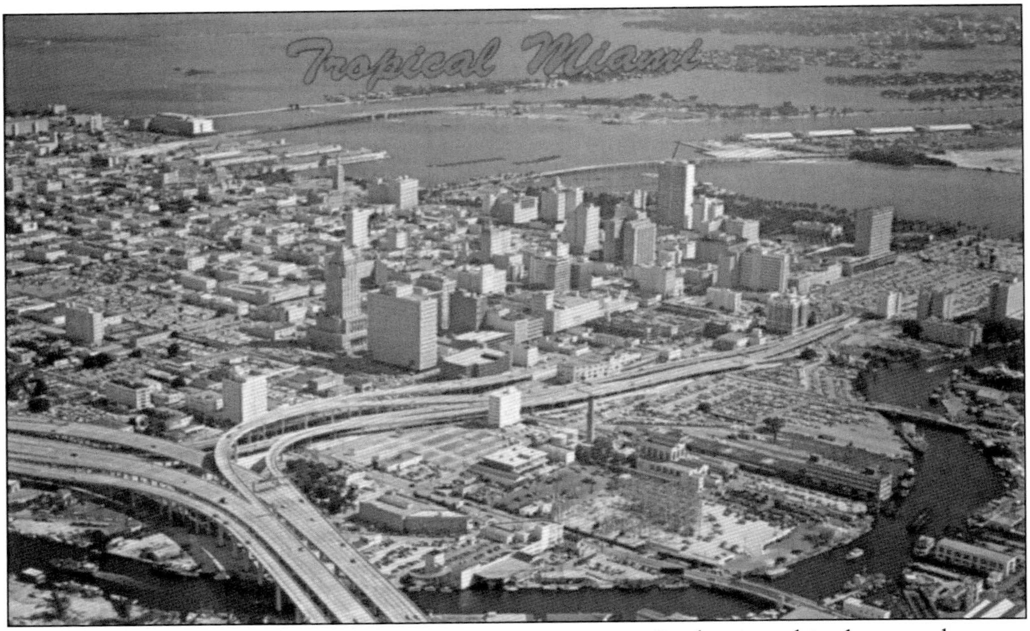

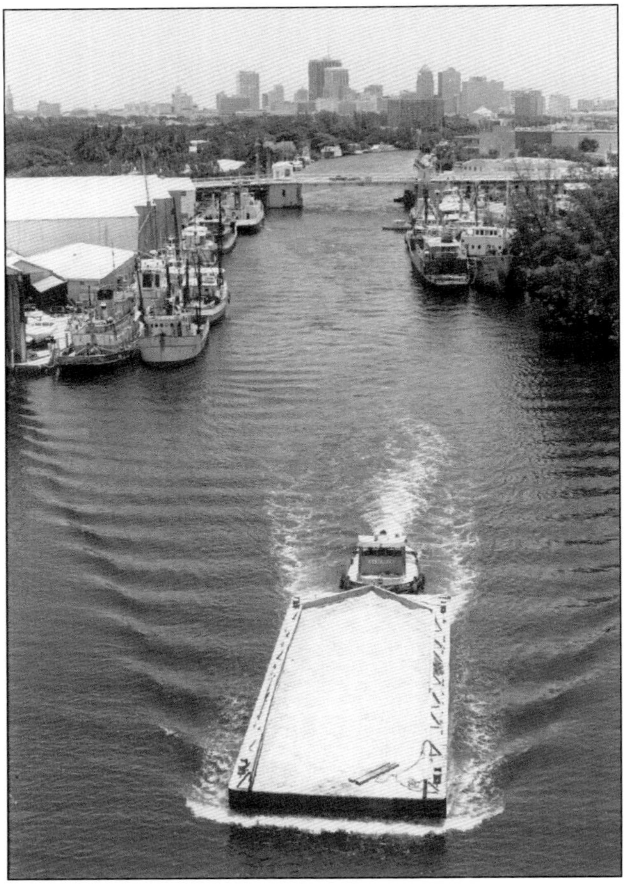

By the time this photograph was taken in the 1970s, Miami was already a large city, but its downtown had declined sharply with the explosive development of suburban Dade County. The river, too, had diminished in the imagination and interest of Miamians, but it remained an important working stream generating jobs and tax revenues. (Courtesy of Larry Wiggins.)

Today, the city of Miami possesses one of the densest skylines in the United States. That was not the case in the late 1970s, however, when this photograph was taken from a point west of the Northwest Twelfth Avenue Bridge. In the foreground of the photograph is the bustling Merrill-Stevens Boatyard, which fell on hard times in recent years and closed its operations. (Courtesy of the author.)

This daunting view of the Miami River from the northeast shows the working river of the late 1970s in its downtown sector. The building complex toward the top right-hand side of the photograph includes active boatyards that have occupied that area on the south bank of the stream since 1904. In the upper portions of the extreme right corner of the photograph stands the redbrick Florida East Coast Railway warehouse, which fell to the wrecking ball in the 1980s. (Courtesy of the author.)

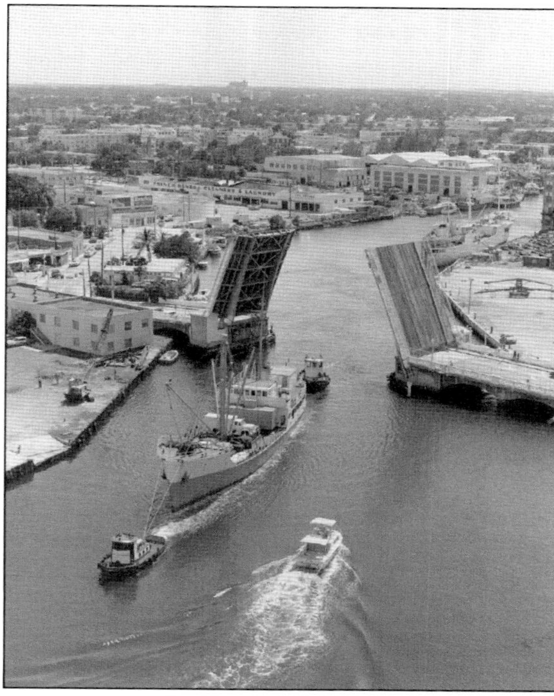

With the Riverside/East Little Havana neighborhood in the background, the south bank of the Miami River from the West Flagler Street Bridge to the Northwest Fifth Street Bridge continued to host several marinas and boatyards as late as the 1970s. (Courtesy of the author.)

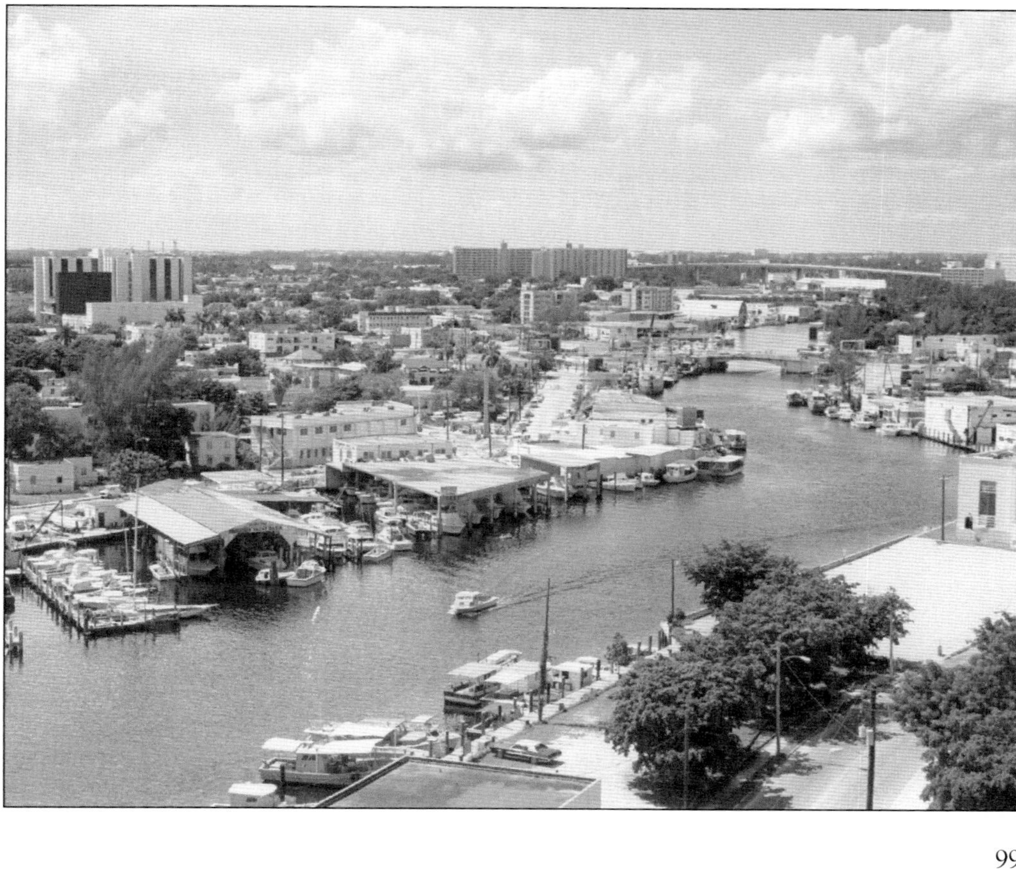

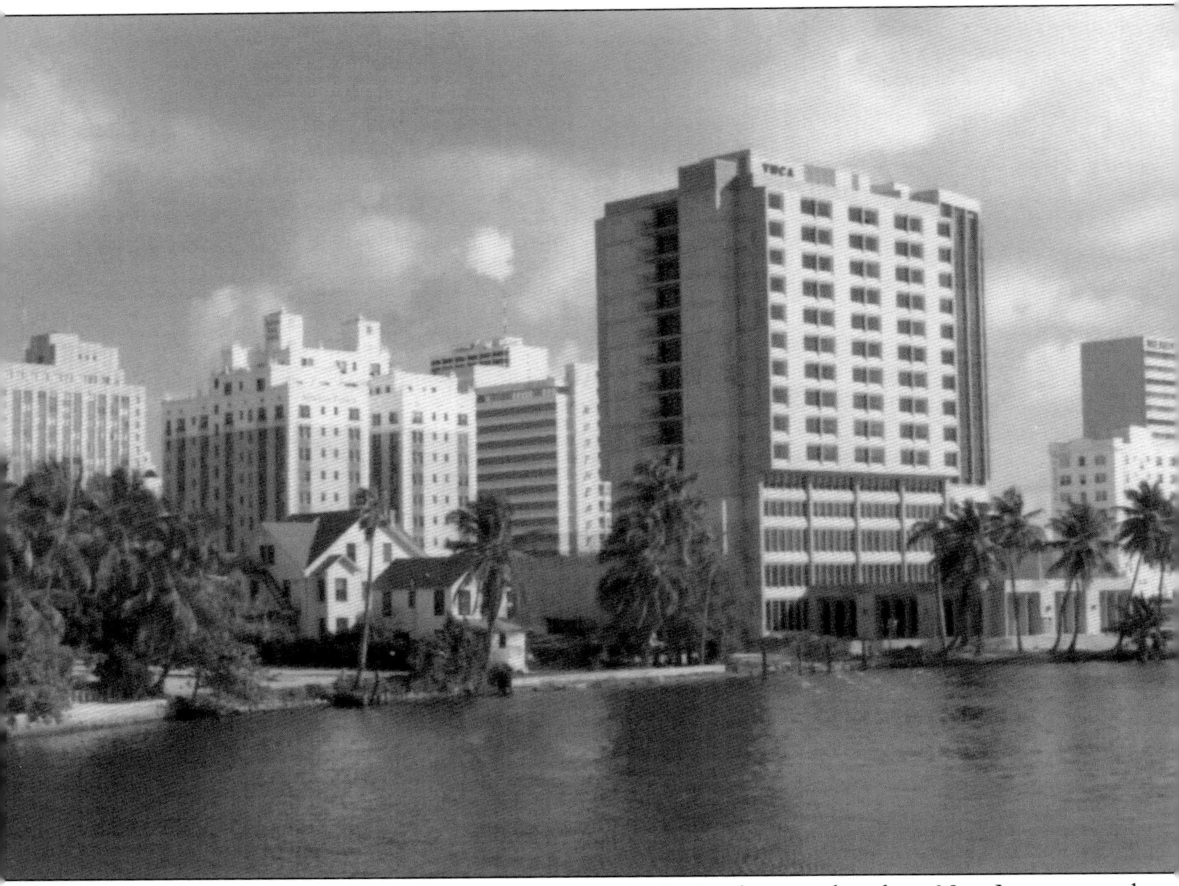

The Rambo House, the onetime home of Elizabeth Rambo, a widow from New Jersey, traced its beginnings to the formation of the Fort Dallas Park subdivision in the early 1900s. Rambo's next-door neighbors were Harry Tuttle, developer of the subdivision, and his family. The Rambo House, seen here in the left center of the photograph, was the last residence to fall to the wrecking ball in 1974. Today, Bijan's On the River Restaurant occupies most of the site. (Courtesy of the Arva Moore Parks Photograph Collection.)

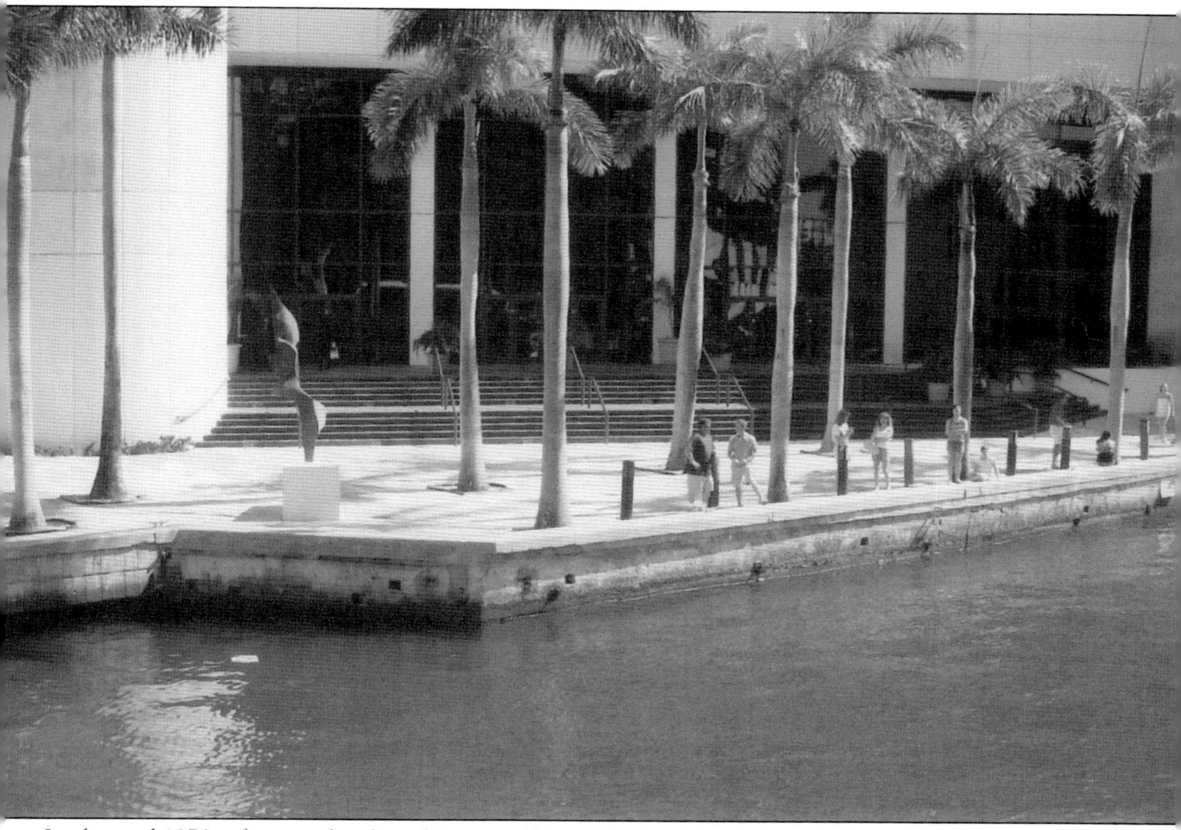

In the mid-1970s, the city developed Riverwalk, seen here beside the rear steps of the downtown Hyatt Regency Miami, as a major bicentennial project. Its completion brought activities and attention back to the river in the downtown area for the first time in many years, as Miamians and Dade Countians had already left the center city in droves for the new suburbs beyond. By the 1980s, however, the Riverwalk was largely forgotten by most Miamians. (Courtesy of the author.)

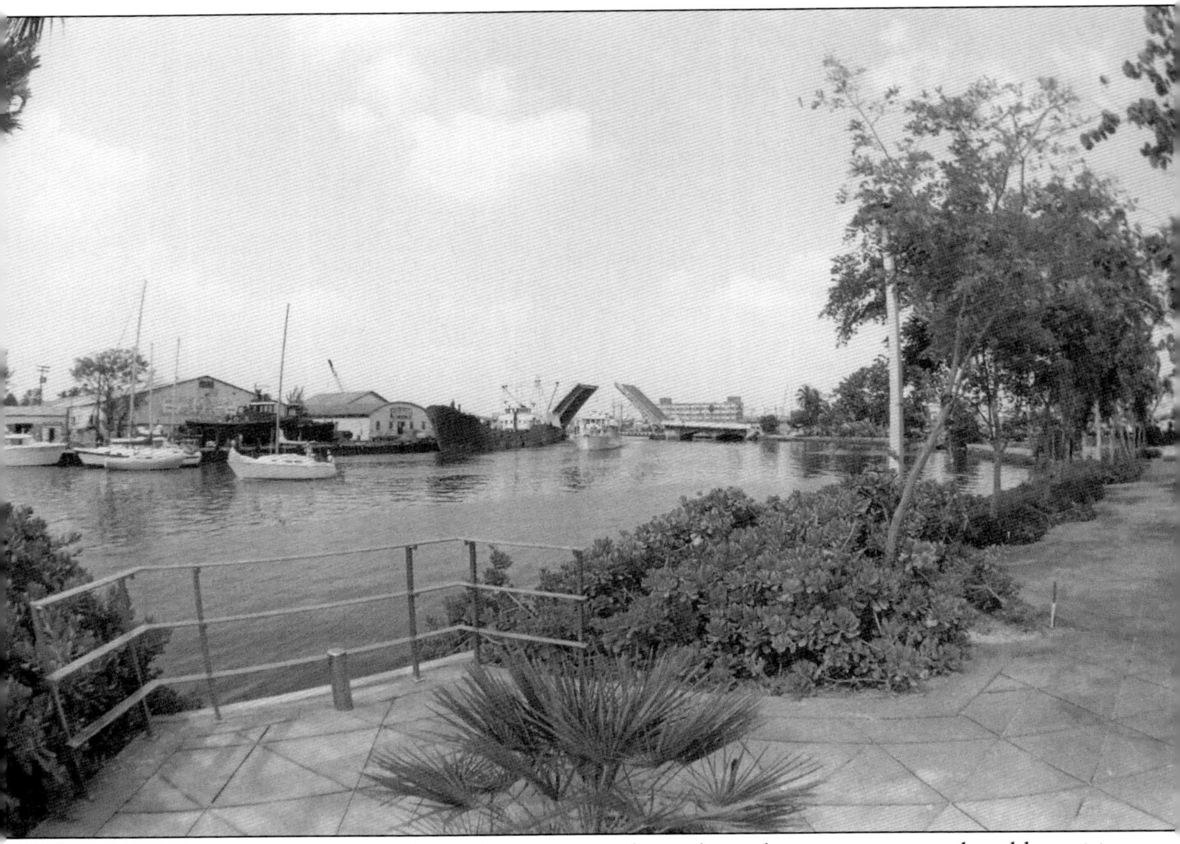

The Bicentennial Riverwalk in the foreground stands in sharp contrast to the old maritime businesses across the water in this early-1980s photograph. Before the end of the decade, those businesses would disappear, and a new Miami would arise on or near those sites by the beginning of the 21st century. On the west or far side of the Miami Avenue Bridge, near the center of the photograph, is the imposing Florida East Coast Railway warehouse, which also fell victim to the wrecking ball in the early 1980s. (Photograph by Miami-Metro Tourism, courtesy of the Arva Moore Parks Photograph Collection.)

As noted, part of the residential base of beautiful Fort Dallas Park had given way in the 1920s to a rising hotel and apartment district, which, by the 1970s, had also fallen victim to the wrecking ball. These images capture the demises of the Patricia and Dallas Park Hotels, two key components of that district. Shortly after their destruction came that of the Robert Clay Hotel. (Courtesy of the author.)

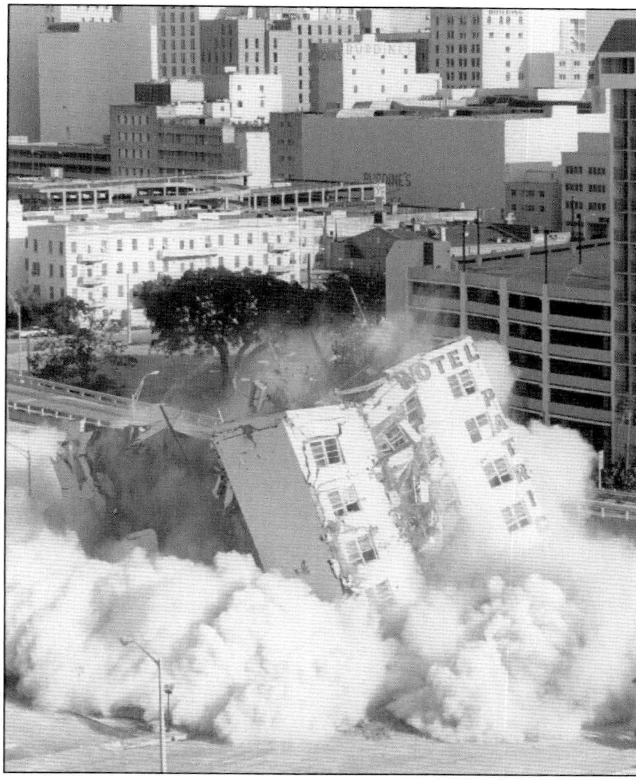

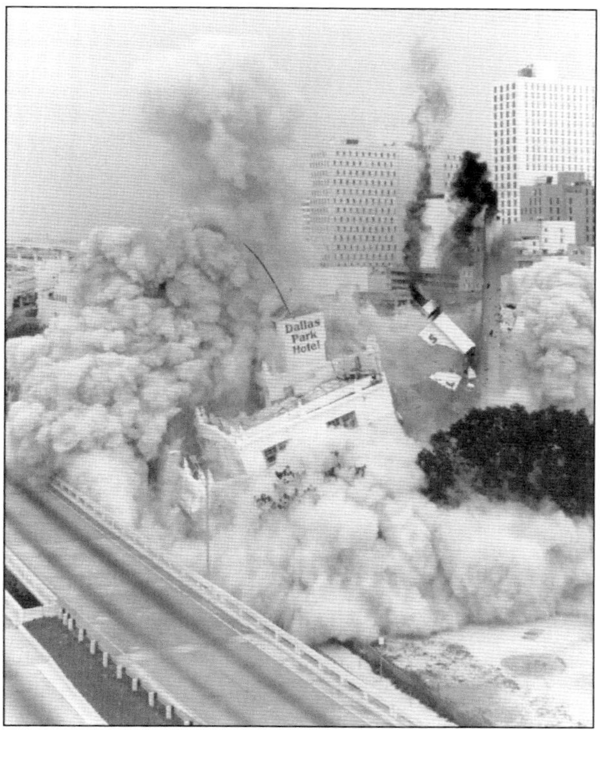

By the beginning of the 1980s, little was left of the onetime proud Fort Dallas Park neighborhood as a new neighborhood began to emerge in that area, marked by the opening of the Knight Center, a Hyatt Regency hotel, and, later, the towering I.M. Pei–designed Centrust Bank building, now called the Miami Tower, on the eastern edge of the old community. (Courtesy of the author.)

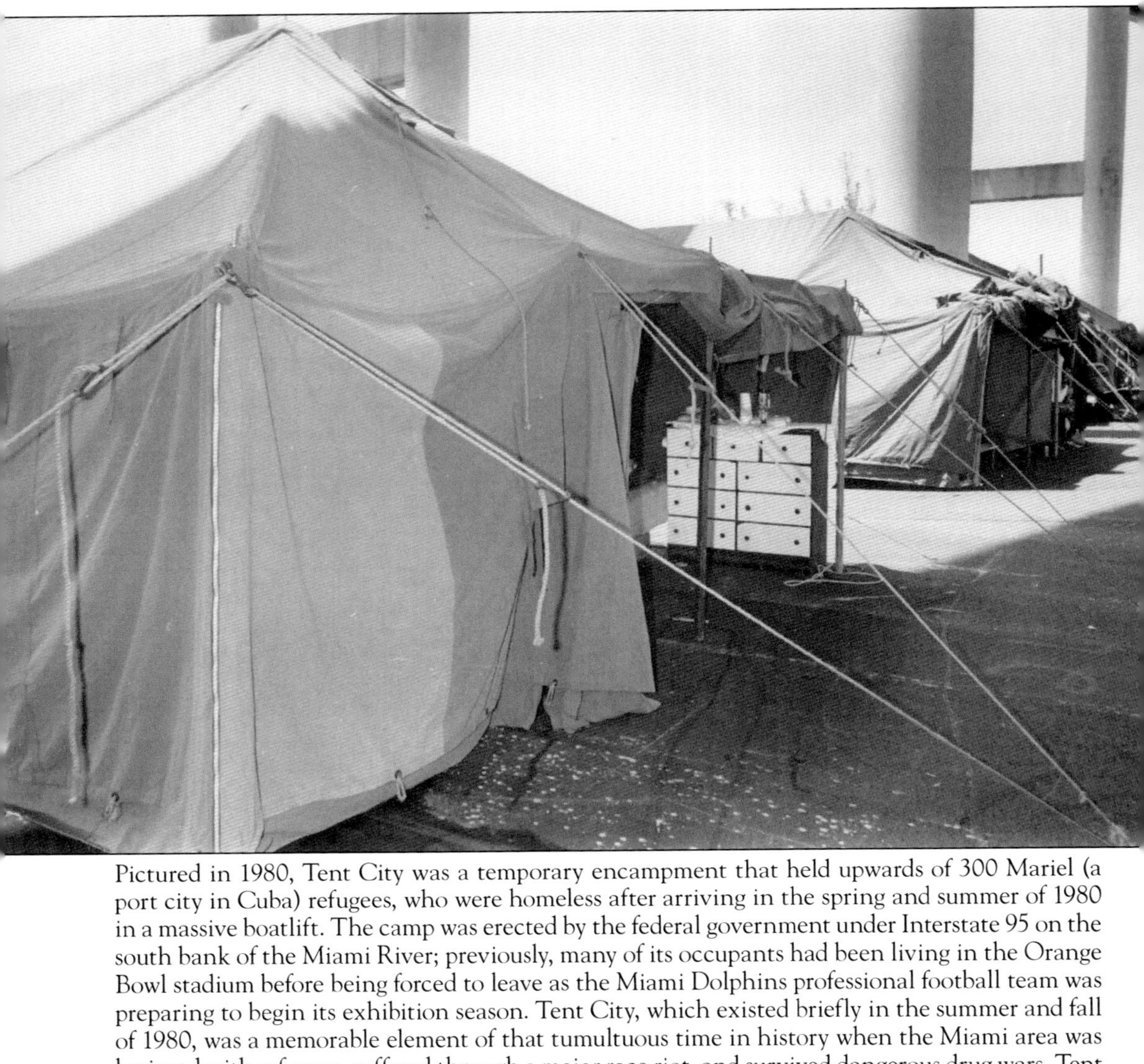

Pictured in 1980, Tent City was a temporary encampment that held upwards of 300 Mariel (a port city in Cuba) refugees, who were homeless after arriving in the spring and summer of 1980 in a massive boatlift. The camp was erected by the federal government under Interstate 95 on the south bank of the Miami River; previously, many of its occupants had been living in the Orange Bowl stadium before being forced to leave as the Miami Dolphins professional football team was preparing to begin its exhibition season. Tent City, which existed briefly in the summer and fall of 1980, was a memorable element of that tumultuous time in history when the Miami area was besieged with refugees, suffered through a major race riot, and survived dangerous drug wars. Tent City also appears in the movie *Scarface*. (Courtesy of the author.)

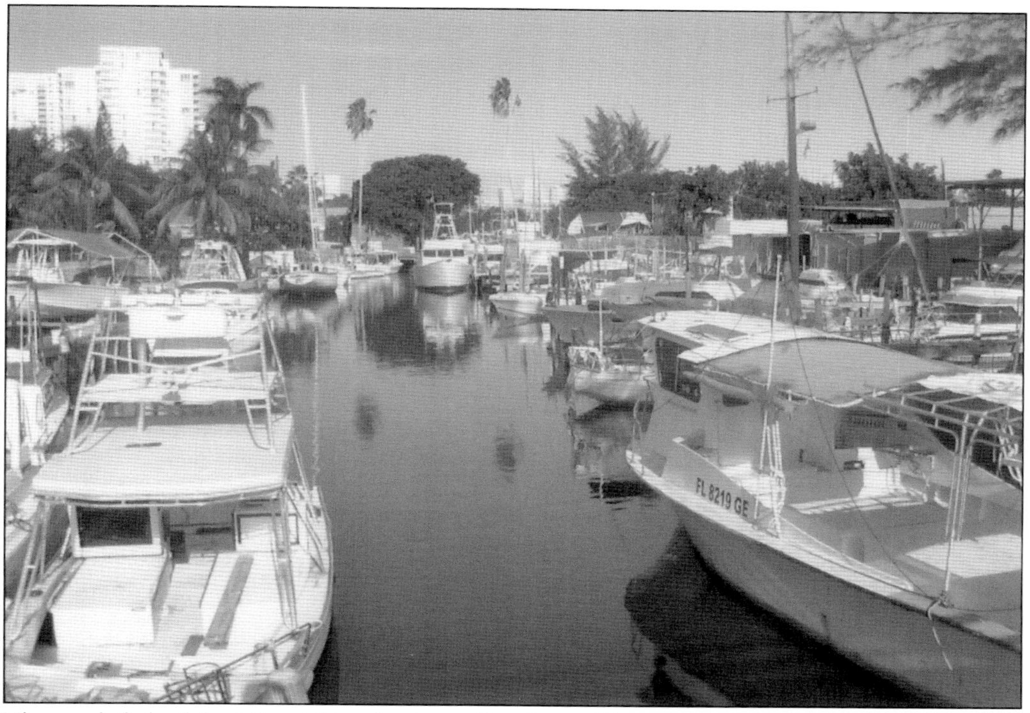

The south fork of the Miami River begins at Northwest Nineteenth Avenue as it breaks off from the main course of the stream. It extends in a southwesterly direction for nearly one mile before ending just past today's Northwest Twenty-seventh Avenue, near Eleventh Street, where it meets the Comfort Canal, which eventually connects with the Tamiami Canal. The river's south fork is dramatically different from the north fork. Where the former once hosted small numbers of settlers and, later, businesses like Allied Marine, that portion of the river stretching from Northwest Nineteenth to Twenty-second Avenues is flanked by Durham Park, a pretty residential community on the north, and by the south shoreline. As can be seen in the above photograph, many vessels are moored in that portion of the river. By contrast, that part of the south fork immediately west of the mooring area, seen below, remains pristine, with heavy foliage hugging its banks. (Both, courtesy of the author.)

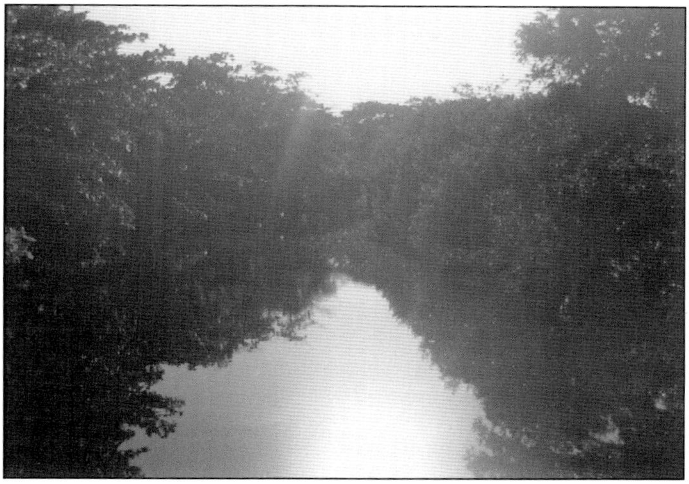

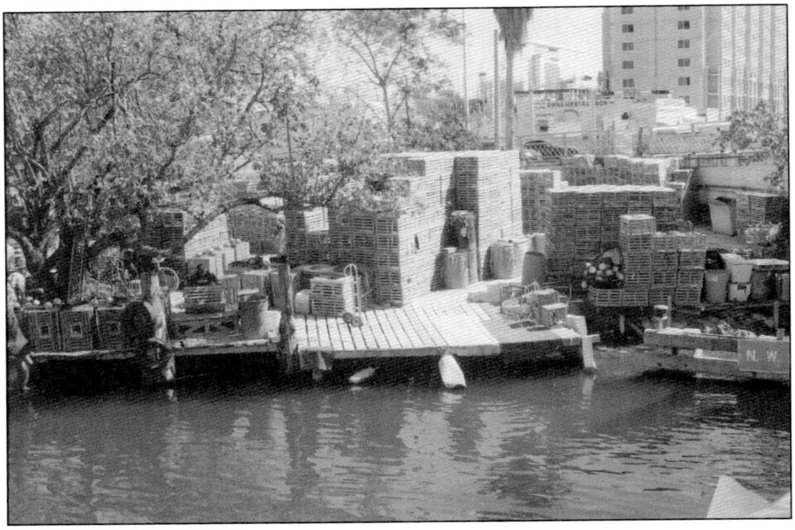

Many fishing businesses are located on the Miami River, such as this enterprise at the entranceway to the Seybold Canal. Note the lobster and stone crab traps. (Courtesy of Elliot Salloway.)

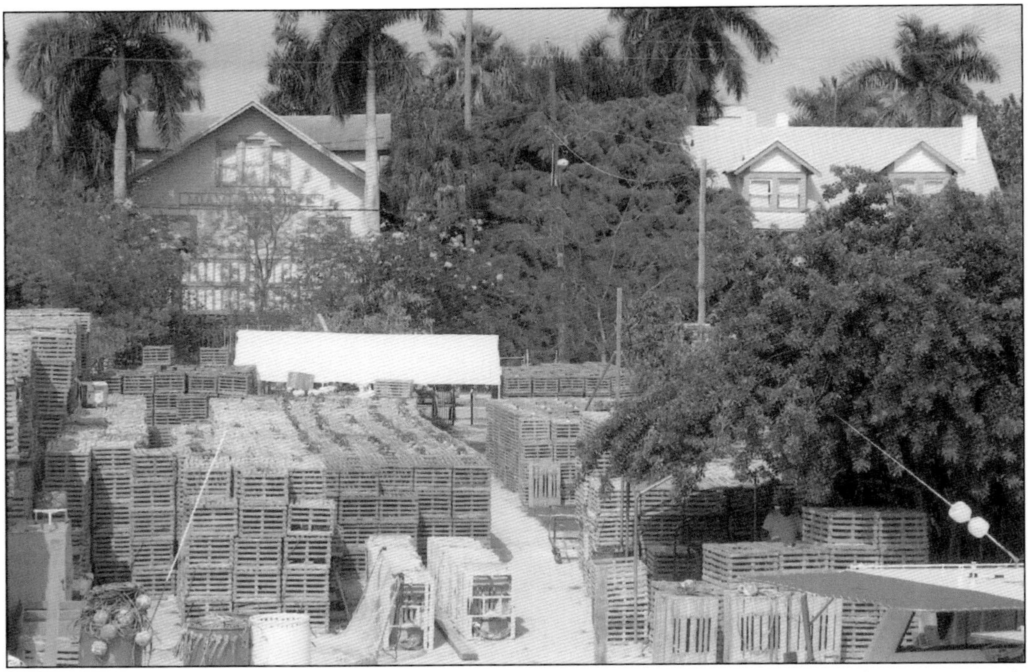

The Prieguez family, who hail from Cuba, have been operating the Miami River Lobster Stonecrab Company for more than 30 years at this venue on the river's west bank, near Southwest Fourth Avenue and Second Street in East Little Havana (originally known as Riverside). In the background is the Miami River Inn, Miami's premier bed and breakfast complex, which has been in operation since 1990. The buildings seen here are more than 100 years old, a rarity in Miami. (Courtesy of Elliot Salloway.)

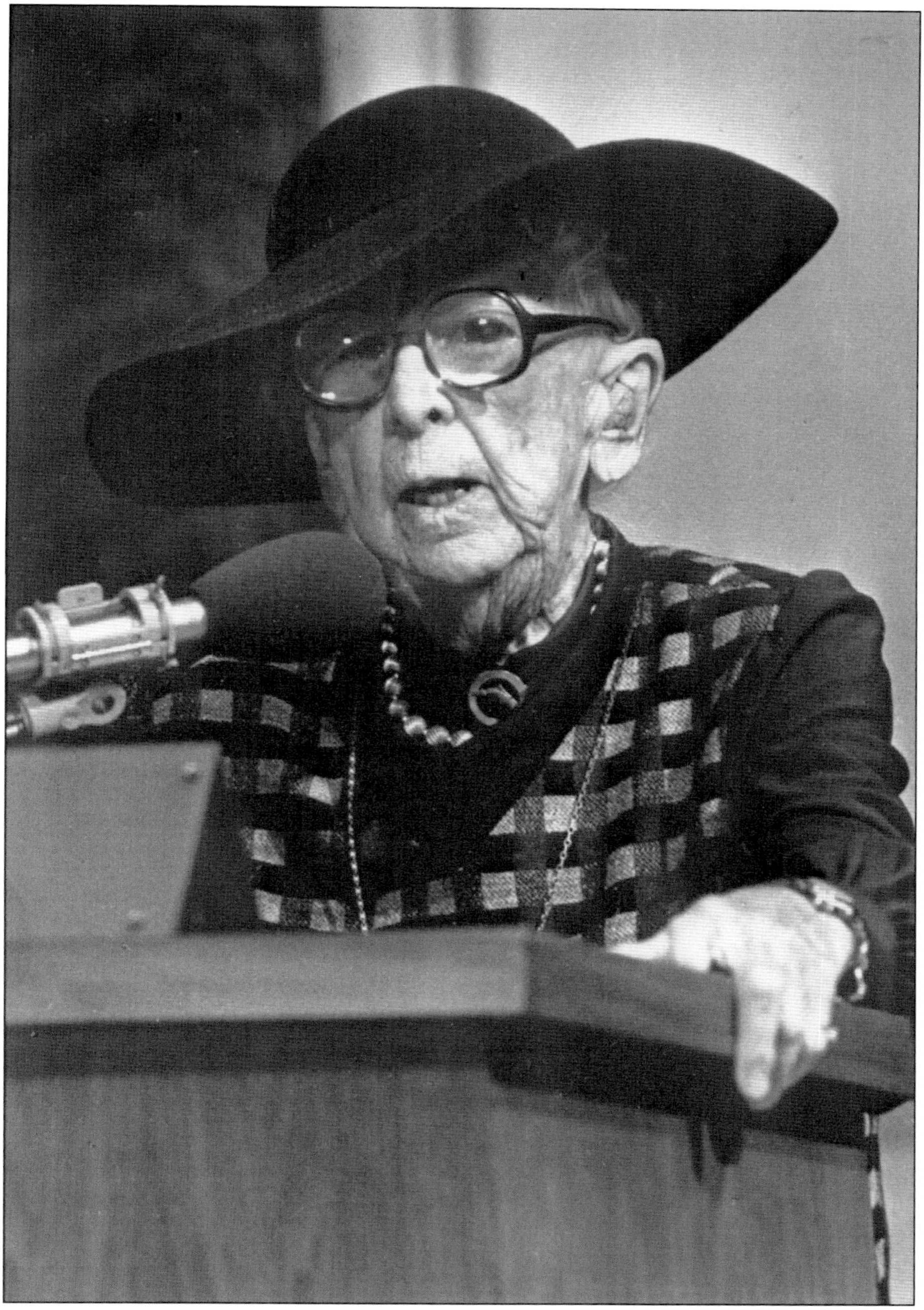

Marjory Stoneman Douglas (1890–1998), the great environmentalist and champion of the Everglades, was among the first to write of the damage visited upon the Everglades by the state's ambitious drainage program. This warning is contained in her influential work *The Everglades: River of Grass* (1947), which grew out of Douglas's idea to author a history of the Miami River. Douglas was familiar with the river, having spent her early years in Miami in nearby Spring Garden. She lived there with her father, *Miami Herald* editor Frank B. Stoneman, from the time of her arrival in 1915 till the early 1920s. (Courtesy of the Florida State Photographic Archives.)

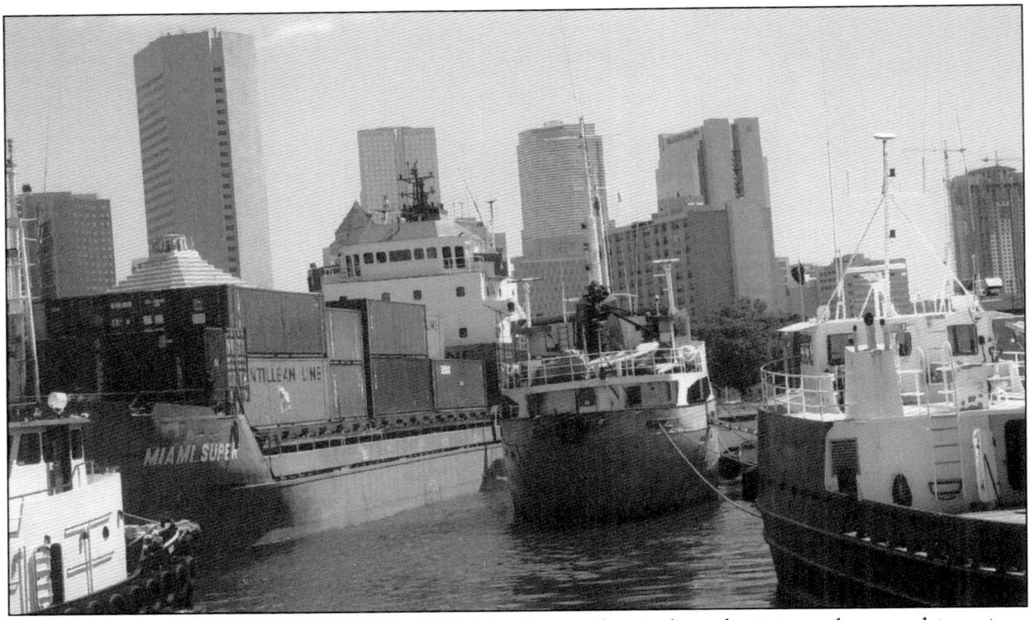

Although the Miami River is little more than four miles in length, it is truly a working river and the fifth-busiest port in Florida. Tugboats are occupied in moving ships in and out of the waterway, and commercial vessels using the bustling stream visit more than 110 ports of call. (Courtesy of Elliot Salloway.)

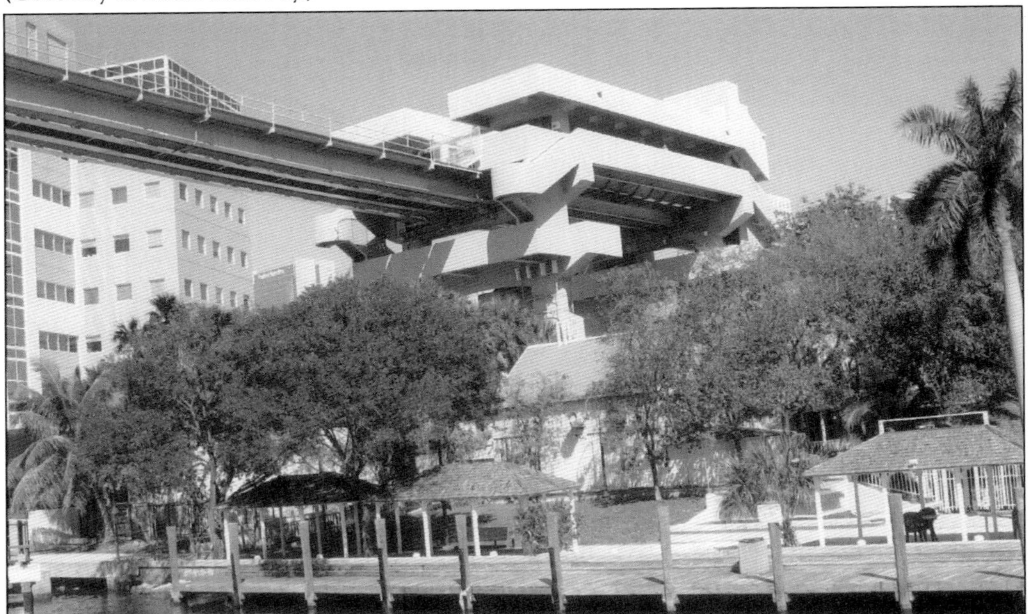

Rising above the Miami River is the Metromover extension, which became operational in May 1994. The station and tracks lie just east of Miami Avenue, the city's first street. A brick chimney is barely visible through the cluster of trees in the right-hand side of the image. This marks the location of the Flagler Palm Cottage, which, dating to 1897, is one of the city's oldest buildings. (Courtesy of Elliot Salloway.)

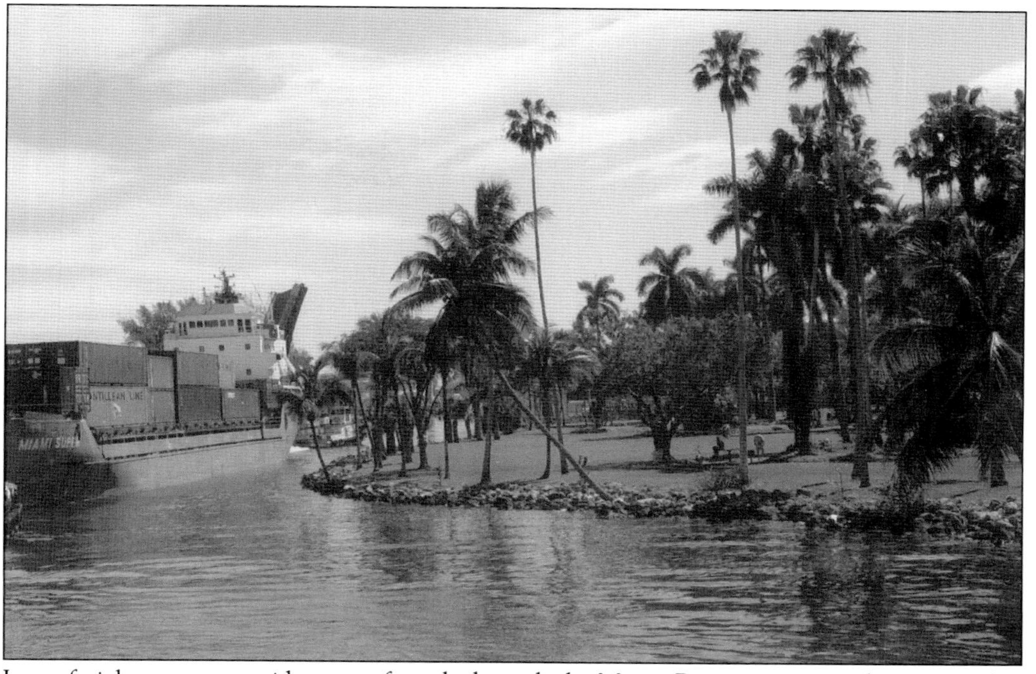

Large freighters carry a wide array of goods through the Miami River to ports in the West Indies and Latin America. The waterway's narrow, winding course has necessitated the employment of tugboats to move these vessels up- and downriver. Everest G. Sewell Memorial Park also appears in this photograph. (Courtesy of Elliot Salloway.)

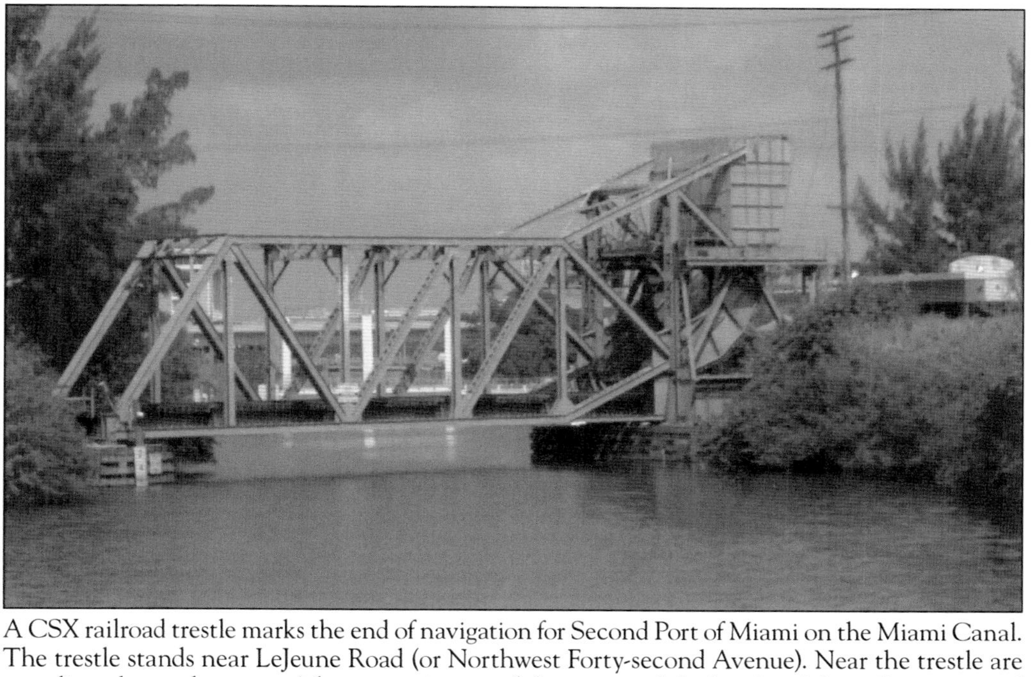

A CSX railroad trestle marks the end of navigation for Second Port of Miami on the Miami Canal. The trestle stands near LeJeune Road (or Northwest Forty-second Avenue). Near the trestle are recycling plants, the county's huge new intermodal center, and the bustling Miami International Airport. (Courtesy of Elliot Salloway.)

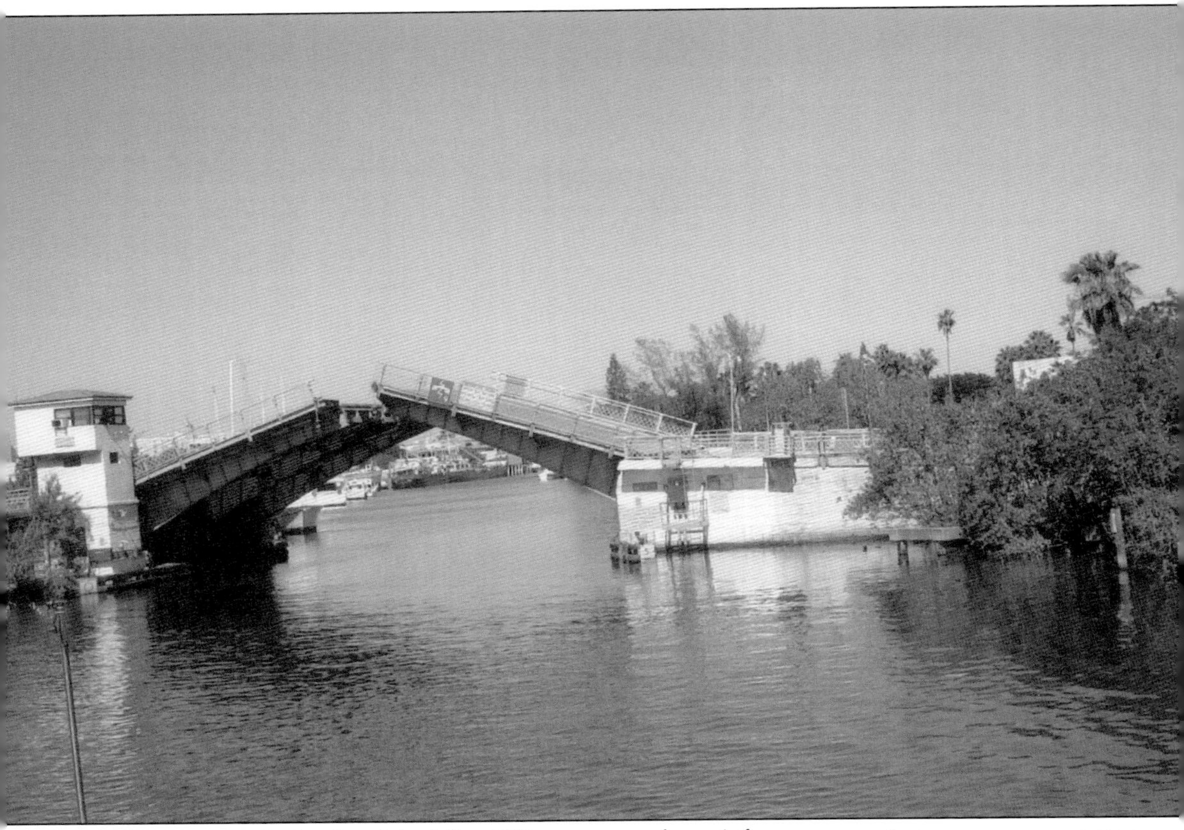

At one time, the banks of the Miami River were verdant. A few trees remain in some areas, as seen here on the north bank of the river, just east of the Seventeenth Avenue Bridge. This photograph was taken in the early part of this century. One of the oldest bridges on the river, this span was built in the late 1920s. (Courtesy of Elliot Salloway.)

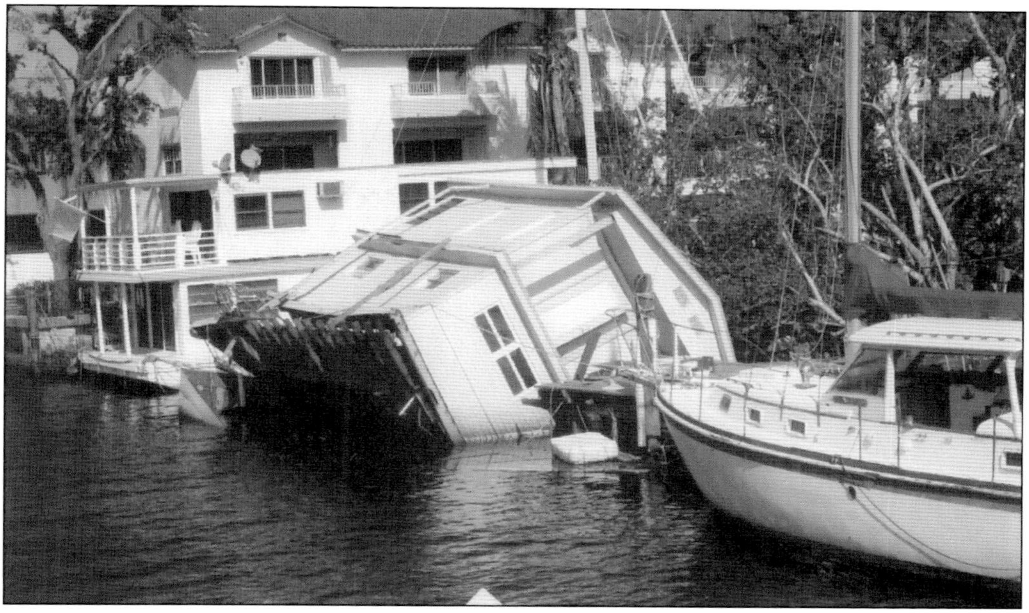

An extensive river cleanup of derelict vessels has rid the stream of many boats in recent decades. In this c. 2006 photograph, a houseboat lies on its side on the southern edge of the Spring Garden neighborhood. In earlier decades, many people lived in houseboats on the river. Today, their numbers have diminished significantly. (Courtesy of Elliot Salloway.)

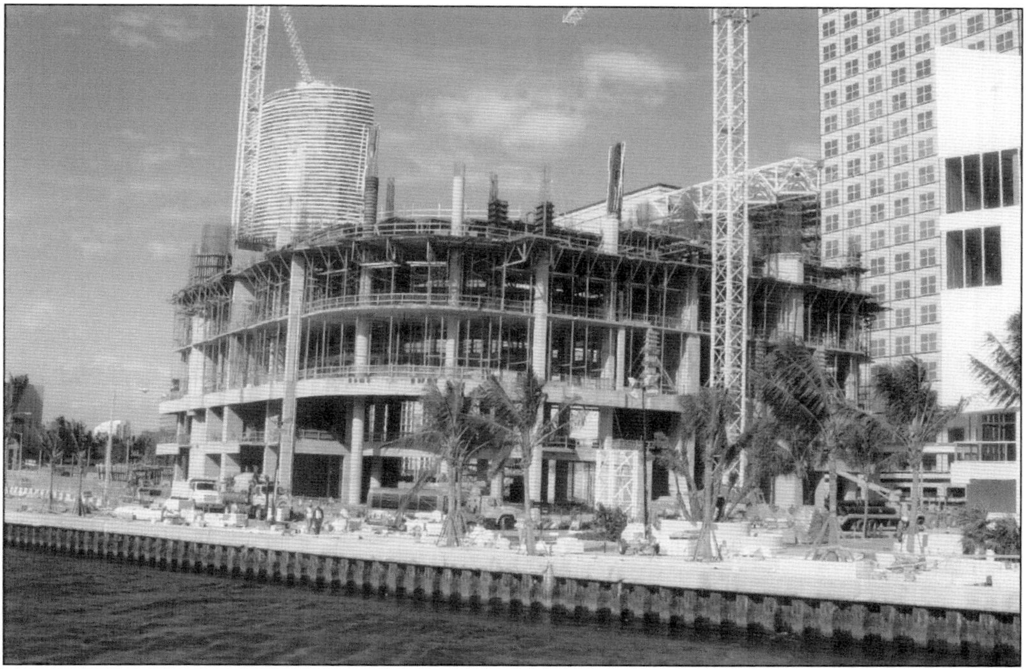

The most recent real estate boom in Greater Miami radically transformed both banks of the river as high-rise condominiums arose there for the first time. This photograph, taken around 2005, chronicles an early phase of construction of Met One, today a tall condominium standing on landfill on the north bank of the river, near its mouth. (Courtesy of Elliot Salloway.)

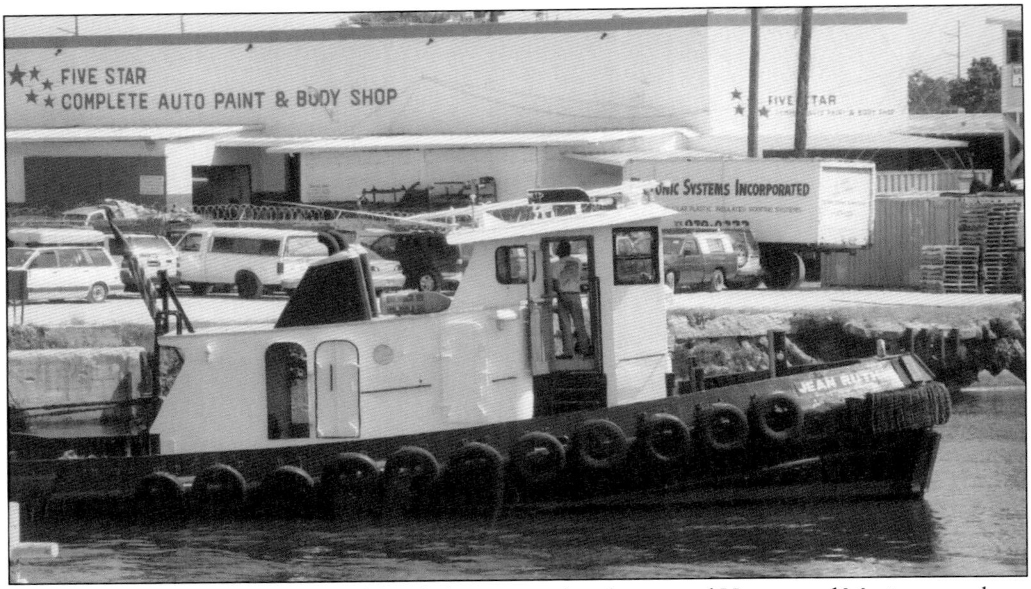

Four generations of the Hempstead family have owned and managed Hempstead Marine, a tugboat operation on the Miami River, for 90 years. The *Jean Ruth*, seen here, is a powerful 55-foot-long vessel with five-foot propellers and two large diesel engines that moves freighters up- and downriver on a regular basis. The business resided for decades on the north bank of the Miami River near Northwest Twentieth Avenue; in recent times, it has operated from a new location on the south bank of the Miami Canal. (Courtesy of Elliot Salloway.)

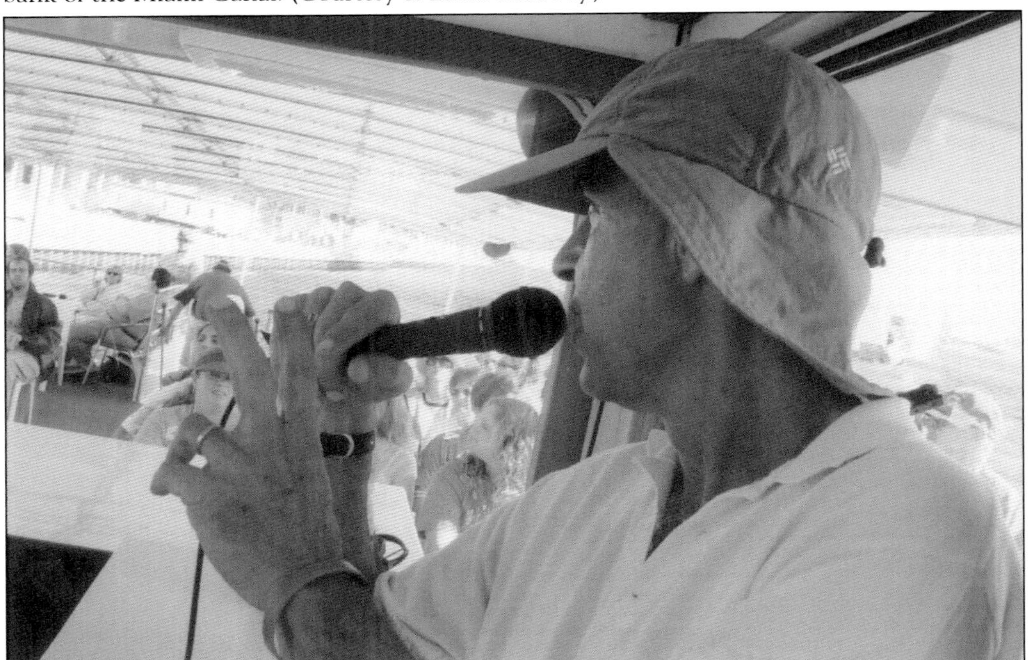

Author Paul S. George offers more than 60 different history tours. Of all of these, explorations of the Miami River are the most popular. People are intrigued by the short but bustling waterway and by the wide array of maritime businesses hugging its banks. (Courtesy of Elliot Salloway.)

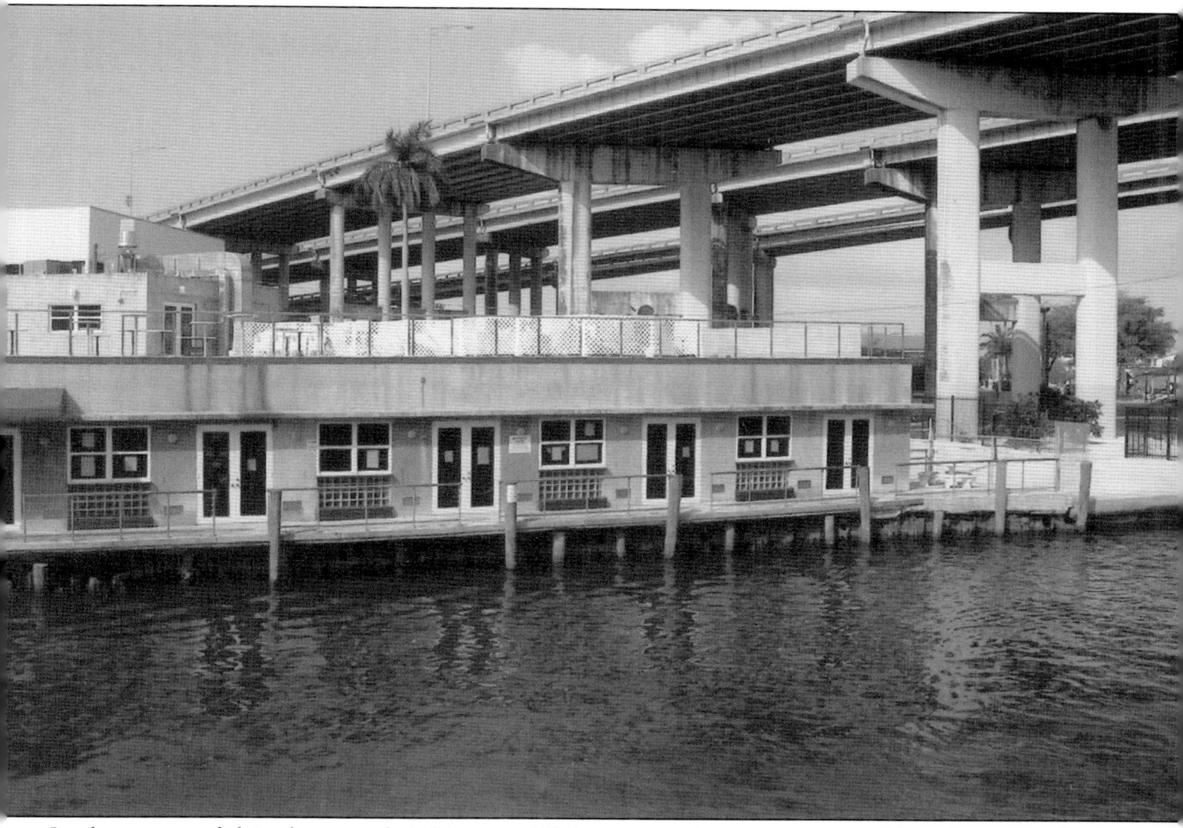

In the center of this photograph is Finnegan's River, a popular restaurant and bar that opened in the early part of this century. Located at 401 Southwest Third Avenue, it affords its patrons stunning views of downtown Miami's dense skyline at nighttime. Behind Finnegan's River stands Interstate 95, which was completed through Miami-Dade County in the late 1960s. The area beneath the expressway served as a temporary home in the summer and fall of 1980 for hundreds of Cuban refugees from the Port of Mariel. (Courtesy of Elliot Salloway.)

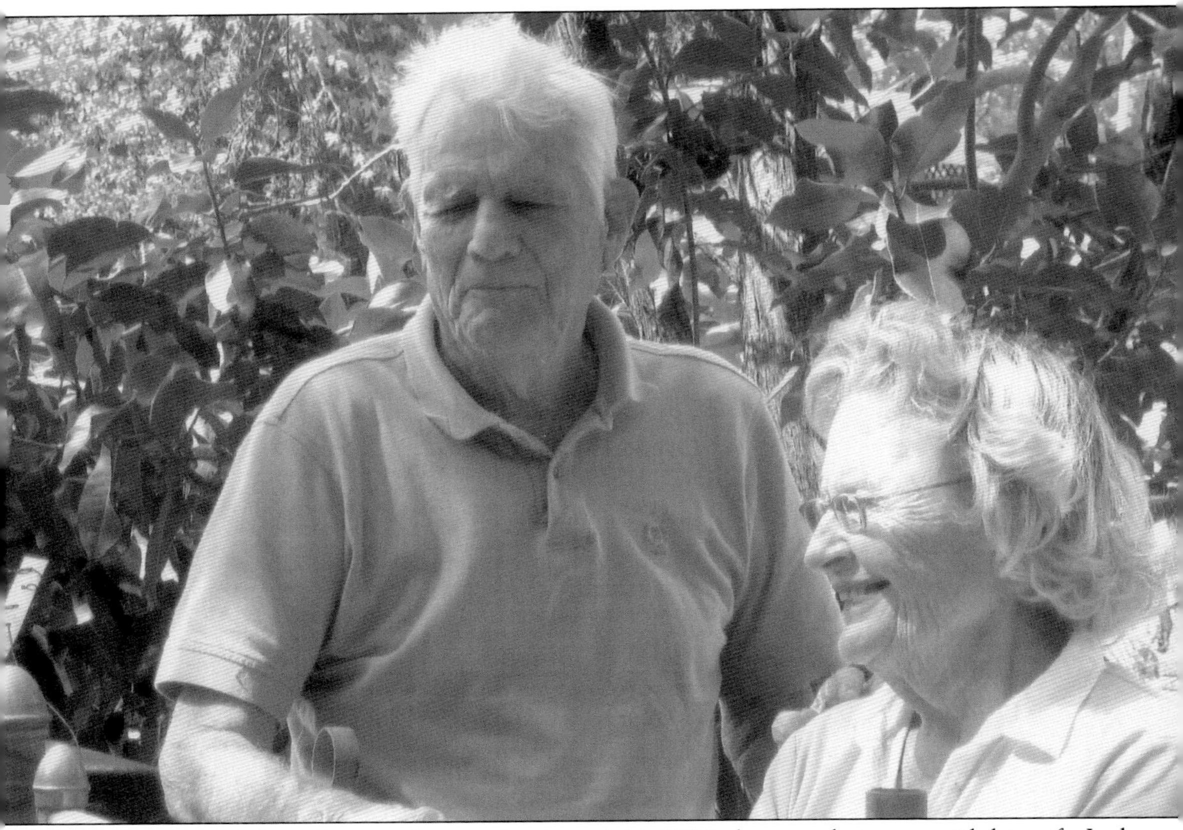

Gardnar Mulloy, 95 years of age at the time of this 2009 photograph, is seen with his wife, Lady Jacqueline Mayer (a member of British royalty), on the grounds of their home in beautiful Spring Garden. This riverine community traces its origins to 1914, when John Seybold, the city's premier baker, began developing it. One of the world's greatest tennis players in the 1940s and 1950s, Mulloy arrived in Spring Garden as an infant and has lived there since then. Mulloy's eventful life includes serving with the US Navy during World War II as a captain of an amphibious ship supplying tanks, men, and supplies to invasion forces on the beaches of Italy and France, earning a law degree from the University of Miami, holding the no. 1 ranking among both singles and doubles tennis players, and being a member of the winning men's doubles team at Wimbledon in 1957. He won four other major professional titles as a member of the winning men's doubles team at the 1942, 1945, 1946, and 1948 US National Championships. Gardnar knows the river as well as anyone. From his boyhood, he remembers diving into the stream with his dog from the Northwest Twelfth Avenue Bridge and swimming downriver to his home. (Courtesy of the author.)

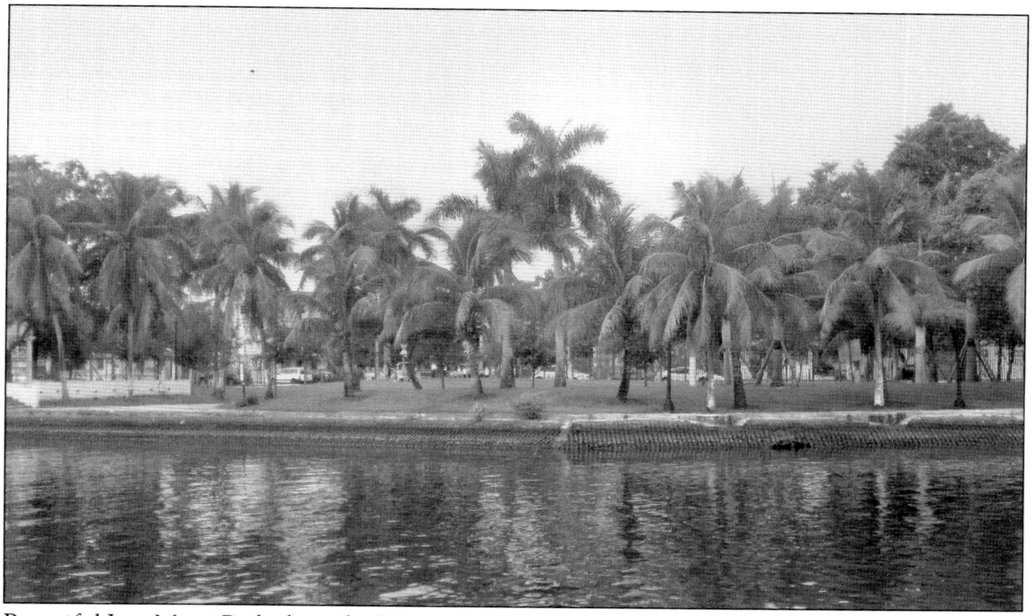

Beautiful Jose Marti Park abuts the Miami River on its west bank and represents the eastern edge of Little Havana. The park opened in 1985 on land that formerly hosted a canoe club as well as Destin Cement Company, which operated there during World War II. In recent years, the park has expanded to include a community center and a gymnasium. (Courtesy of Matthew George.)

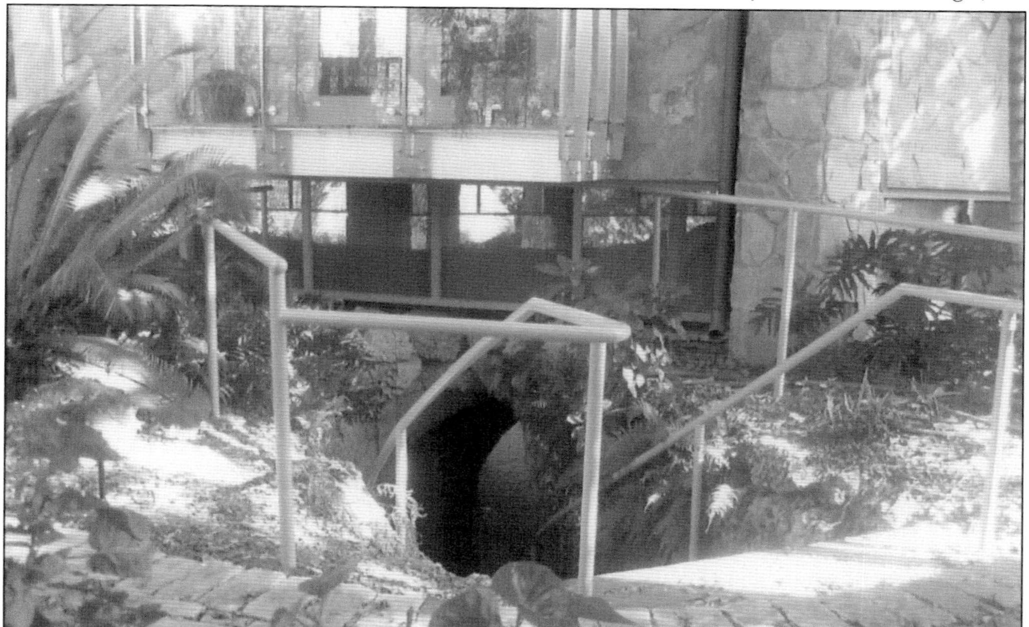

Among the most celebrated river-related elements of the Miami of yesteryear were the Indian Caves, solution holes in the limestone ridge above the Lawrence Canal, which were enlarged by the hand of man. The Miccosukee Indians, who own the property containing the caves, have erected atop them a large embassy house, a beautiful stone-and-glass facility, buttressed by steel pillars rising above the caves. (Courtesy of the author.)

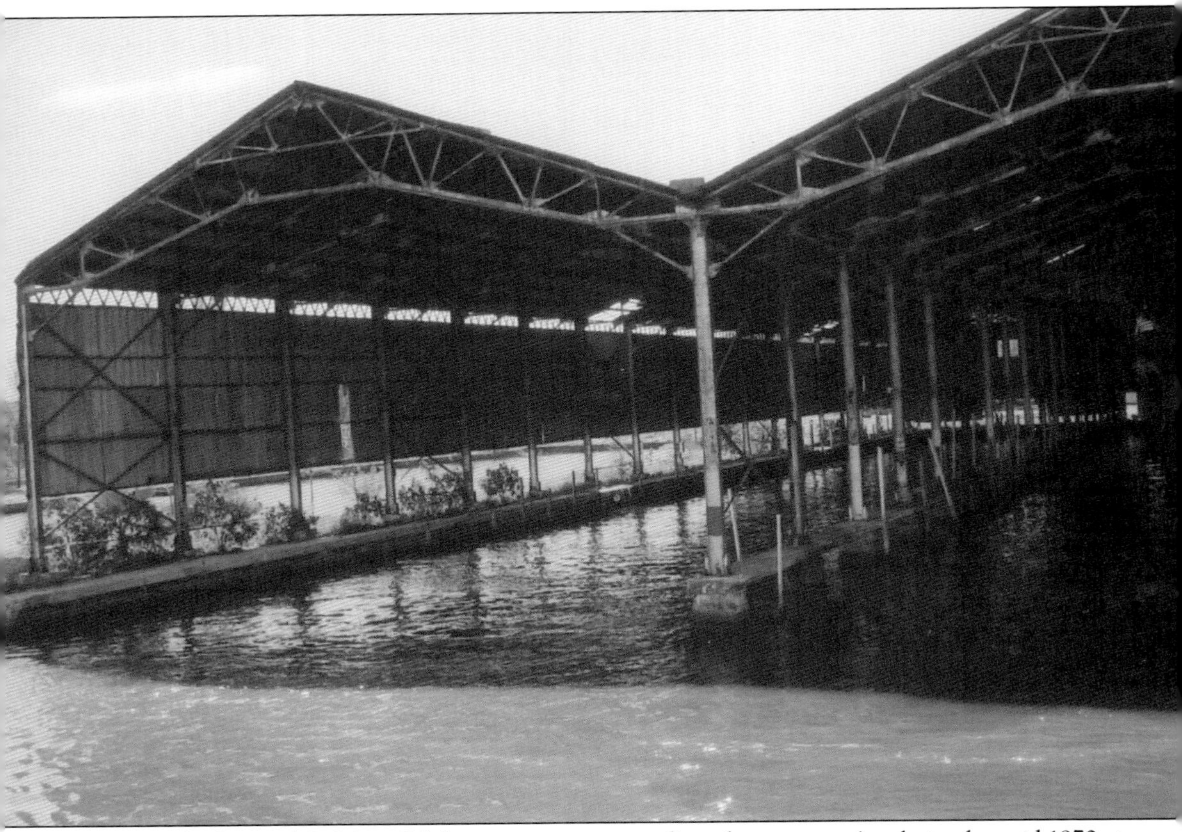

This shed served Belcher Oil for many years preceding the company's sale in the mid-1970s to Coastal Oil. Tugboats and other types of vessels were moored here. Today, many boats rent mooring space in the sheds, which are located on the south bank of the Miami River near Northwest Twenty-fourth Avenue (a site that, 100 years ago, hosted orange and grapefruit groves). (Courtesy of Elliot Salloway.)

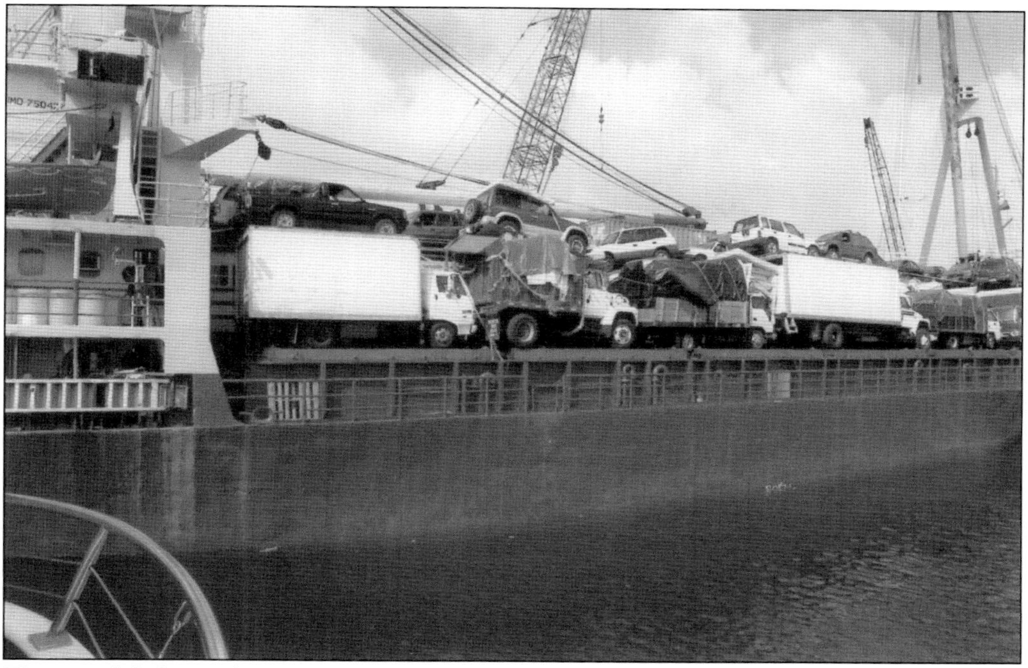

This vessel, laden with cargo to be delivered to a port in the Caribbean, typifies the business of the Miami River. The ship's cargo on deck is often sold by the captain and his crew as a business venture apart from the vessel's major task of transporting cargo. (Courtesy of Elliot Salloway.)

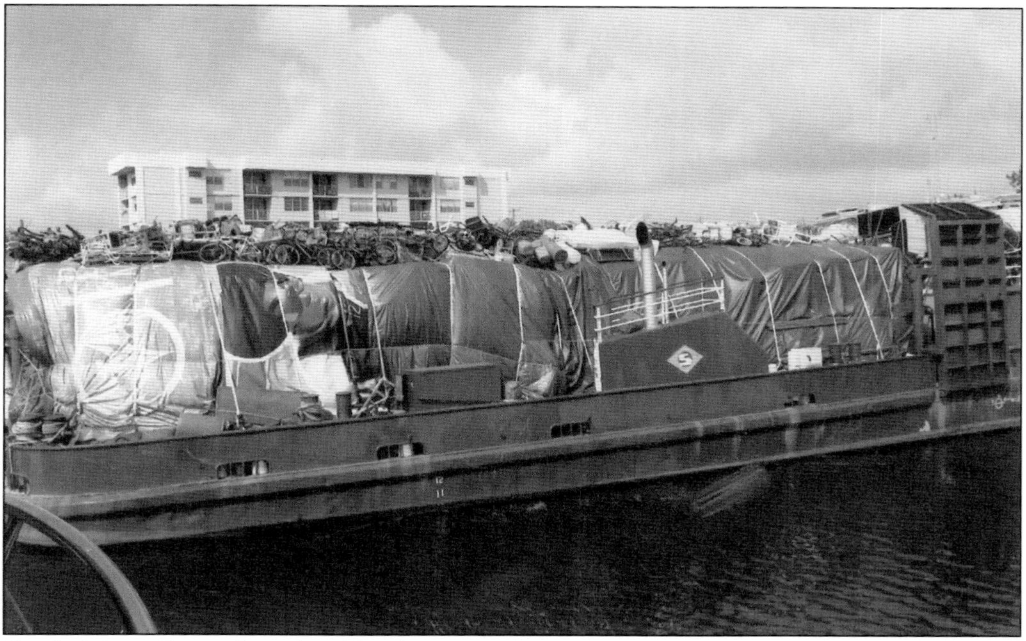

On the Miami River, the sight of freighters, such as this one bound for Haiti, filled with discarded bicycles, refrigerators, receptacles, and even cars and trucks, is a common one. The south bank of the Miami River hosts large numbers of vessels bearing these goods for sale. (Courtesy of Elliot Salloway.)

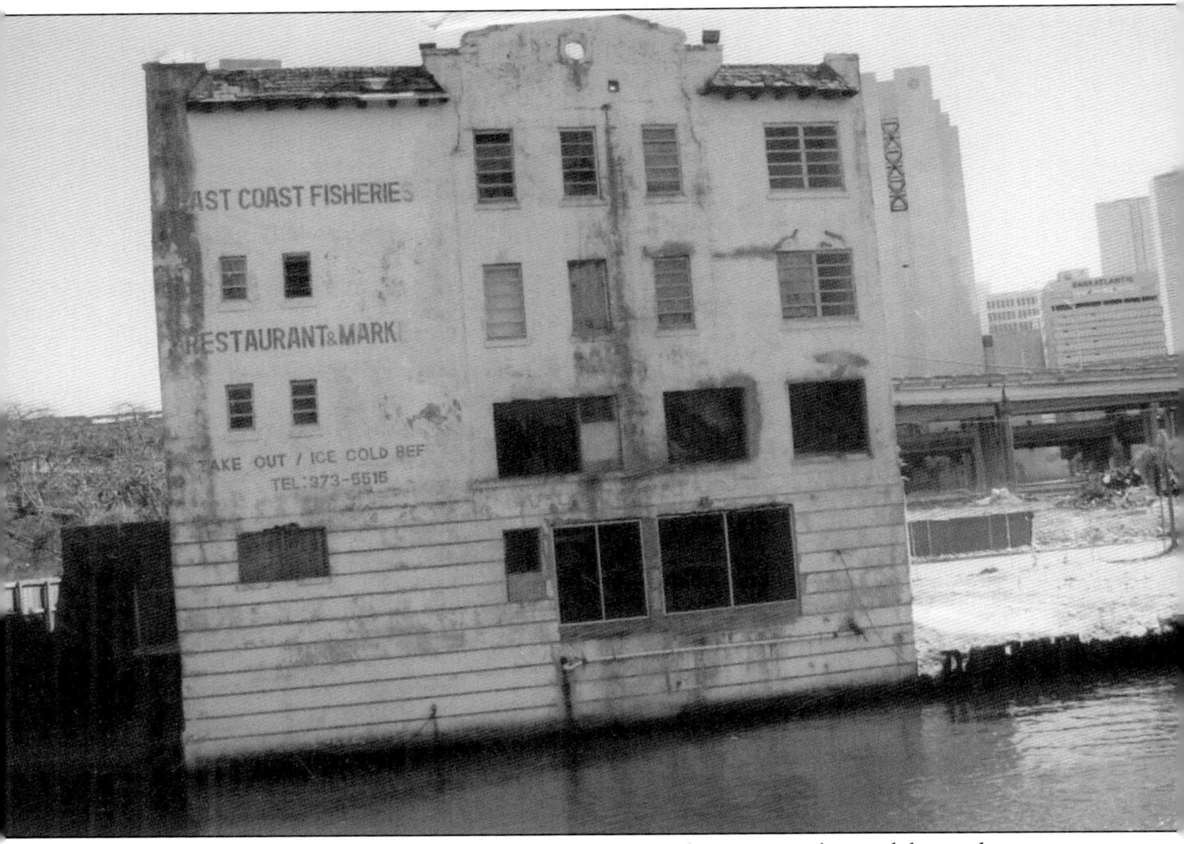

The building in this photograph housed East Coast Fisheries, a market and, later, also a restaurant that served Miamians and visitors for more than six decades before it was closed by the City of Miami for numerous code violations in 1999. Even when downtown was at its nadir as a destination for food and entertainment, the restaurant thrived. In an earlier incarnation, the building, constructed in 1918, was said to have been a house of prostitution. Located at the western edge of downtown's Flagler Street, it was razed in the early part of the 21st century. (Courtesy of Elliot Salloway.)

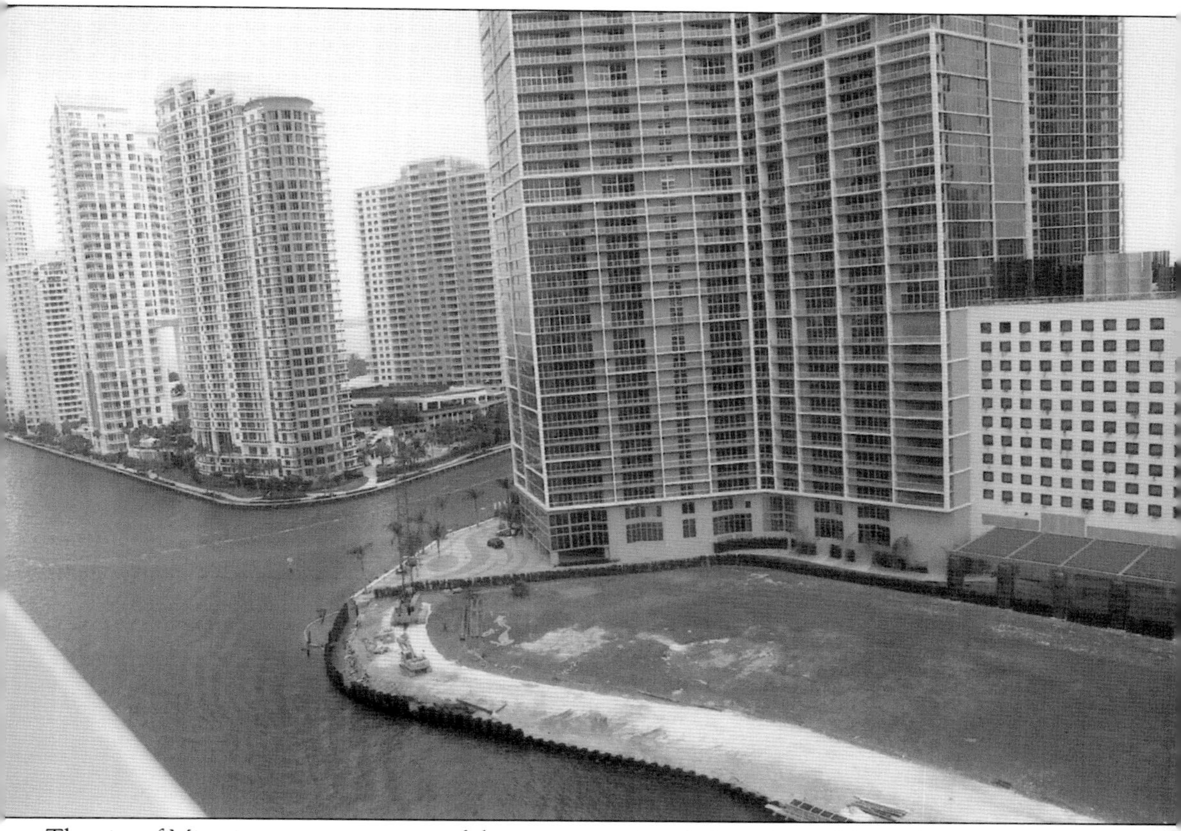

The city of Miami now possesses one of the most imposing skylines in the United States. In this photograph, taken around 2007, Condo "King" Jorge Perez's massive Icon Brickell complex hovers over the famed Miami Circle archaeological site. Behind it, to the east, stand several additional condominiums and apartments on the northern edge of bustling Claughton Island. (Courtesy of Elliot Salloway.)

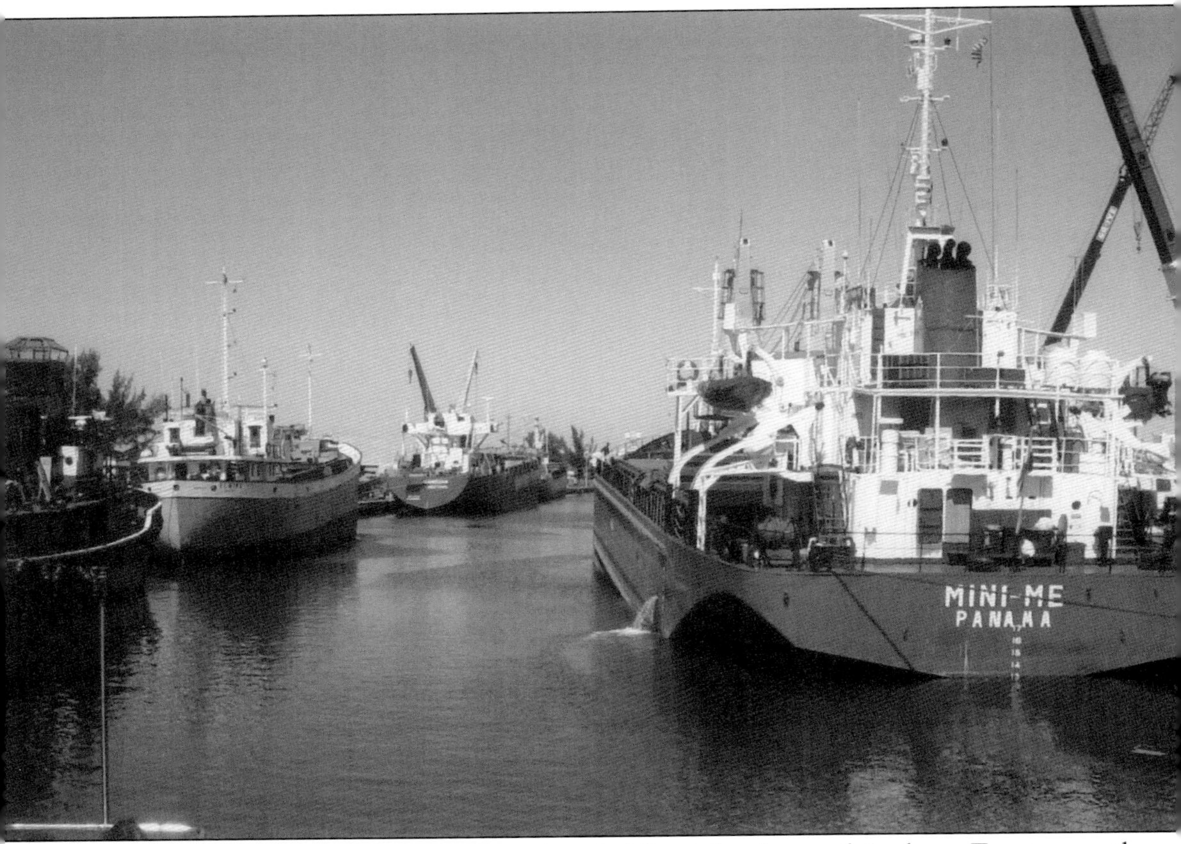

The busy Second Port of Miami is located on the Miami Canal, west of Northwest Twenty-seventh Avenue, in unincorporated Miami-Dade County. Vessels originating here visit 110 ports of call in the West Indies and Latin America. When construction of the canal began in 1909, no one could have foreseen that this waterway, created to drain the Everglades, would become one of Florida's busiest ports, responsible for more than $4 billion annually in trade alone. (Courtesy of Elliot Salloway.)

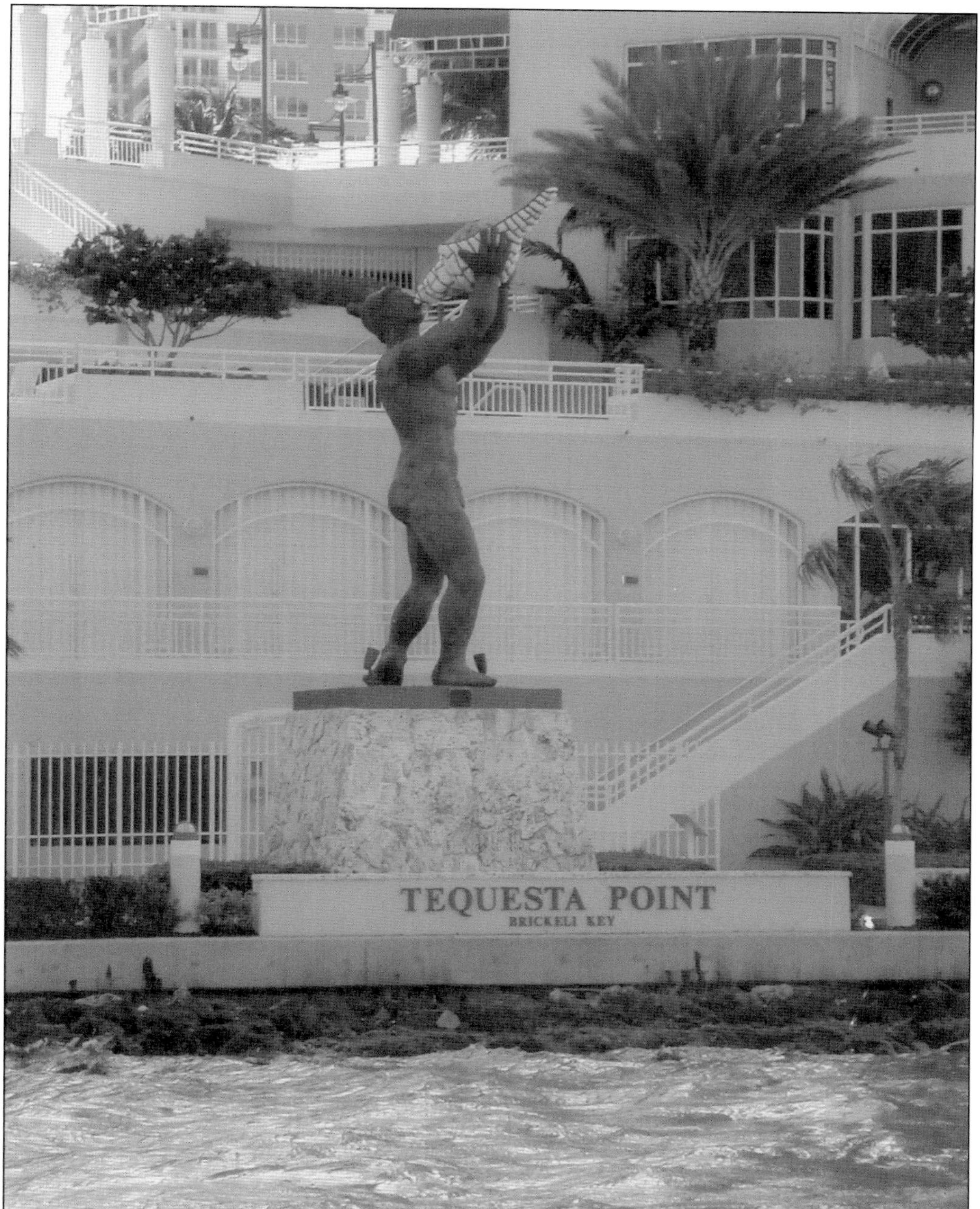

Manuel Carbonell, a beloved sculptor known for his work in the Miami area and elsewhere, created this bronze statue of a Tequesta Indian, representative of the original inhabitants of the Miami River. Carbonell executed the sculpture for the condominium and apartment towers known as Tequesta Point. It sits on the northeastern end of Claughton Island, overlooking the entranceway to the Miami River from Biscayne Bay. Seen here, the Tequesta Indian blows on a conch shell to alert his confederates that there is a shipwreck on the nearby reef, which represents the northern end of the Great Florida Reef. (Courtesy of the author.)

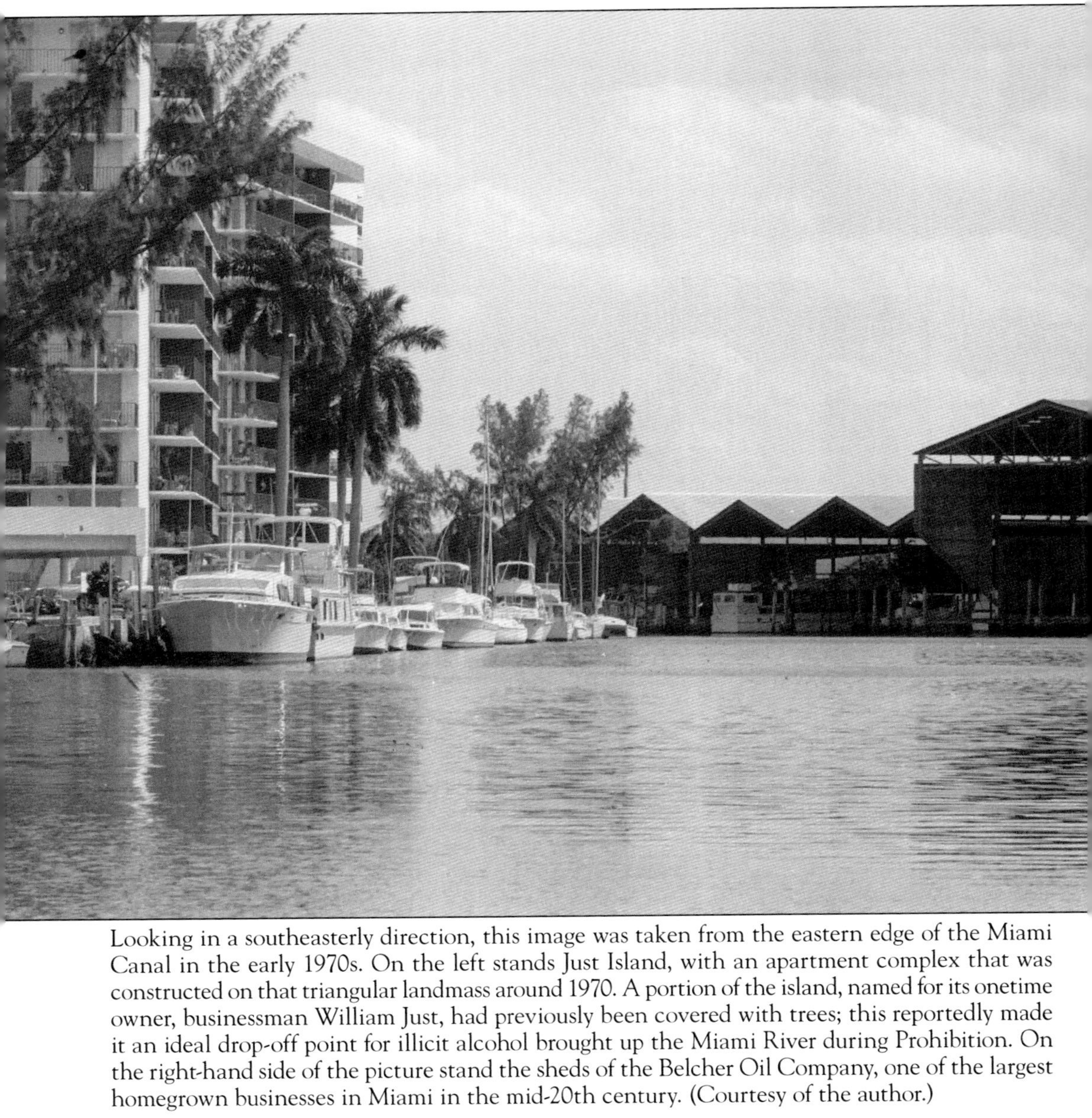

Looking in a southeasterly direction, this image was taken from the eastern edge of the Miami Canal in the early 1970s. On the left stands Just Island, with an apartment complex that was constructed on that triangular landmass around 1970. A portion of the island, named for its onetime owner, businessman William Just, had previously been covered with trees; this reportedly made it an ideal drop-off point for illicit alcohol brought up the Miami River during Prohibition. On the right-hand side of the picture stand the sheds of the Belcher Oil Company, one of the largest homegrown businesses in Miami in the mid-20th century. (Courtesy of the author.)

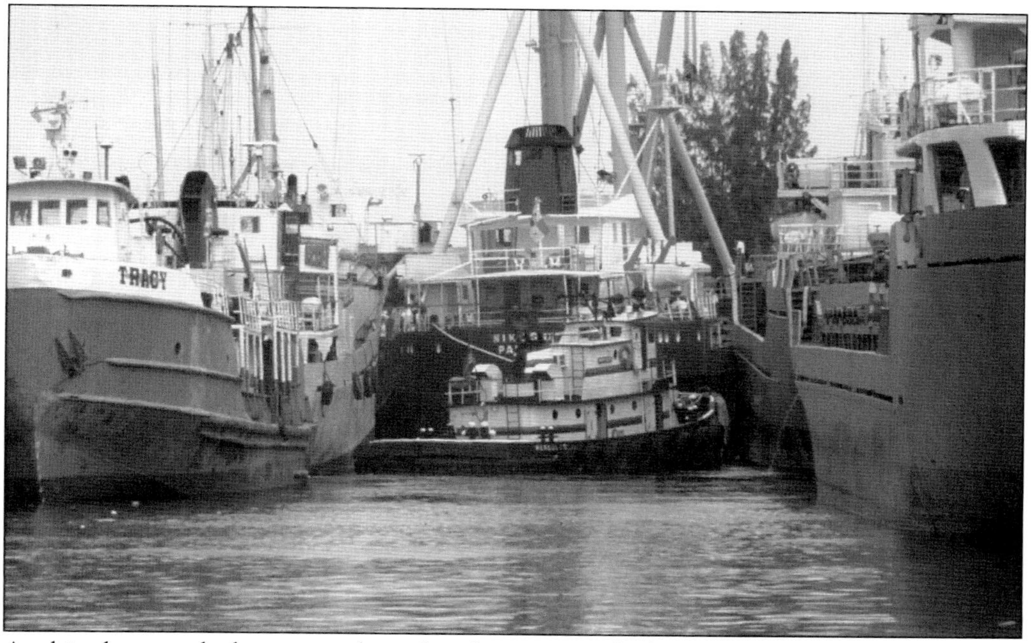

As this photograph shows, on a busy day, the passage of a large freighter through the narrow waterway known as the Miami Canal can be challenging. (Courtesy of Andrew Melick.)

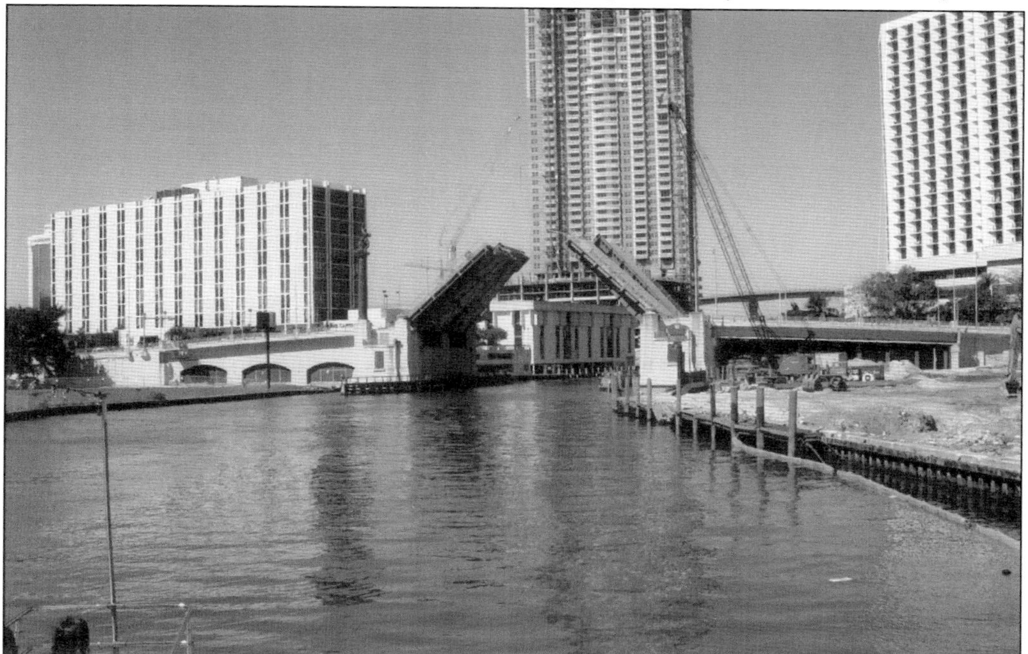

The boom was well underway in the early 2000s when this photograph, looking west from the mouth of the river, was taken. The upraised span is the Brickell Avenue Bridge. On the right is the north bank of the stream, which, at the time of this photograph, had recently been cleared to prepare for the construction of the posh Epic Hotel and condominiums. (Courtesy of Elliot Salloway.)

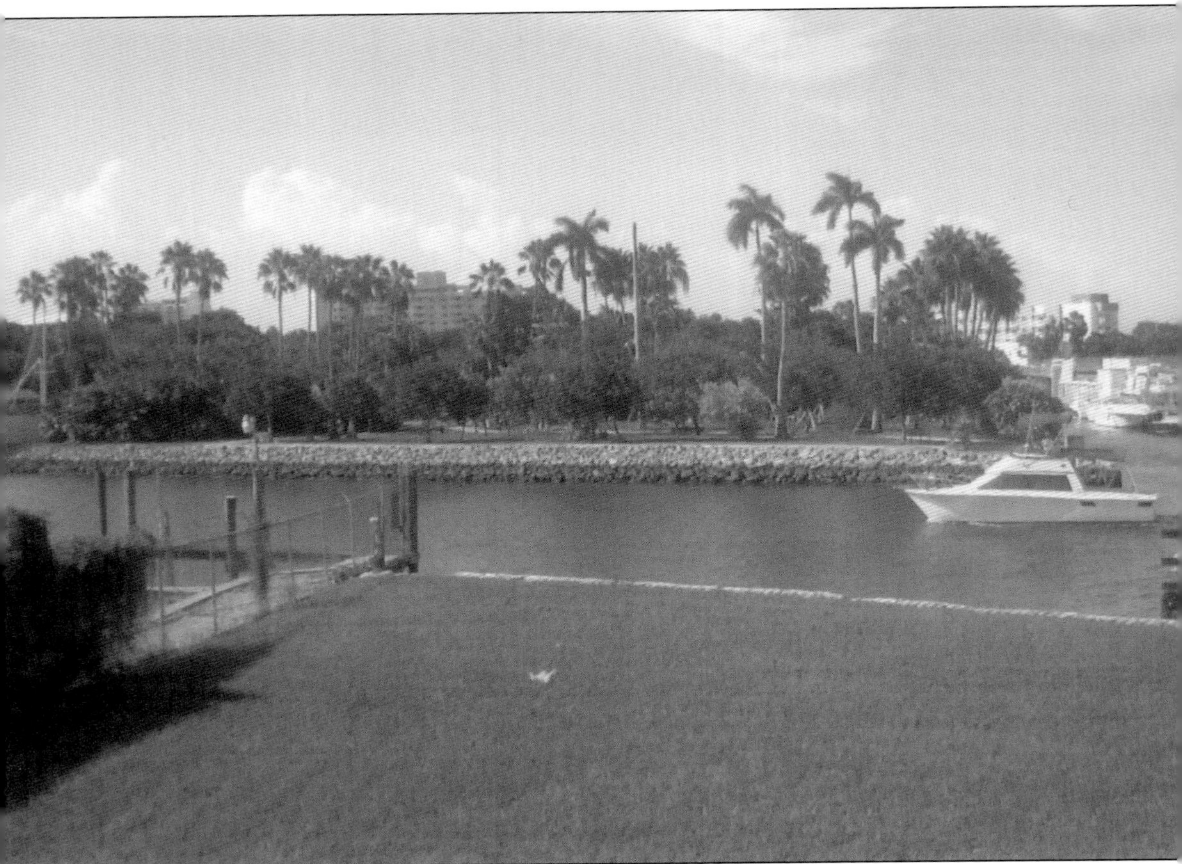

Beautiful Spring Garden Point Park, a recent addition to the City of Miami's park system, is viewed here from the south bank of the Miami River. In the early 1900s, John Seybold, the developer of Spring Garden, planned to build a home for himself and his family on a portion of the future park site; that dream, however, did not reach fruition. In 1999, an active neighborhood group, working with the Florida Community Trust and employing Florida Forever Funds, purchased the land for the city for the purpose of creating a beautiful waterfront park to be enjoyed by the public. Alligator Joe's famed alligator and crocodile attraction of more than a century earlier once occupied a portion of the property that now constitutes the park. (Courtesy of the author.)

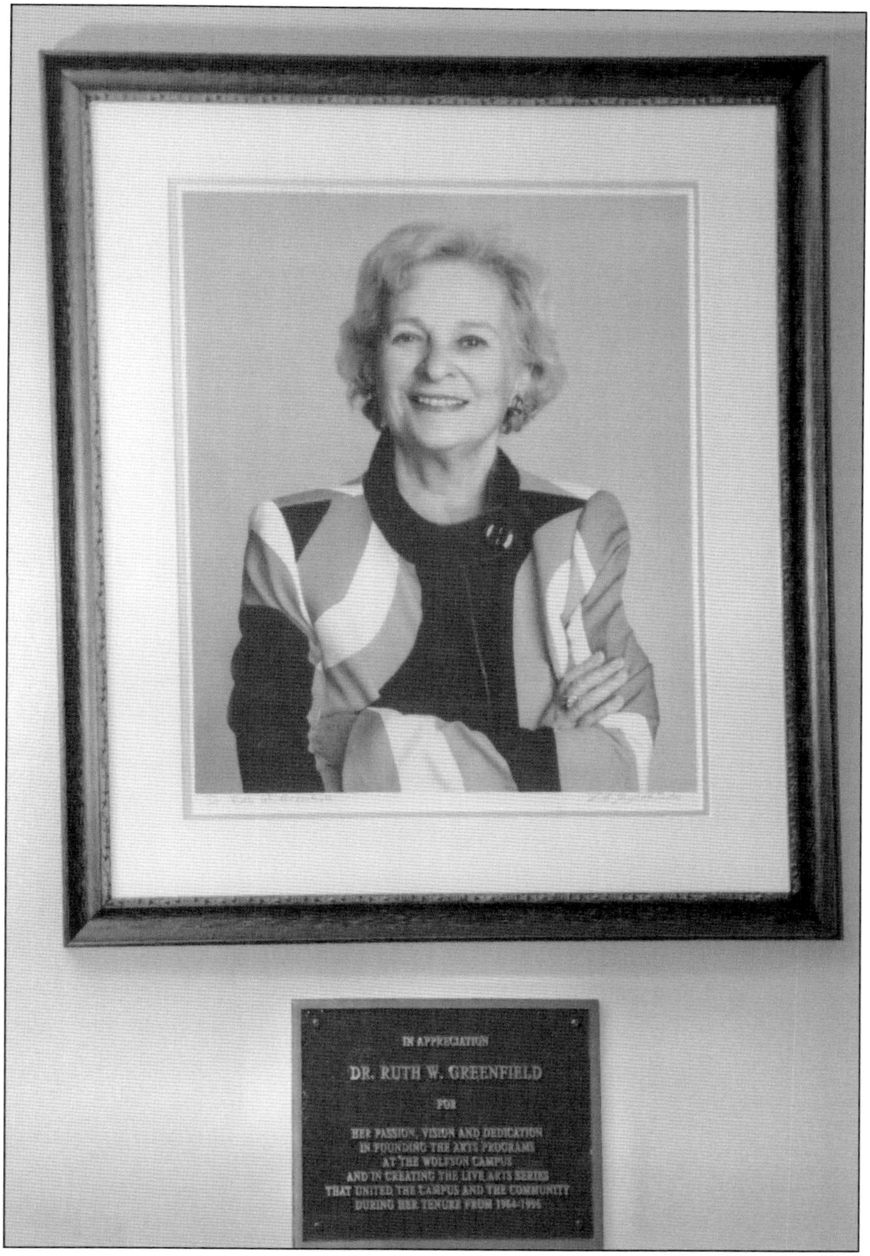

One of the jewels of the historic riverine neighborhood of Spring Garden is Dr. Ruth Greenfield, who settled there with her family, the Wolkowskys, nearly 90 years ago. Greenfield was, among other things, a musical prodigy. At the outset of the 1950s, she opened the Conservatory of Fine Arts, the first integrated conservatory of music in the South (she received death threats as a result of it.) When downtown Miami was dying in the 1970s, she staged the Lunchtime Lively Arts Series (free presentations on the steps of the county courthouse, on West Flagler Street, and in the recently restored Gusman Center) in an attempt to help revitalize the downtrodden quarter. The Lunchtime Lively Arts Series was attended by throngs of downtown workers and shoppers for nearly two decades. (Photograph by Timothy Greenfield-Sanders, courtesy of Ruth Greenfield.)

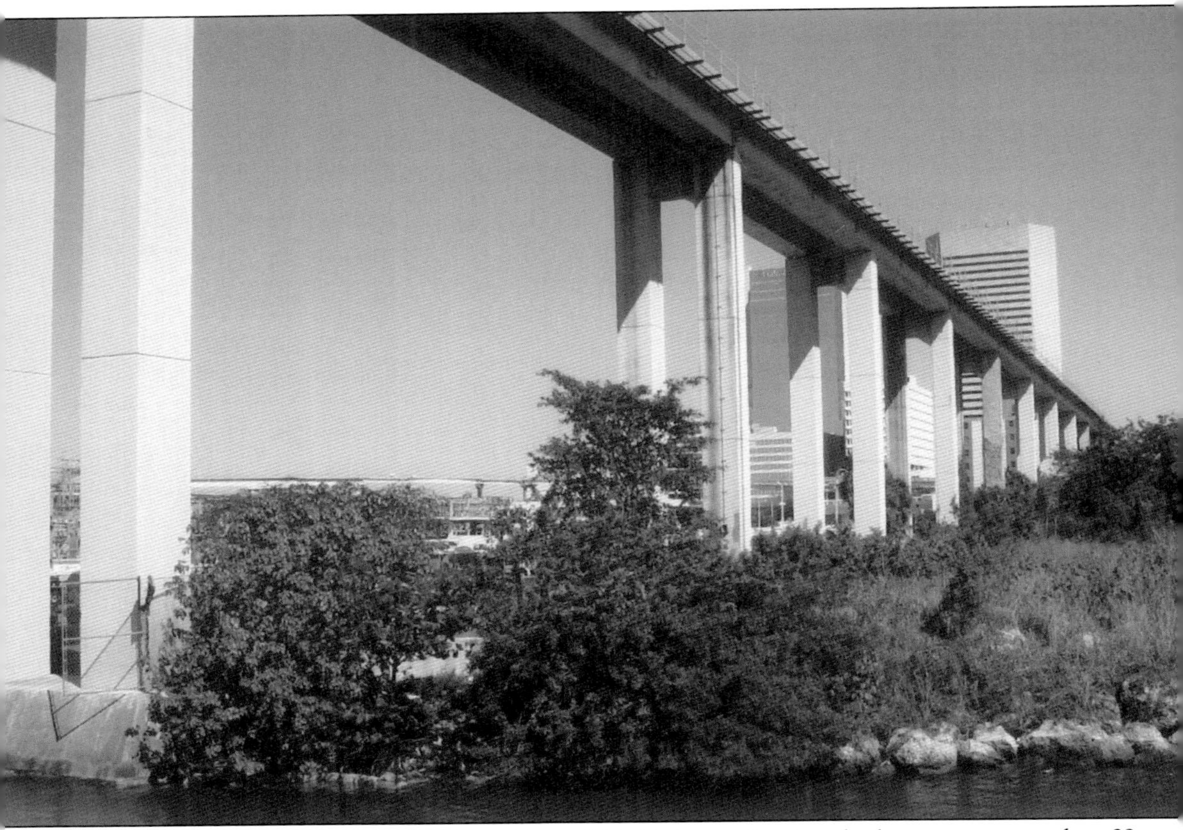

Metrorail runs high above the Miami River. This high-speed train, which traverses more than 22 miles of Miami-Dade County, began operating in the spring of 1984, running from the Dadeland South station to downtown. Immediately east of the Metrorail tracks stood the Florida East Coast Railway right-of-way. It was that railroad's entry into Miami in April 1896 that helped transform a wilderness into an incorporated city just three months later. (Courtesy of Elliot Salloway.)

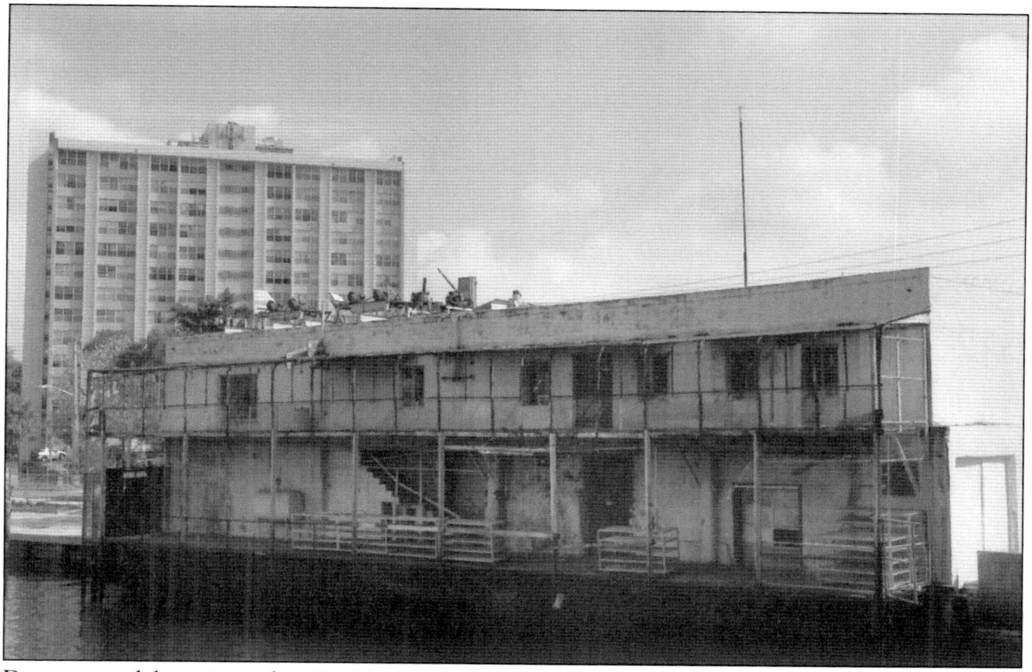

Dormant and decaying today, Captain Tom's Fish Mart, which billed itself as a "Seafood Department Store," was a popular seafood restaurant and retail/wholesale business located on the western edges of downtown Miami at river's edge. Named for charter boat captain and civic activist Tom Newman, the business flourished in the middle years of the 1900s. One of Captain Tom's unique attractions was the proprietor's promise to provide an interested party or parties with a cane pole to catch their own fish. If, after dropping a line into the murky, mullet-filled waters below the second floor restaurant, the fisherman were lucky enough to catch a fish, the restaurant would fry it for him or her. Captain Tom also pledged to his customers, through an inscription in the masonry wall near the building's entrance, that he would charge a fair price for anything he sold them. (Courtesy of Elliot Salloway.)

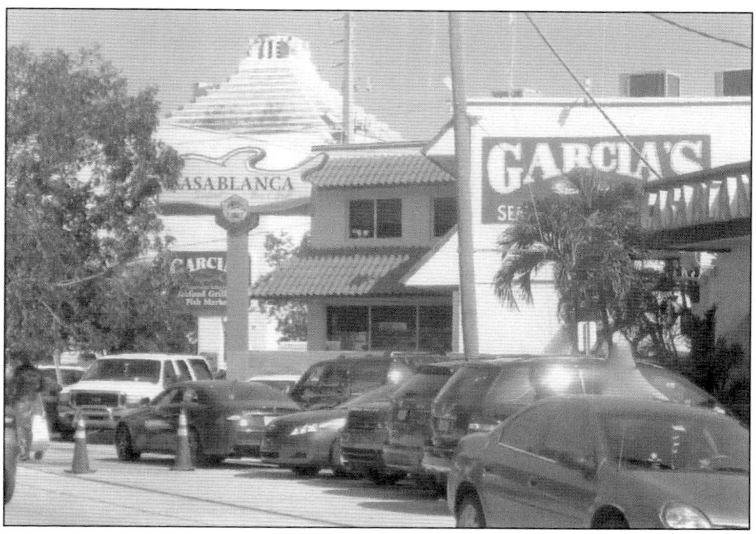

The Miami River has long hosted restaurants. Today, two of the most popular restaurants on the river are Garcia's and Casablanca, standing side by side on the east bank of the stream at the confluence of Northwest Fourth Street and Fourth Avenue. (Courtesy of the author.)